Elemental Tales

A Multi-Genre Stone Soup Anthology

Exploring the World through
a Tapestry of Elementals

Stories by members of Stone Soup

Jeanne Felfe

Parallel Pathways, LLC

St. Charles, Missouri

Published by Parallel Pathways, LLC
PO Box 502
St. Charles, MO 63302 (United States of America)

Publisher's Note: This compilation of short stories is a work of fiction. Names, characters, places, and incidents are a product of the authors' imaginations. Locales and public names are sometimes used for atmospheric purposes. Any resemblance to actual people, living or dead, or to businesses, companies, events, institutions, or locales is completely coincidental.

Book Layout © 2017 BookDesignTemplates.com
Elements quote© Victoria Erikson, used with permission
Flourishes provided by Lauren Thompson, http://nymphont.blogspot.com

Library of Congress Control Number: 2019932745

Elemental Tales — A Multi-Genre Stone Soup Anthology -- 1st ed.

Publisher's Cataloging-in-Publication Data

Names: Felfe, Jeanne, editor.
Title: Elemental tales : a multi-genre stone soup anthology / Jeanne Felfe.
Description: St. Charles, MO: Parallel Pathways, LLC, 2019.
Identifiers: LCCN 2019932745 | ISBN 978-0-9670185-3-9 (pbk.) | 978-0-9670185-4-6 (ebook)
Subjects: LCSH Short stories, American. | BISAC FICTION / Anthologies (multiple authors) | FICTION / General.
Classification: LCC PS3605 .L3775 E54 2019 | DDC 813.6--dc23

Dedicated to writers the worldwide who simply love sharing tales mined from their imaginations.

The stories included in this anthology are the result of eleven authors responding to a prompt to write a story that included one or more of the earth's elements. The results are delightful. We hope you enjoy them.

It is one thing to touch a flame and know it is hot, but quite another to jump into that flame and be consumed by it. — Adyashanti

All know that the drop merges into the ocean but few know that the ocean merges into the drop. — Kabir

Don't dismiss the elements. Water soothes and heals. Air refreshes and revives. Earth grounds and holds. Fire is a burning reminder of our own will and creative power. Swallow their spells. There's a certain sweet comfort in knowing that you belong to them all."
—Victoria Erikson

"The Earth turns to Gold, in the hands of the wise." — Rumi

Dedicated to writers the worldwide who simply love sharing tales mined from their imaginations.

The stories included in this anthology are the result of eleven authors responding to a prompt to write a story that included one or more of the earth's elements. The results are delightful. We hope you enjoy them.

It is one thing to touch a flame and know it is hot, but quite another to jump into that flame and be consumed by it. — Adyashanti

All know that the drop merges into the ocean but few know that the ocean merges into the drop. — Kabir

Don't dismiss the elements. Water soothes and heals. Air refreshes and revives. Earth grounds and holds. Fire is a burning reminder of our own will and creative power. Swallow their spells. There's a certain sweet comfort in knowing that you belong to them all."
—Victoria Erikson

"The Earth turns to Gold, in the hands of the wise." — Rumi

Contents

The Sun Shines on The Brave

Magical Realism
Water and Air

Morgana McCabe Allan

Beth

Growing up around Max was like growing up with the wind. Age seven and an orphan by all accounts, he drifted into my life. He was always on the move, fleeting in every encounter. Nothing gave him permanence in the world, no roots or dreams, until—at 14—he found sailing. In the space between sky and sea, he became a man, strong and capable. With his sometimes-blue/sometimes-grey eyes that carried the weight of storms and his slow, deliberate smile radiating sunshine, he commanded the attention of everyone who met him. He was the horizon and everything else to me.

At first, he would spend days, and later—as he gained experience—weeks, flying across the seas with wings made of cloth. At seventeen he was possessed by the love of an old yacht he affectionately named "The Brave". Her hull creaked secret lullabies to him, and he worked endlessly, earning money by carefully repairing old gear, to make her his own. Unkempt and with a perpetual scent of sea air, I couldn't help but shed tears over him; I grew ever more in love, though he paid no attention to me. Somehow, his passion for the old boat made him seem reliable in a way he had never been before. He cherished her, and she, in turn, made him purposeful and direct.

When we were 18, sipping fresh cider under an autumn sunset, Max asked me to sail to America with him and kissed me for the first time. I never wanted to breathe anything but him ever again. It was a powerful thing that burned wickedly through me destroying the minutes we were not together.

"The Sea and the Sky are Lovers such as us," he used to say. "Great gods destined to an eternity together."

I didn't stop to fear the enormity of such relationships nor the danger. Instead, we called ourselves *the brave*, and my head filled with destinies, fates, and the spirit of the endeavour.

At 19, after repeatedly breaking my mother's heart, we finally set sail from Arisaig. We made the portentous acquaintance of dolphins that first day, singing all of our shanties and hopes to the vast blue-grey around us. Those creatures delighted the child in me, playing in the wake and riding the bow wave. Mothers and babes leapt high into the sky, hanging for a moment in the air, before plunging back into the deep; a sign that they did indeed belong to both worlds.

With nothing to do but grow up, we meandered then, taking in these new islands, shedding our old lives. I changed more than I could have imagined, inside and out. Calluses grew like barnacles as we hauled, again and again, the woven snakes I had not yet befriended until gradually they differentiated into discrete ropes and then tamed again: mainsheet, kicker, genoa halyard, all named. At rocky points, we caught mackerel with a simple hand line Max made. His hand over mine, he taught me how to tease the fish. It seemed they queued up to die, so eagerly they took those little hooks. They were easy food, and Max dispatched them with such precision and care that there was grace in it. Death, I learned, could be beautiful.

By the time we reached Barra, our second-to-last stop before the big sea, the fishing people there treated us as real voyagers. They respected Max's preternatural sense for the wind and gave us homegrown vegetables and their own fine brew to take with us on our journey.

"Remember us when you are famous!" They laughed, hugging and patting us as fiercely as their own close kin.

Max plotted our course from Barra to St. Kilda—the last outpost before the long ocean passage to the Americas. Sails full and the wind at our backs, we soared under rainbows and Northern Lights—unstoppable—until our entire existence keeled in the point where air and water meet. Becalmed, without even a ripple in the world. An ocean of glass brought us the first taste of the bitter turbulence all lovers must learn to expect.

Other partners. Past loves. I had never imagined, though I should have, of course. But whilst I was loving him to madness, those feelings had clearly not always been returned. It shouldn't have mattered, and it didn't. But it did. When the wind came back, it was an ill one, changeable and flighty, and even The Brave grumbled along.

We finally reached St. Kilda days later than anticipated and anchored to rest, but there was still something foul in the air. An apprehension that neither of us could put words to, yet tainted everything, and we hardly spoke or touched for seemingly end-less days. I felt sick to my stomach. The world coloured grey and we faltered, unwilling to set off without some omen to release us from spiralling antipathy. After—I don't remember how many, maybe five—nights of intimidation by the awesome majesty of that last bastion of island carved out of time itself, we drank the Barra brew. We shouted like gales, howled and cried everything out in the looming shadow of the terrifying sea stack men once braved to feed their families the precious eggs and fledglings perched amongst the cliffs. When we came together again, it was with the tempestuous force of that great god and goddess of old. The horizon was restored.

When we woke late, it was to the full cacophony of the island's treasured bird population. Max's face glowed with astonish-ment; Minke whales surrounded us. It was their feeding, chasing schools of fish to the surface that invited the cawing frenzy. The fish oil released in their killings made the air thick

with promise. Life and death hung together, equal partners, in the space between sea and sky, but we saw only one, Max and me. We were blind to the other.

"The sun shines on The Brave," he sang, his smile back in all its glory, and never so deeply had I believed him.

We hooted and whooped, and revelled at life, and set off under blue skies. In another universe, another Max instead said, "We don't have to do this. We aren't ready," and we agreed to postpone—to return home—pride be damned. And when that other Max and Beth embraced, she too believed in her omen that she was making the right choice. Even yet, retrospect gives me no insight. Destiny is fickle, and fate makes no sense.

The night of the whales, the storm of sagas came in, worthy of Thor, or Zeus, or at least the Old Testament. Perhaps those ancients battled that night for control, raising waves like mountains, great columns of water that crashed over the foredeck, relentless as battering rams. With them came legendary winds that ripped through the ocean and sky, tearing holes in the universe. We battened down, like the guillemots and shearwaters, but even with the hatches shut tight, the water found hidden weaknesses, breaching what had been our refuge, revealing it a fragile and treacherous illusion. Ropes broke free, whipping the hull with their hard metal fittings. The Brave keeled, groaning, crying, under the strain of staying together. And I was beyond useless, curled in a ball, vomiting and vomiting, rattling around inside myself like loosed marbles.

"What can we do?" I screamed over the roar, though, of course, I could do nothing.

Max, eyes harder than I'd ever seen, put his oilskins on. "The sun shines on the brave," he said. Up he went then, torch in one hand and a clip in the other to attach onto the deck.

Only as the world calmed a little, and far too late, did I possess the sense to realise he had not returned. I raced onto the deck, imagining him injured somewhere, but he was gone. In disbelief I circled again and again, expecting to find him clipped on to something. Somewhere. Anywhere.

I scanned the water for a sign of him. I screamed for him, over and over, through the brutal mix that was neither sea nor air, that nearly drowned me where I stood, and left my throat tasting of blood. Endlessly, even after my voice ran out, I screamed into that late May night, demanding the crescent moon and the sea return him to me.

As the elements calmed and the first rays of light broke through, I saw those red streaks on the deck. Blood, where he must have hurt himself, maybe hit the winch or the boom, and then gone overboard. I searched then even more frantically, everywhere a hundred times each, for his red life jacket. Maybe he was okay. Maybe he needed rescuing. *Maybe he was okay.*

I tried to bargain with the Sea and the Sky then, half of one pair to another. Return him to me, and I will do anything, give anything. They did not reply. Nor did the dolphins, nor the whales. I was alone. Lost in a sea of my own making. A sea where I could drown in my mistakes a thousand days over but never summon the will to end it all. The vomiting continued, and I imagined it was the violence of my grief expelling itself.

Time was irrelevant when they rescued me; I had given it up entirely. If I were to guess, it could have been a week, but it's hard to say when we provisioned for two who were eating, not one who was starving of grief. They told me he saved me—something he had miraculously fixed up there in the storm, that salvaged The Brave and me. His body was never recovered, lost in all but memory. My bargains would not stick, it seemed, because he first made one of his own. I found I had no choice but to live, whatever it might mean, because that was the price.

Next came blankets, and hospitals, and news crews. Never stopping to breathe because the sea scent of him still filled my lungs, and I would not relinquish it. Next came my body pitching as I tried to move on land, adapted to life in the margins between the deep water and the vast sky, rejecting the return to "Before Max". Next came the certainty that without him I could neither go forward nor back. And yet, eventually, an unequivocal push arrived. The doctors gave me the all clear of course, but for one detail.

"Congratulations, you are pregnant."

At first, I thought I felt nothing. Later came hope and loss and the feeling that he remained buried deep inside me, all welling up and soaring through me, beating me like hot needles or hard icy hail. Guilt that my first thought was not of joy and love. I didn't know what to feel—there was no guidance on the right order to it.

Nevertheless, somehow in those months, I live on. The Brave and I, brave life together, albeit lashed to a pontoon. We are unable to leave the sea, unwilling to sail without you. Your soul is everywhere; neither the winds cutting through us nor the waves washing around us can ever disperse you from my life. You linger in the meticulous polish of the deck boards, the stiff rise of the mast, the smooth curves of the hull, and my growing belly. Conceived before everything changed. Before the night I realised I never knew you. Before the night when I knew you best.

In time, those goddesses who bless us still deliver us a daughter, Max, and she is everything you have ever loved and more. Naming her is hard because part of me wants to name her Storm, or Gale, or Kilda, and revel in excruciating pain every time I look at her. A terrible part of me almost hates her, but that is grief, and I have to believe it will pass with time—she is all I have left of you to hold. In the end, I call her Skye, for the love we found there, for the dolphins and their infants that hang ever so briefly between the water and the air, as we did once.

Her first word is Daddy, and it is so hopeful, so tentative and loving, it breaks my heart forever. Of course it is Daddy, for I talk of almost nothing else. She cannot miss a father she has never met, yet your loss pours out of her, for I have inadvertently filled her tiny vessel with nothing else.

Her first steps, and all those which follow, are towards the sea. An old seal basking in the sun watches her with soulful eyes, as though he too were a parent, committing to memory each moment of squidgy little feet wobbling over soft sand. We see him many times, those next quick years. In a blink, she is three. For the first time, we catch mackerel with the line you left us, my hand over hers, joyously throwing them to him "for him share them." He waves a mournful farewell with soft, murmuring calls, as we toddle home hand in hand that evening. It is the last time we see him. Perhaps he finally realised, our world can never be his.

After that, everything capsizes again and cannot be righted.

"I need a brother or a sister," Skye announces.

Everything falls in on itself, and I don't know how to climb back out. Grief never leaves, it only changes. And so it goes now, as I am confronted with the writhing faces of all the other children we might have had. The many sons who would have looked like you and carried themselves with the same broad-shouldered, good-natured assurance of someone who can rely on their own hands to mould the world around them. Or looked like me and marvelled at your capacity to read water like poetry. All the possible daughters, every one of whom would have loved you as fiercely as I do—then, and now, and forever. The one gets lost, momentarily, in the shadows of the invisible others. I am face down, crying gritty tears when she comes to me with two daffodils in an old chipped cup.

"This is all we need, Mama. One is you. The other is me. This is The Brave." She gestures to the cup, smiling your exact same smile.

My body aches, my heart bursting with more joys and pains than I have words to put name to. She cradles my head as though I were the child and reminds me, "It's ok, Mama. The sun shines on the brave." And I fear the tears that come will drown us both.

She is five, and we finally set sail for she cannot be contained any longer. She hears the voices of the same old gods who spoke to you, inherently knows their rhythms. Her heart was not forged on this earth, and it is a force to be reckoned with. All of the ocean is hers; all of the wind falls under her spell.

She is seven, and the whales come, my first and only humpbacks. Such rare visitors to Scotland, yet they come for her. She is so brave in this world that is always filled with echoes of you; they must have heard the bittersweet song in her soul. She is so courageous I am awestruck, and in every fibre I know you died for her. You and I were never "the brave". Our beloved vessel was only ever wood and cloth. She is "The Brave". Her eyes are your eyes, and her wavy hair has every colour of the autumn sun within it. Every day, even the hardest ones, I have something to live for, when each drop of the sea is you and the heavens howl your name, taking you away from me again and again. I live for her, just as you gave your life. What is love, in the end, if not the ability to sacrifice?

And so, here we are. We have made our lives upon the beach, where I wait for you still, Max, in the spaces between tides and breaths. There is a whole graveyard of sea glass, driftwood, and broken nets strung into art, all dedicated to you. We sing the songs of these islands, and I still don't know what to feel. But the people here are kind to me, for they too have lost many loves to the beautifully dark and terrible clash of the Lovers.

Every morning I wake to exquisite pain; my nightmares are real, and yet my dreams remain only that. As my body ages, the shape of your memory always folds perfectly into it, whatever the

contours. Each new line brings new grief at what we should have shared; how we would have grown old together. I know now what the dolphins and the whales were trying to say: there is a price for living between the water and the sky. Maybe they are the spirits of lost souls, existing between worlds, between everything and nothing.

We were young, Max, and knew it all, except to know better. We listened to the wind and sea and heard their call to adventure, but we did not heed their grieving tears. I have only stories of you, My Love, to give to our daughter but, despite it all, there is beauty in life, and the sun shines on us still.

Max

Beth came into my life at seven, like a new moon rising, invisible, and yet a force to be reckoned with. When she looked down at the world, already beneath her feet, she was unfathomable. Only in time came the little revelations.

From that very first day, I loved her, and I made a plan. "A man has to be dependable and skilled," my old man always said, before I ran away all those years ago. Sailing seemed like a good fit, but I've never hurt myself so many times doing anything—every damn tool slipped into my skin at least once. Ropes pinched and burned me, and I don't have enough numbers to count how many times I sent myself into the sea, arms and legs flailing. It did change me though, knowing the wind and water that way, just like she did.

The next step came easier: "No fine woman would settle for a life with a man without means," Father said, "and money is just a process of trading time." It was time with her and I regretted that, but it purchased a future that dutifully arrived: a small ship for me to call my own. The Brave, I named her, and she could go anywhere. All she and I needed was a first mate.

It took weeks to provision and even longer to steel the guts, but finally, after years of lining everything up, I asked Beth to come with me. To make a life of adventure. I remember exactly, the way the sun caught her wild, flyaway hair; the pale silver of her loosened blouse; the sound of my blood in my ears. In my head, I chanted, *If she says no, I'll laugh it off as her loss, leave now and never come back.* But she was coming! Only after I was mentally rechecking the final itinerary, did I hear what she was actually saying "... and of course we'll need to wait until I finish my studies, and naturally we will need time to plan, and save, and pack ..." Somehow the words "I've done it all, I've thought of everything" stuck in my gullet and would not come out. Becalmed is not the same as calm.

The waiting was tedious. I had nobody to say goodbye to, and everything I wanted lay ahead, not behind. Weeks dragged into months, and her mother's shadow clung to everything. I was never bored of Beth, but I was bored, and I made a mistake. Two mistakes, I suppose, if you include not confessing my sins to her. It was me who opened the door to everything that was to come.

When we set sail, I thought to leave those errors behind me, a man renewed by having everything he ever wanted and more. We grew together, became something greater than I imagined possible, a single entity born to fly across oceans, The Brave, me, and Beth—body, heart, and soul. I took in less of the people and places than I should, spending my time captivated by the luminescence that exploration gave her. A goddess, carved into full flesh.

Then the truth hit like lightning and split us apart. I tried everything, never found the right thing to say or do. The storm that came after hunted us from the rough edge of the world. The gods made it, just to test me. A punishment. Love is sacrifice. When the wave came there was no time to do anything; it hit like a train, carrying me with it into the maelstrom.

It was the curse that washed me up on the shore. Ancient and terrible. My seal skin fit badly over my human soul, and my love for Beth would not diminish, no matter my mother's ministrations or my father's admonishment. There was no release in swimming, no delight in catching fish. Only searching. Until, one day, I finally found her, rafted up with a bairn in her arms. Every day I watched them, guarded them by night. It seemed she had metamorphosed, at least as much as I, into an uneasy visage of motherhood. My own parents urged me daily to give up or take the child's life for myself. Meanwhile, I plotted and schemed, determined to find a way to take both of them.

Water and wind change everything, even hearts and minds. The little one caught a fish of her own one day, on my true and trusted selkie line. At first, my heart soared, "She is mine" echoing in every chamber. I almost leapt out of the water right then and raced to them, seal skin be damned. Then it hit me, just like the wrath of the gods: taking them into the bosom of the sea meant cursing the little one's magic and cursing Beth twice over. All the hours we had and the lifetime more they could still have flashed in equal measure. A life of being something completely, instead of neither and both. Or I could offer them in-between-ness and danger, and misery. I rolled under as the cord that drew me to them snapped back, a fierce whiplash to the soul. It was long time for goodbyes.

Inside, I am just a shadow now, my magic fading and with it myself. One day soon, I will be nothing but an ordinary seal. For now, I watch the passage of the moons to see the many outlines of Beth's delicate face and cry for our daughter, who I will never know. There is beauty in death, My Love.

THE END

Morgana McCabe Allan Ph.D is an interdisciplinary researcher specialising in women and their interactions with the physical environment, things and people. Her work explores the transition to motherhood and the maternal investment in infant life, and she has a number of academic publications. A lover of folklore, fantasy and magical realism and deeply connected to the stunning, isolated beauty of her native homeland of Scotland, she is an explorer and adventurer at heart. This is her first short story and first time bringing all of those passions together. It is hoped it will become one of many.

morganamccabeallan.com
https://www.facebook.com/MorganaMcCabeAllan/

Windsong

Fairy Tale/Fantasy
Earth and Air

Kerry E.B. Black

In a town where everyone's skin shone like burnished mocha and their hair fell straight and dark as afternoon shadow, Maurya shone pale as the underbelly of a toad. Her wispy hair flew like errant stratus clouds. Pink streaked her light-sensitive eyes, and she stumbled through life unable to see clearly. Troubles and guilt etched age upon her.

As a grown woman with skin wrinkled as birch bark, Maurya wore her differences like a shawl wrapped about her. She kept her eyes downcast not only to prevent headaches from the light's glare but also to avoid the neighbors' disgusted looks or frightened glances. Instead, she befriended birds and chattered with them to pass the days of "inane usefulness" required to live in her tribe.

Everyone had to do their part to keep things running smoothly. Maurya nurtured mushrooms and herbs, and a woman with a stout heart named Leesa from the nearest village sold them for her. Owls and bats kept the nights from crippling her with loneliness. Maurya told them adventurous stories, and she visited her mother's grave where she left nosegays of apology. "Sorry you died. I wish I knew you. Everyone loved you."

Nobody loved Maurya, not even her father, the wealthiest and oldest man in town. His work harnessing wind power earned him esteem and holdings, but he could not bear the sight of his daughter.

"You stole her from me, the only being I've ever loved. I'll never forgive you." Since he proved as good as his word, Maurya had fled his household when she grew to adulthood and never returned.

Perhaps stating Maurya was unloved was incorrect. Maurya enjoyed the friendship of a few herb dealers, and she didn't mind being ostracized from gossip. Besides, her bird friends loved her. She spent most of her time among their delightful chatter and hurried antics.

As she walked to work, a cheeky chickadee hopped among the sparse branches along the path. When she arrived, an angry crowd surprised her. The chickadee flew from the scene with a flurry of feathers.

"Where is she?" the town busybody asked, thrusting her pointed chin into Maurya's face.

The woman's teenaged son, Albert, sneered around his mother's bony shoulders.

Maurya stepped back. "What're you talking about?"

Albert chuckled, his stringy black hair veiling his angular face, but the busybody's skin darkened and her voice raised.

"White Buffalo. What have you done with her?"

Maurya wiped the spray from her cheek and ignored the taunts from the gathered townsfolk. She walked into the mushroom cave. A circle of fungi had formed, but hoof prints and moccasin marks smashed the closest mushrooms into the compost. Maurya bent and touched the ruined crop.

"Could it be?" she wondered aloud. Her fingertips tingled as though she'd touched a tree minutes after lightning struck. She straightened, wiped her hands along her backside, and motioned in a warding symbol. She blinked into the crowd. "I think I know where she's gone."

The town's chief, Maurya's Uncle Tomas, tottered up to loom over her. His breath smelled of garlic. "Since it's your place that lost her and your mind that knows where she'd be, you'd better find her."

The crowd shook fists, glared, and growled with displeasure. Uncle Tomas leaned closer, intensifying his malodorous presence, and whispered, "Don't blow this, woman. You know what that creature means to the town."

He clapped a heavy hand on her shoulder and turned her toward the crowd. "Maurya will return your White Buffalo or not return at all."

The sight of her angry neighbors standing atop manure-rich compost in the underground light embedded on her psyche. Gangly Albert crossed his arms over his chest as a secretive smile cracked the planes of his face. His mother shook with rage. The others' expressions mirrored her obvious sentiment.

They really hate me. She tucked a lock of silvery hair behind her ear and pushed aside the thought. *I need a plan.*

She pulled from Uncle Tomas's grip and walked straight-backed through their disgust.

"I'll be on my way," she said. No point disavowing her involvement in the disappearance. They had their scapegoat, and until the sacred animal returned, they would allow Maurya no peace.

She gathered a bag of supplies, frustrated by the trembling of her hands. "Who cares what they think of me?" she asked a curious robin. "If I can be of help, I'll help White Buffalo." She bid any bird friends in the vicinity best wishes and walked out of town.

Along the way, a tawny-eyed beauty fell in step beside her. Maurya recognized the girl as Leesa's daughter Annalee. As a child, Annalee would stare at Maurya when she brought her wares, but Leesa cuffed her ear and demanded an apology. The child complained, "I've never seen someone so like a spirit."

Maurya had bent to the girl's eye level. "Touch me. See? I'm flesh, just not the same lovely color as you."

After that, Annalee had helped carry Maurya's baskets. She'd grown into a forthright and bold young woman.

As they walked, the girl's chin thrust forward with brash confidence. "Where are you going?"

Maurya shrugged her pack higher onto her shoulder. "To retrieve White Buffalo."

Annalee's harsh laughter frightened a flock of starlings. "You? But you're at least a hundred years old."

Maurya glanced sidelong at the youthful speaker. Strong arms of a farm girl. Lithe legs of a dancer. Sun-kissed, pretty, and brimming with health. "Thanks for noticing."

"Seriously, and aren't you blind or something?"

Maurya adjusted her wide-brimmed hat and internally prayed the sun protection she'd applied would last. "Only during the daylight hours."

"Really? This reeks of a bad idea." Annalee scratched her chin and frowned. "I'm curious. Do you think she's been kidnapped?"

"No. I think she left of her own will."

"Then why bring her back? Maybe she's happy where she is."

Maurya said nothing.

"Answer this. How are you getting her back if you manage to find her?"

Maurya shrugged. "Hope she'll listen to reason."

Annalee doubled over with barking laughter. She wiped away tears. "Yeah, that'll do it." She removed a knife and a strip of rawhide from an interior jacket pocket and cut a piece to tie back her waist-length hair. "Right then, guess I'll be coming with you."

Maurya froze in place and the hairs rose along her neck at the presumption. "You weren't invited."

"Yeah, well, the way I see it, I'm more likely to be able to return with White Buffalo." Her head bobbed with the confidence of youth and health. She lifted the pack from Maurya with ease and rested it on her back. "She's more likely to listen to someone closer to her own age, not some relic." She rested a hand on Maurya's elbow. "No offense intended."

Maurya rubbed her sore shoulder and squinted into the painful glare of day. Who knew how long the journey, and a sighted, able-bodied companion might come in handy, even if she was a willful chit like Annalee. Besides, the recent image of the neighbors brought a lump to her throat. Annalee would be company during a lonely time. "But of course. We'll buy some additional provisions on the way. And you'll have to tell your mother where you're going."

A group of blue jays squawked the news from the treetops, and wrens danced into bushes as they passed. Although unaccustomed to small talk, Maurya found she enjoyed Annalee's chatter as they crested a series of hills. Their conversation reminded her of birdsong.

As the afternoon wore on, Annalee wiped sweat from her brow. "Why's White Buffalo so important, anyway? I mean, we have other buffalo."

Sun exposure had scorched Maurya's skin despite the poultices she'd applied. She poked at a blister. "White Buffalo is descended from the first White Buffalo Woman. All buffalo call the first White Buffalo their ancestor. The first brought our traditions. She brought medicines to heal and taught our people to grow good foods. She taught us to burn tobacco as fragrant conduits for prayer. When famine fell upon our lands, she sacrificed herself so we could survive. We ate her meat and used her skin for our clothes. We crafted her bones into vessels and weapons and painted her skull for the magic she brought." She slathered balm onto her reddened arms. "Our White Buffalo is a symbol of the first White Buffalo Woman. She restores hope for the people and brings promised miracles."

Annalee pulled dried fruit, cheese, and a loaf of bread from their satchel and ate. "You know, I don't understand something. Since White Buffalo is so important, shouldn't the warriors seek her? Why'd they send you?"

Maurya ripped a hunk of bread and chewed. "I don't know, but I couldn't stand by. If I can help, I will."

When Annalee removed a jug of thick milk from its ice packing, Maurya took it from her. "Not this." She offered a canteen of lemonade instead.

After they finished their meal, they continued.

As the sun set, Maurya found her destination. Seven blackened stones stood in a circle, taller than the tallest of men. Maurya and Annalee spoke in whispers away from the sacred site.

Annalee hunched into the shadow of a rowan tree. "Is this the Giant's Dance of the Flame-haired people? Should we be here?"

Maurya studied Annalee's face. "It is, and if we're blessed, this will be our doorway to White Buffalo."

Annalee paled and gulped. "We're going to the Summerland?"

"I believe we'll find White Buffalo there. Hopefully she's not eaten anything." She fixed the girl with a serious gaze. "Please remember, no matter how tempting, you must not eat anything offered you during our time there."

Annalee's hand moved in a warding gesture. "I'll remember."

"Good, because if you eat even a single seed, you'll never be able to survive on normal food again. You'd be trapped." Maurya searched the pack and handed Annalee a bottle. "Before the moon rises, we'll coat our eyelids with this sweet oil. It'll allow us to see through glamours and recognize the invisible, but it's best to keep your vision secret. Okay?"

Annalee nodded.

"And you must be on your best behavior. Good manners will keep you safe. Promise me."

"Yes, I promise."

Maurya nodded. "Don't forget." She reached into the satchel and pulled four bowls and the jug of cream-rich milk. She set the bowls in a circle and filled them with cream and a piece of bread. While she worked, she hummed an old tune she'd heard from her avian friends during her lonely childhood.

The moon cast silvery light over the scene, and Annalee shivered.

"We'll be fine if we remember the rules," Maurya said.

A snowy owl made a silent landing in a nearby maple tree. Maurya smiled a welcome. "Hello, friend! We seek admission to the Summerlands. Have you any suggestions?"

It cocked its head and blinked brilliant amber eyes. With a hushed swoop, it launched and glided into the circle.

"Hurry," Maurya called to Annalee, and they followed the owl into a new, shimmering curtain in the center of the standing stones. Dew moistened their skin and they grew disoriented.

The owl stretched and formed into a tall, pale man wearing a cape of white feathers. He bowed, then blinked huge amber eyes. With an eerie, echoing voice, he said, "Welcome to the Summerlands, Sister Stratus. Good wishes."

Maurya tilted her head, a queer smile upon her lips. "Sister Stratus?"

With a swirl of feathers, he became a mini-whirlwind and regained his owl shape.

Maurya bowed. "Well, thank you!" She watched his retreating form and muttered, "Wonder why he called me Sister Stratus?"

Gentle breezes wafted floral fragrances, setting their hair adrift.

Annalee's face shone with wonder. She touched a strand of Maurya's hair. "Maybe because your hair looks like the stretched clouds of summer afternoons?"

A golden sky bore cotton-thick clouds, but high above, stratus stretched like strands of taffy. The tinkling music of a brook guided them down an embankment and into an emerald glen where people pale as spirits glided in a graceful pattern, an age-old dance set to the rhythm of the seasons. Maurya fought a pull to join them and held Annalee back.

"Don't disturb them. We've got to find White Buffalo."

Annalee's lip jutted out like a thwarted child's. "But it's so beautiful."

Citrus trees mixed with evergreen to make a delightful scent. They crunched fresh russet and yellow leaves underfoot while being crowned with floating spring cherry blossoms that tangled in their hair.

"So many contradictions," Maurya whispered. "Seasons living in unordered harmony."

A myna bird clicked its sunshine-bright beak and repeated, "Contradictions." It tilted its head as though waiting for Maurya to say more.

She cleared her throat. "My, you're a pretty bird. Have you seen White Buffalo? She's from our land."

The bird's throat expanded. Its trilling song commanded attention. Its black bead eyes shifted to a path through a copse of white-blooming trees. Maurya sensed the message. *That way, but be wary.* Maurya smiled her thanks and took her companion's arm. "Let's go."

Moss made their footsteps springy. The sound of a fair made them hurry. In a clearing, a market with a garden of bright booths beckoned.

Clay-like creatures with misshapen hands accepted coins and nodded thick heads. Their language reminded Maurya of a rock slide, deep and grating. They offered their wares to all, but one took an interest in Annalee. The goblin smiled, revealing decayed teeth. His breath reeked of deep, sulfur-filled caverns.

"Try some of my wares, pretty lady." He held a persimmon in one knobby hand and a pomegranate in the other. "Just picked this morning."

Lush, ripe, and sweet-smelling, Maurya never saw such delectable fruit. Her mouth watered. The sounds of the market fell away into a delicate chiming. The goblin's voice grew gentle, and its features softened. The air shimmered and filled with petrichor.

Annalee licked her lips and reached. Her eyes glazed with longing.

A flash of black and orange in the trees, and the myna bird repeated, "Contradictions."

Maurya rubbed her eyes and felt the oil she'd placed there. A drop infiltrated her left eye, and it watered and burned. Her vision blurred, and tears poured over her cheeks. Through her blinking, Maurya's vision clarified in the injured eye, while what she saw from the oil-free eye remained idyllic. The goblin's nasty grin turned triumphant as Annalee raised the fruit to her lips with the intimacy of a kiss. From her unglazed eye, Maurya saw Annalee smile, unaware of her peril.

Maurya lunged as fast as her old body allowed. She slapped the fruit from Annalee's hands. It splatted on the ground, spilling candy-sweet nectar. Annalee protested. The goblins converged, angry, thrusting fruit into the women's faces.

The myna swooped into the market to gobble the fruit, startling the assembly. Maurya grabbed the girl's hand and ran, lips pressed tight against the goblins' continued assault, pressing fruit into their faces. The women pushed their way through the onslaught. Juice ran over their cheeks and chins, sweeter than honeysuckle. Maurya fought the impulse to lick the stickiness and prayed Annalee remembered as well.

All at once, the goblins stopped their holus bolus attack and fell back. The creatures bowed until their noses scraped the ground.

Maurya paused, suddenly nervous. She thought they must have crossed the boundary of the goblin territory, but what caused the horrible creatures to stop their assault?

The goblins grumbled as they returned to their posts.

Maurya's knees wobbled, and she resisted an urge to run. With dread, she turned to face what cowed the goblins.

She gasped, hands covering her mouth. Giants pushed up from the earth, as though the ground birthed them. An imposing king and queen surrounded by an entourage of looming, walking stones regarded them from their great height. The queen's voice crunched like gravel. "I heard you'd come."

Maurya inclined her head as much to show respect as to disguise her confusion.

The king stepped toward her, and the earth shook with his movement. "But why have you come? You don't belong here, daughters of men."

Maurya trembled, but she met his stare.

The giant did not blink its marbled eyes.

"We've come to bring White Buffalo home."

The queen frowned deep crevices into her craggy face. "Why? She came of her own accord."

Maurya discretely wiped the goblin fruit from her face.

Annalee cleared her throat. "Begging your pardon, your ... uh ... queenliness." She fiddled with the hem of her shirt and ahem'ed again. "But why'd she do that? She's revered at home, a beloved symbol of hope and inspiration."

The queen loomed over them. "Here in the Summerlands, we've always prized white cattle. It's something of a game to us, capturing them for our own." Her bulk blocked the sky. "Besides, she's in love with my son."

Maurya and Annalee exchanged startled glances.

The queen continued. "Since she arrived here, though, she's not eaten. My son is distressed and worries himself into sickness because of her."

Maurya elbowed Annalee, and the girl closed her gaping mouth.

With a creak and pop, Maurya straightened her spine. "I'm sorry to hear of his sickness. Maybe I can be of help?"

The king's face darkened. "How could a daughter of men help?"

Annalee raised a finger and stepped forward. "Excuse me, but Maurya's pretty amazing. She grows herbs and mushrooms. Nobody else's plants possess their healing powers. It's like she infuses them with magic. If anyone can help your son, it's Maurya."

Maurya blinked back her surprise and struggled to keep her face composed. Nobody had ever said anything so kind of her or her crops.

Annalee leaned in to whisper, "Don't look so surprised or they won't believe me."

Ah, Maurya thought. *A clever ruse*. She smoothed her furrowed brow.

The king narrowed his eyes with suspicion, but the queen inclined her massive head. "If you're able to help, I'd be grateful."

They followed the rocky court into the rift their passage made in the ground. As they descended deeper into the earth, Annalee grabbed Maurya's hand like a child seeking comfort. They passed through hallways and great chambers until they reached a fissure.

"He's in there," the queen said, and they took their leave.

"Do we knock?" Annalee whispered.

"Who's there?" a pettish voice called. The women stepped into the room. A smaller version of the imposing giants reclined on a black marble couch, arms above his head. A stench like rotting corn emanated from his bared feet.

Annalee gagged and raised a hand to her nose. Maurya shot her a warning look.

The young giant rolled to his elbow. His words slurred together, like pebbles sliding. "What do you want?"

Annalee placed her fists on her hips, but Maurya said, "Your mother worries about you. What ails you?"

He sat up with a grunt and leaned closer to Annalee. "You're pretty."

Annalee frowned.

"Not pretty." He stood. "Strong. Interesting. I think I like you."

Annalee crossed her arms over her chest. "Huh. Do you mean like you like White Buffalo?"

He sat again and glared. "The cow doesn't like me. Thinks she's too good for me. Wants some pretty-boy fairy, I guess, but not me." He rubbed his eyes and turned away.

Maurya stepped closer and placed a hand on his shoulder. "I'm sorry. What a disappointment."

He sniffed. "It was all a lie so she could get to the Summerlands, I guess."

"Did you help her come here, then?"

"Yeah. I saw her in the moonlight last Midsummer. Couldn't get her out of my mind. Her friend said she fancied me and wanted to visit."

"So you formed a mushroom circle in my cave."

He nodded.

"Who's her friend?"

"Don't know his name. Sorry."

Maurya slid to sit beside him, and he rested his head on her lap. She gasped at its weight, but with deliberate strokes, she smoothed his moss-like hair. She hummed a mourning dove's song as she thought.

Annalee sat on the floor cross-legged beside their pack.

"Annalee, will you please bring me my cloak?"

Annalee retrieved it from the bag. The prince sat up and blinked back tears. Maurya unfolded her handiwork and spread it on her lap. "I've been sewing this all my life." To the rough side of the leather she'd sewn feathers molted by her friends. "It was a way to belong somewhere, to the only creatures who bore my company with grace." She traced a flicker's delicate neck feather and fingered the sturdy point of a hawk's flight. "It's awfully big on me now that I'm old and shrinking." She chuckled. "I fear it might be tiny on you, but if you'd like, I'd give it to you as a gift."

His mouth gaped cavernous. "Why?"

Maurya studied him. "I sense we're a lot alike. Yearning for something we can't have." Her smile deepened the lines in her weathered face.

His fingers trembled as he touched the cloak.

Maurya whispered, "It has a secret. You know birds hide well, blend in to become a part of the landscape?"

He nodded.

"When you wear this, you'll blend in, kind of invisible." She patted his hand. "Would you like it?"

"Yes, I would. Thank you."

"Let's try it on, then."

Although the cloak encompassed Maurya, it only fell from his shoulders to his waist and did not meet in the center.

Annalee said, "It looks very nice on you."

He tipped his chin toward his chest, a blush rising in his muddy skin. "Thank you."

Maurya squeezed his hand. "Do you feel a little better?"

He stole a glance at Annalee and blushed deeper. He nodded.

"Good." Maurya stood. "We must find White Buffalo now. Do you know where she is?"

He stood. "Yes. I'll take you there."

The women exchanged a triumphant glance. "That's very kind. Thank you."

He led them above ground, through a spearmint field peppered with grazing sheep. They passed a vineyard and a Grecianlooking temple where laughing nymphs danced in vats to make grape juices and wines.

Annalee's stomach growled, and she licked her lips.

"Have one of the hand pies from the satchel," Maurya said.

Annalee frowned. "No, thanks."

The prince placed a finger to his lips. He pulled the cloak tighter about himself and blended in to the stand of linden and hawthorn trees. The women followed, careful to stay quiet.

In a clearing swayed White Buffalo, longing evident on her features as she stared at a young man leading in a foot race. The other participants strained to catch him, but his fleet movements outstripped them. The crowd of beautiful beings ringing the track erupted in cheers. The victor dipped a bow, flashing a broad, winning smile. White Buffalo's sides heaved with a heavy sigh.

The rock prince whispered like shifting stone, "That's the second son of the Air King. His name's Ariel." He glanced at Annalee. "Everybody loves him."

Annalee looked up at the rock prince with a half-smile. "What's the big deal, anyhow? So he's fast. I bet I could outrun him." She puffed out her chest and pointed to Maurya. "She's probably smarter than him, and I am certain you're stronger."

The rock prince all but disappeared into himself as a blush enveloped him.

A trumpet blast ripped through the air, followed by the gentle tinkling of invisible instruments. With her oil-coated eye, Maurya witnessed tiny fairies blowing into the bells of foxglove. To her uncoated eye, no such whimsical scene appeared. A group of twelve took the field. Maurya shielded her eyes, since the fair folk glowed, and the glow hurt. At the center reigned a female with skin paler than Maurya's. Her silver hair haloed chiseled features, and she moved with fluid grace. Flanking her, armed males shone bright as full moons. Hundreds of luminous moths fluttered around the assembly like enamored snow flurries.

The rock prince whispered, "The Court of the Air and their sylphs."

The woman in the center settled a silver medal around the victor's neck. Ariel made a courtly bow, and the crowd applauded. The woman clapped her hands, and they broke into a raucous dance. The lady and her entourage glided away from the crowd to a stand of birch trees.

Seizing the distraction, Maurya rushed to White Buffalo and threw her arms about her neck. "Friend, you've been missed."

White Buffalo stomped her foot and shook her shaggy head. "No, not one of you! Not a daughter of men. Leave me! I don't belong with your people. I belong here." Her gaze returned to Ariel.

Maurya followed her line of sight. With her uncoated eye, Ariel shook hands, a perfectly formed person. With her coated eye, she saw a whirlwind without measurable form, not human in the least. "I'm not here to lecture you about responsibility. I'm simply overjoyed to see you."

Annalee stepped forward. "You're missed, White Buffalo, but," she said, leaning conspiratorially toward her, "is he why you're here?" She pointed to Ariel.

White Buffalo gulped back tears. Ariel had dipped a dryad until her ivy-tangled hair touched the ground and kissed her with passion.

Maurya wiped her right eyelid, hoping her old skin rejected enough of the oil to be of help. She needed a drop.

Annalee humphed. "He's not worth it, White Buffalo. You outclass him, you know."

White Buffalo's eyes widened in surprise. Her nostrils flared with indignation. She stomped. "You don't know him."

With her coated finger, Maurya poked White Buffalo in the eye. White Buffalo recoiled with a roar, blinking furiously. Hooves flashing, she reared, snorted, and shook her head. She glared at Maurya. "Why'd you do that, old woman?"

"I'm sorry. I thought you had a fly in your eye."

The party had stopped to observe, and White Buffalo shifted her weight from side to side, head low.

Ariel stepped forward, bringing with him a scent of rain. "White Buffalo, isn't it? Are you going to introduce us to your friends? Children of men, aren't they?" He walked around them, and as he circled, Maurya and Annalee's hair tossed and tangled with his breeze.

"They're not my friends." White Buffalo raised her head and gasped. Maurya imagined her surprise. With one eye, Ariel appeared as an Adonis, but he was only a swirl of mad-capped atmosphere. She stepped back, mouth wide with surprise.

Ariel rounded on her. "What's wrong with you, you stupid cow? How dare you stare at me like that?"

Annalee leapt before White Buffalo and pointed a trembling finger at Ariel's chest. "How dare *you* speak to her so disrespectfully? Back off, you blow-hard!"

Ariel retreated a pace, but then closed, using his greater height to menace the smaller woman. "Look here, you're an outsider." He raised his hand as though to strike.

Maurya's arthritic hips creaked as she stretched to stop him, but Ariel's hand froze above his head, captured in the newly visible grip of the Rock Prince.

The Rock Prince growled like an avalanche, "Don't you dare strike a lady. Not in my presence."

Ariel unraveled a bit when he considered the Rock Prince's face. He pulled his hand from the prince's grip and backed away toward Annalee and White Buffalo.

White Buffalo butted him with her horn. "Watch your step. You could have hurt my friend."

Annalee wrapped an arm atop White Buffalo's neck.

Ariel shook his head and swept through the crowd who shrugged and followed him.

White Buffalo blinked at them, head lowered. "I've been a fool."

Annalee kissed her cheek. "Who hasn't been a fool for love? Would you like to go home now?"

A tear trickled over White Buffalo's snout. She licked it with a soft, pink tongue. "This feels like home."

Annalee sighed. "I understand. Everything's more vibrant here. Prettier." She blushed and looked up at the Rock Prince. "More interesting."

The Rock Prince sidled closer to Annalee.

"Besides, I can't talk at home. I guess that's why nobody ever asked what I wanted." White Buffalo sniffed. "Well, almost nobody."

Maurya's head snapped up. "Almost nobody? Please, White Buffalo, who listened? Who helped you? Who was your friend and accomplice?" She recalled the townsfolk standing atop the compost, hate in their eyes. One had smirked. The son of the busybody. "Was it Albert?"

The Rock Prince stiffened. "Albert said you loved me."

White Buffalo had the good grace to look ashamed. "I love the Summerlands."

The Rock Prince grumbled, "I gave him a handful of diamonds to tell you how to get here."

White Buffalo shifted her weight and whispered, "Thank you." She lowered her large, bovine eyes. "I never meant to hurt you."

Birdsong filled the awkward silence.

Maurya pondered. "We can tell the town elder you're happier here. The elder can seek recompense for your loss from Albert, since he's responsible for your flight in a way, and he is in possession of a small fortune as a result." Maurya patted White Buffalo. "They will have to understand. Everyone should have a say in how they live their life, even a sacred being."

White Buffalo blinked back happy tears. "Thank you."

A reveler vaulted by with a fragrant tray. Maurya's stomach rumbled.

"May I have something to eat from the pack, please, Annalee?"

The girl recoiled as though the food in the pack had rotted. She thrust the satchel to Maurya.

Realization dawned on her, and Maurya gaped. "Oh, Annalee, you ate some of the goblin fruit, didn't you?"

"I licked my lips. One lick." Annalee's cheeks colored.

Maurya looked skyward. "That's all it takes. One lick. One seed. Just one."

Annalee's voice shook. "So I'll never be able to eat normal food again?"

"Not from what I've read."

"What'll happen to me?"

Maurya did not meet her anxious gaze. "If you can't get goblin food, you'll waste away. Starve to death."

The Rock Prince knelt before her. "Never fear. I'll bring you food every day."

Annalee set a hand on his shoulder. Tears collected but didn't fall. "I couldn't ask so much of you."

The Rock Prince straightened, his gaze fixed on Annalee's face. "It would be my pleasure."

"Maybe I could find a home here, you know, so I wouldn't be so far away." Annalee smiled at the prince.

Maurya chewed her lip. "You're both grown. I can take a message to your mother if you want, Annalee, and tell everyone your wishes, White Buffalo."

"Why go?" Annalee clasped Maurya's hands in hers. "Didn't the elder tell you to either bring back White Buffalo or not return? White Buffalo wants to stay. I want to stay. Why don't you stay, too?"

Maurya blinked, realizing the light in the Summerlands did not cause her eyes to ache. "And do what?"

"What you did at home, I suppose." Annalee squeezed her hands. "But here, you wouldn't be alone. We'd be together."

The Rock Prince and White Buffalo nodded.

"How would we get the message to the others?"

The owl who had guided them to the Summerlands swept from a linden tree and landed at her feet. "I would be your messenger, my friend. You've always been kind to me and to my people. Please write the notes, and I'll deliver them."

Annalee giggled as she wrote two letters, one to her mother and one to the tribe on behalf of White Buffalo.

"Don't come looking for us, because we are much happier here in the Summerlands. We are independent beings and will make and live with our own life decisions, thank you very much." Annalee's eyes sparkled. "What do you think, Maurya? Are you staying with us?"

Maurya reached for a blueberry resting atop a laden tray. As she popped it into her mouth, she smiled.

THE END

Kerry E.B. Black writes from a butter-yellow bungalow sinking into a swamp along the Allegheny River. This lover of fairy tales attended Penn State University and has worked several "day jobs" to support her writing habit, including journalist, membership and event coordinator, horse groomer, karate instructor, tutor, and pharmacy tech. Hobbies of this confirmed bibliophile include world travel, costume design, archery, gaming, and of course reading. Please follow Kerry at:

https://kerrylizblack.wordpress.com/
www.facebook.com/authorKerryE.B.Black
https://twitter.com/BlackKerryblick
https://www.amazon.com/Kerry-E.B.-Black/e/B00IKURGVS/
https://www.goodreads.com/author/show/17521186.Kerry_E_B_Black

Muffled Gold

Mythology
Metal

Avery D. Cabot

Present

B y gods. What in Hades am I going to do? I struggle not to bite my fingernails. It's not a very manly thing to do. A king's nails should be smooth and well-polished. Not all raggedy and torn.

Just *fuggetyfudge*.

Look at her.

What am I going to do? She's so ... gold. This was not what was intended to happen. I swear to all of the gods from Zeus to Hades, I never intended to harm anyone, least of all my baby.

I walk around her, sizing her up and down. Really, her likeness is striking. Each strand of Arianna's thick dark curls has been replaced by a wisp of gold thread waving in the breeze. Her once bright brown eyes and pretty pink mouth are round with surprise, glimmering like the sun. She is so life-like, I half expect to feel the elastic give of her skin by brushing her cheek. My fingers trace her face, but there is no give. She is solid and cold. How can someone with such a warm heart be so frigid?

This is a complete and total disaster. I know ... Maybe I can convince people a statue was made of the child? The people love Arianna. They may appreciate a statue in her likeness they can worship. They could make offerings to the statue to win her affections. Surely they would never really think it was my daughter. How long before they grew suspicious? When would they notice Arianna was missing? A day? A week? Could I convince them she wasn't missing at all? How long could such a charade continue? But still ... I'd miss her.

I need to stop pacing and biting my nails. Panicking isn't getting me anywhere. It's time to breathe and think, but the more I try to calm down, the more erratic my breathing becomes. A wave of nausea hits me picturing the mob coming to dethrone my sorry behind. Perhaps it's well deserved.

I break out of my reverie when I hear footsteps slapping on the marble floor. They are going to see the monstrosity which was once my beloved daughter, and they will immediately know

what I have done. How could they not after the events of the last week? My heart is beating in my temples as I try to regulate my breathing to calm myself. It's not working. There is only one thing left to do.

I suck in my protruding gut, bend my knees and grunt, and try to lift the solid gold mass. Though Arianna is a mere four feet tall, she barely lifts off the ground. I drop her back to the floor, the sound echoing through the empty hall. Arianna had been light as a feather. Gold is heavy like the lead in my stomach.

Fuggetyfudge.

Panting while leaning on my child's head, I need to think fast. I whip off my robe, leaving my toga behind, and cover her. It's a pathetic attempt to hide the little statue, but I'm out of options. If I manage to survive this, I'll find a better way to move her. I hear the usual sounds of people moving around the castle, going about their everyday tasks. Hopefully, no one important is approaching Arianna and me, and if they do, they won't stick around.

I see the shadow before the man. I'm screwed.

Deo approaches, body erect, chin raised, and a haughty grin as always. I hate Deo. He thinks he's so much smarter than me just because he's my head advisor. Someday I'm going to scream at him. Deo may be better at ruling a country, but I'm the one with the royal blood. He's got nothing on me. Well, unless he figures out what I've done to Arianna. I'm smarter than he thinks. I know he wants to be king. *Not happening.* He's not next in line for the throne. Arianna is. Or was. If Arianna is out of the way then, yes, I suppose he could be a contender. He'd be thrilled to know about my blunder.

"Your Majesty." Deo forces himself to bow to me, but really it's barely more than a head nod.

"Deo." My voice sounds casual. I lean on Arianna's head to be certain my robe can't fall off. I hope she can't feel my weight. For the first time, I consider the possibility she may still be aware of the world around her.

"I've come to check on you. How are you and your ... *condition?*" Deo snarls the last word with derision. He grins, showing every tooth in his narrow mouth, but it looks more like a sneer than a smile. He doesn't need to say he's been enjoying my situation, waiting for catastrophe to strike. Determined not to let him have the satisfaction, I will figure out how to cure Arianna before he learns what has happened.

"It has been dealt with." I lie.

"Good. I will inform Queen Callista. She will be most pleased. Will you be joining her for dinner?"

Why the gods would my advisor be passing information on to my wife? There are messengers for this purpose. My eyes narrow as I examine his expression closer. He gives nothing away, though. He has been much too interested in my *condition* as he calls it. I smile, but it doesn't reach my eyes.

"No. I'll be dining alone."

"For shame. Arianna will be most disappointed. She was looking forward to dining with both her parents this evening."

"I am certain the child will be fine, Deo. Don't you have more important matters to attend to? I expect your daily report to be on time today." My chin rests on the palm of my hand, where my elbow leans on my robe. I feel ridiculous.

Deo raises his eyebrows. "I have never been late, Your Majesty. Is everything all right? You are standing funny. Do you need the physician?"

"I am well, thank you. You would be good to inform the queen I will not be at the meal this evening."

It's not like I'll miss having dinner with Ice Goddess Callista. It's clear my daughter received her exquisite beauty from her mother, but she got her charm from me. My wife has the personality of a snake. I gladly avoid her as much as possible lest I end up having to bed her again in an attempt to produce a more worthy heir. I'm perfectly happy with Arianna as my prodigy. She is a bright, lively child who has already won the hearts of her people at a young age, and I suspect she'll be a worthy ruler someday.

If she can ever speak again.

Fuggetyfudge.

How did my life slip into this disaster? All I wanted was a nice gift for Arianna. Something fun. A little golden ball or something of the like.

Deo continues to stand erect as an arrow. He doesn't even shift his weight. Never trust someone who can do this. He's not stiff like a soldier. It's more like he's showing off his perfect posture. Deo is long and lanky, with bones and angles protruding everywhere. He's handsome in his own way. Women fawn over him, but he never seems to notice. They fawn all over me too, but I'm the king. They'd fawn all over me if I had two heads and no teeth.

I need Deo to go before he decides he wants to see under my robe and discovers Arianna. There is nothing further to discuss as far as I'm concerned, but he remains standing there, silent.

"You are dismissed." Yes. Definitely dismissed. Please go away before I fall over or my robe slips. Somehow Deo has failed to notice there shouldn't be anything here to lean on, proving he isn't as smart as he thinks he is. Or he is playing with me so he can find out later. Either way, I want him to leave.

"Of course, Your Majesty." Deo gives his typical head bob and turns away. He knows better than to turn his back on royalty, but I let it go this time. I welcome the opportunity to stand up straight. My back aches, and my knees are about to give. He can't know what's under the robe, but I'm sure he believes it's another casualty of my *condition*. He has to be hoping it's the final catalyst to tear me down once and for all.

He stops as he reaches the door to make his exit. His upper lip curls. "You know, Your Majesty, if you needed my assistance in anything—especially anything regarding your condition—my only purpose is to serve you."

Did I mention my palms are feeling sweaty right about now? "You have always been a most faithful servant, Deo. I assure you, you're the first person who will come to mind if help is needed."

"I have been doing some research of my own. I believe if you speak to Dionysus directly, he can—"

"We both know I'd be risking offending him. I'd be better off living out the rest of my life dealing with the consequences of this curse than angering a god. Now, again. You are dismissed."

Once he is gone, I consider again how to move Arianna to some place where no one will find her. I figure I am not going to be able to go it alone. I am many things, but physically strong isn't one of them.

I go to move my robe and realize it too has turned to gold. Why didn't I think of this? Now, not only is my daughter's beautiful face covered with a solid gold robe and I'm not sure it can be removed, but I've made her heavier. I rub my hands across my face.

What if she is still breathing? Is the robe going to suffocate her? Is Arianna even alive? What if—

I break down in unmanly sobs, not caring if anyone sees. Well, except for Deo, but he's not anyone. Little Arianna is my world. Or she was. I love her to the sun and moon and back again. She is the only person I enjoy being around. She loves me as me. Not as a king. Not as a man of undetermined wealth and power. I'm just her Baba who plays ball with her after the evening feast, tells her a bedtime story every night, tickles the bottom of her feet and tucks her in. I can't go on without my baby girl.

I'm not good at many things. I'm definitely not very good at being the king. Oh, my advisors treat me like there's a clue in my head, but we all know Deo is running the show, and he's biding his time until he can figure out how to place my crown on his head and take the credit. Here is what I am good at. Parenting. Or was. I guess I suck at parenting too.

I never should have accepted the wish from Silenus. Anyone with half a brain knows wishes come with consequences. Anyone with half a brain knows this, but clearly I don't even have a quarter of one. Especially when I am drunk.

I swear, if there is a way to restore Arianna, I will never drink wine again. Not even if Dionysus, God of Wine himself, comes to pay me a visit. Ten days of feasting and drinking is not a healthy way to live. I don't recall much of those ten days, either passed out or living in an intoxicated haze, but I'm certain I did other regrettable things. I have this vague recollection of calling Callista a dried-up barren hag and possibly bedding a couple of the maids. Could have been a mere dream, but it would explain why my wife has been icier than normal.

Strangely, it was Deo's idea to throw the feast for Silenus. I hadn't even recognized him as a close follower of Dionysus, but Deo had. You can count on my advisor to know who is who in the world of important people. I think he's been climbing the social ladder since he was a mere babe in his mother's womb. I don't even care for parties, but when Deo says we need to honor someone, feast it is. Deo made all the arrangements, and I pretended to host it. I thought the party went well when Silenus wanted to thank me with a wish, but now I think I shouldn't have accepted it. Or should have made my wish when I was completely sober. Deo pushed me to accept the gift as soon as possible. He didn't make any wish suggestions. I think he knew no matter what I wished for, the results would end up disastrous.

I wished for gold.

Like I don't have enough already. It sounded like it would be fun.

Now everything I touch turns to gold—my bed, my food, my clothes, and even my daughter.

Fugg-et-y-fudge.

I pull myself up with resolve, determined to fix this myself. Deo wants me to come to him for help so he can take one more step closer to usurping my kingdom. I won't let him. A different man in my position would shut the bugger up with a big hug and watch his veins harden into metal more valuable than my advisor's advice, but I can't bring myself to do it. I will figure out how to restore my precious daughter all by myself and prove to everyone I'm not an ineffectual boob.

Arianna, Two Weeks Prior

These parties are sooo boooring! I don't even like Mister Silly-nus. He smells funny. Like Dee-oh's farts. No one says anything, but Dee-oh toots all the time. I try not to giggle, but it's so hard. I don't think Baba likes the parties either, but he has to go to them. I asked him if he'd play ball with me. I always have my ball. He said he had to go to the party. It's what kings have to do. I'll understand when I'm a grownup and a queen.

Can you imagine being a queen? Everyone is going to have to listen to me me me. No one listens to me now because I'm just a dumb kid. Dee-oh says I won't be queen, but Baba says I will. Dee-oh says I have to have a brother and he'll be king. I don't want a baby brother. Boys smell. Except Baba. He smells nice, like warm olives. The green ones are my favorite.

I try to steal just one more olive, but Mama slaps my hand and gives me her evil look. If I eat too many she says I'll plump up, which is bad for some reason. I need to be a pretty princess. I'd rather be a tree-climbing princess. I like to climb the olive trees and look out over all of Baba's kingdom. Mama doesn't like it.

There are lots of grown-ups at the party, but no kids for me to play with. Even my nanny, Lindy, isn't looking at me. She is letting one of the guards stick his tongue in her mouth. It's so gross! Lindy warned me earlier to be on my best bee-hay-ver. Silly-nus is very important, she said. He's friends with a real god. Who cares? Gods are boring. Especially the God of Wine. Wine is yucky. I can't even say his name, and I'm good at saying big words.

I try not to cry when Mama smacks my hand. I'm trying to show Dee-oh I can act like a queen. I stand straight and stick my chin high in the air until my neck hurts. I walk away from the big plate of olives and move into the crowd. It's hot and stuffy, and I don't like the way the grown-ups keep bumping into me like I'm not really there. Lindy still isn't paying attention to me, so I head to the garden outside. I like the pretty doorway. Baba said it's called an archway.

The garden is my favorite place. The boh-gan-villy are my favorite flowers. They have big pink petals. I like to pick them and put them in my hair. There's a big stone well. Lindy says I'm not big enough to fetch water from it, and it's not proper bee-hay-ver for a princess. I don't care. It's fun. Water tastes better when you drink it from a well bucket. Bet you didn't know.

The rope to the bucket is prickly on my hands, but I lower it anyway. I don't like it when grown-ups insist on helping, so I ignore the pain. Splash! The wood touches the water, and I scoop some up. I smile, feeling essited as the bucket comes back up. I'm ready to drink it without even getting a cup when I notice a big ugly frog sitting on the edge staring at me. It has big yellow googly eyes. Green warts cover the gross slimy thing, and his long tongue slithers over his lips like he's going to lick me. The little hairs on my arms are sticking up, and I feel cold. I give the bucket a good hard shove so both it and the frog go splashing back down the well. I hear Lindy's voice calling me and head back inside.

"Where, by Gods, have you been, little girl?" Lindy scolds me and roughly takes my wrist. Her small sharp hands are cold and they hurt, but I don't cry out. "The king has been requesting you."

I grin now and skip alongside Lindy. She no longer needs to hold my hand so hard. I want to see Baba. Maybe he'll play ball with me. I'm tired of the stupid well and the gross frog. Baba looks tired. His eyes are red and his skin is pink, but when he sees me he smiles a real smile. Not the fake ones he gives to people he doesn't really like, like Dee-oh and Silly-nus. He scoops me up in his big arms and pulls me into his warm soft chest. I don't usually like hugs, but Baba is different. He's Baba.

"Where has my girl been? I've missed you."

I try to give him my biggest smile. The one showing every one of my little pearl-like teeth. "I was at the well."

Baba laughs. "I'm sure Lindy was not pleased!"

"She didn't catch me."

"Well, good thing."

"Baba, there was a big ugly frog sitting on the bucket. It was staring at me. I think it wanted to eat me."

Baba narrows his eyebrows trying to look mad. I think he's going to laugh instead. "Now calling the frog ugly isn't nice at all, Arianna. We must treat all creatures in our country as special and beautiful or they won't want to live here."

I hear a snort. I lift my head from Baba's broad chest and see Dee-oh. "Frogs are far from important, Your Highness."

"Not true, Arianna," Baba corrects Dee-oh. "Frogs are as important as any of the gods' creatures, and it is our job to be kind to them and care for them."

"I don't care. The frog was still gross."

"Arianna." Baba's voice says enough. I pout and wrap my arms tighter around him.

"The frog is gone anyway. I pushed him back into the well."

"Next time you see the frog, I expect you to say you're sorry and invite him to the feast."

"But Baba, I'm not sorry."

"You will be sorry if you don't."

"Okay, Baba." I wipe a tear from my cheek. I don't like it when Baba scolds me.

"Now, how about a pastry?" Baba reaches for a slice of flaky dessert soaked in honey and covered with nuts. "We won't tell Mama."

My lips are sticky and sweet, and I lick my fingers after the last bite. Silly-nus is heading our way. I wish I could hide, but can only bury myself so deep into Baba. I can smell Silly-nus before he reaches us.

"Your Majesty." Silly-nus has a weaslley voice. He doesn't bow like others do. He looks like a dumb horse. Lindy explained it's because Baba isn't his king, and they are equals. I don't care. I like it when people bow.

"Silenus, please come sit with us. You've met my daughter, Arianna, of course."

"Yes, several times."

Silly-nus doesn't look at me. I don't think he finds me very interesting. I'll show him someday. I'm the most fascinating person in the world. I stifle a yawn. I'm also the sleepiest person in the world, but I won't say so. I don't want to go to bed.

"She's a most lovely child, and you should be proud. I just wanted to thank you for your hospitality. My time here has been exceptional, and Dionysus will be most pleased when I inform him of your kindness."

"The gratitude is all mine," Baba responds. "I must thank you for being kind enough to grace us with your presence."

Silly-nus bows. "With the graciousness of Dionysus, I want to offer you a gift to show my appreciation."

"Very honorable of you, good sir, but if I drink one more goblet of wine I will most certainly have issues."

"Then it is a good thing I do not plan to give you wine, unless of course you wish it. I am granting you one wish—any wish you desire, and I will make it come true."

A wish! I pop up from Baba's chest, essited at the news. I've always wanted a real wish. I wonder what Baba will request.

Maybe toys for me! Or new ribbons for my hair. A new ball would be the best. A gold one!

"A wish? What use do I have with a wish? I am the king. I have everything I could possibly desire."

"Everyone desires something they can't have, Your Majesty."

Baba's eyes lower and the corners of his mouth turn down as though this makes him sad. Why would a wish make him frown? It only lasts a second and Baba's face brightens into a smile. "I know! Arianna, what would you wish for?"

I answer right away. "I want a new ball. A golden one. My old one is yucky."

"It's a brand new ball," Baba says.

"But it's red. I've had lots of red balls. I want a golden one. I wish everything was gold. It's my new favorite color."

"Well, all right. You heard the girl. She wants a golden ball. She wants everything gold. Make it so I can make her wish come true."

"As you wish, Your Majesty."

Present

Near the kitchen, there's a cart my servants use to transport heavy items around the castle. As soon as my fingertips brush the handle it transforms to gold, but fortunately the wheels still function. The cart is heavier than it would have been if it had remained wood, but it at least is in working order, right? Gold is stronger than wood, and will most likely better handle the weight, too. If I can lift Arianna just enough to place her on it, I

should be able to wheel her into the closet in my dressing room until there's a better plan. I only have to be able to lift her a foot, but last time I tried I only managed a couple of inches before she almost landed on my toe. And what if I topple her? Making her upright will be near impossible.

I am able to remove my solid gold robe from over my daughter's head. I'm guessing this is possible because it had transformed at a different time. I'm still learning how this curse works. Lifting the robe makes my fingers ache, but I am relieved to see Arianna's face is unchanged. I'm not certain what I had expected to see. I leave the robe on the marble floor. Arianna is my only concern.

I bend my knees and wrap my arms around the child's middle in an embrace. I wish I could breathe warmth into her and she would melt into me. I pull in a deep breath and lift.

Nothing.

Not an inch.

I lifted her further before.

I let go and pace the room, stretching my fingers. I head back to her, put my knees into it, and try again. I let out a grunt and feel her lift just a smidge. Not enough to even come close to success. I release her again, turn my back on her, and slide to the floor. I rest my head in my hands, trying to fight off the desperation. I need help. Someone is sure to enter the hall sooner rather than later.

I could have Deo retrieved.

He'd know what to do. He'd have Arianna restored again in no time. At what cost? My crown? Would he finally tell everyone

I'm not capable of ruling over them? It's been a matter of time until he does. I'm fooling myself to even try.

No.

I'm not going to let Deo get in my head when he's not even standing here. What would Arianna do? Arianna may be small, but she is fierce. She wouldn't give up before she even tried. I can't let her down. If Deo takes the crown she'll lose her birthright.

I could call on a lesser servant. How can I be certain they'll keep my secret? A cruel king might cut their tongue or worse to prevent gossip. I'm not a cruel king. This is something I need to do myself. I stand again, resolved to be successful this time.

I embrace her tighter than before and put my back into it though I may injure myself. I pull her toward me, hoping she won't topple and crush me. By sheer adrenaline, I manage to lift her and barely slide her onto the cart. I want to dance. Maybe kiss someone. She is firmly standing on the cart, waiting for me to push her to a safer location. I lean in, plant a kiss on her cool cheek, and push the cart, silently praying to the gods no one will be in my way. I decide she should be left on the cart in case I need to move her again in a hurry. I am panting from the exertion, but I smile. It is good to take care of my own problem for a change.

I remind myself nothing has been fixed. I've bought myself some time while I think about what I'm going to do, but remain completely clueless. I barely know how to dress myself and have to figure out if it is even possible for her to be human again. I realize my dressing room may not be safe come morning when I need to be dressed by one of my manservants. I don't trust them to keep quiet any more than I do any other servant. Deo has ears everywhere. It occurs to me not for the first time—I am not a man with many true friends.

I look into my daughter's expressionless eyes. "I love you, darling. Baba will fix this. I don't know how, but I will. I hope you don't know what's happening, but if you can hear me, it's going to be all right. I need to leave you here, but I'll be back. I promise with all my heart." I kiss her cheek again. I swear there's a tear in her eye, but I blink and it's gone.

Arianna will be fine where she is for now. I will leave her to contemplate my next move. If I am lucky she'll be human before I ever have to change my clothes again. I head back to the halls where I hear Lindy's voice calling her charge.

Fuggetyfudge.

Arianna, A Week and a Half Ago

I don't like sitting in the throne room. It's boring, and my chair makes my bum hurt. Baba usually says I don't have to. He says little kids like me belong outside playing. I'm not a little kid. I'm all grown up, but I'd rather go outside so I don't say anything. Today he said he wants me inside like a good little princess. He promised I'm going to love it. Mama is sitting next to me. She looks mad, but she always does.

There are always lots of people in the throne room and it's hot. They all want something from Baba. No one is there just to be his friend. I think being king must be lonely. It's hard to have friends when you're a princess, too. Lindy acts like she's my friend, but I know she isn't really.

We are all waiting for Baba to make his entrance, when the doors swing open and a trumpet plays. He is standing there, hands high in the air, feet spread apart, and smiling. He glides into the room almost like he's dancing. I've never seen him so essited before. Baba twirls, his robes flying around him like a flower. I wiggle my bum to the end of my chair to get a closer look.

"Ladies and gentlemen! Feast your eyes on my amazing magnificence! Of all the kings, there has never been a more powerful one than I!" The people clap for Baba as he steps up to the dais where his throne waits. "I can do something the rest of you can only imagine!"

This isn't like Baba at all. I'm essited, but also a little scared. I'm not sure I like this. I glance at Mama. Her face hasn't changed. She looks like the angry statue of Hera in front of the castle. Lindy says Hera is mad because I never bee-have. Is Baba being bad?

"Deo, bring me something! Anything!" Baba shouts. Deo brings him a stone goblet filled with wine. Bowing, he hands it to him. As soon as the goblet touches Baba's fingers, it begins to shimmer. The color slides from a cool grey to bright gold. I pop out of my chair, jumping up and down, before Mama pinches me.

The rest of the people in the room cheer loudly. I have to cover my ears. Everyone starts yelling, asking him to do it again, each one wanting him to touch something belonging to them. I see

Silly-nus in the crowd, and he doesn't look happy. I remember the wish he promised. Baba needs to say thank you for the gift, but he's not paying any attention to the strange man. Silly-nus moves toward the door and leaves Baba and the rest of us to play with all of the new gold.

Baba makes his rounds, turning a thing or two into gold. Some people who ask are ignored, and others he finds on purpose. Even Mama is interested now, but when Baba catches my eye, everyone else may as well disappear. Even Mama.

"Arianna, darling. I did this for you. Where is your ball?"

I feel in my pocket and pull it out. I don't want to give it to him. I wanted it to be gold before, but now I like it the way it is. I don't want it to change like the way Baba has. I shake my head.

"Arianna, listen to your father." Mama's voice is stern. I hand him the ball, and it turns into gold.

"I love you, sweetheart. You may run along and play with your ball. Just make sure you come in for dinner."

A ball of gold does not bounce. It clinks and rolls away. My red ball bounced. I want it back. I rub my arms even though I'm not cold. I reach to pick it up and decide I don't want it anymore. I throw it into the well and listen for the splash.

"Ouch!"

I jump. There's no one out here but me.

"Is this your ball?"

"Who's there?"

"Me."

I see the frog from a few days ago. He is holding my ball in his mouth.

"Gimme! It's my ball!"

"Not anymore. You threw it away. It's mine now."

"It is not! Baba made it just for me. No one else."

"He made it to show off."

"Did not!" My face grows hot. "Give it back!"

"Hmmm. Why should I give it back?"

"I was playing with it."

"How does one play ball all alone, Princess?"

I look at my feet. "Baba plays with me."

"I'll bet he can't even touch you without turning you to gold. You need new friends."

"How'm I going to find new friends? I'm not allowed to leave."

"I'll be your friend."

"You can't be my friend! You're a frog!"

"And you, Princess, are rude."

"Am not!"

"Prove it."

"How?" I fold my arms across my chest and pout. I need to get the ball back or Baba will be sad.

"Let me keep the ball you threw at me."

"I didn't throw it at you. I was trying to see if it would bounce in the well."

"Oh, please." I think the frog rolled his eyes. "Anyway. You give me the ball and be my friend. If you truly act as my friend, letting me share your meals with you and sleep in your bed, I will give

you your ball back, because I know it's what a real friend would do."

Shivering, I imagine a slimy yucky frog in my bed. What if he tries to kiss me with his gross tongue? I am not sharing my dinner with the frog. *No way.* I picture Baba sad and want to cry. I nod, promising to be friends with the ugly frog.

Present

I don't like Lindy, but at least Deo doesn't like her either. She's Callista's girl. If I had my way, Arianna wouldn't have a nanny at all. I want to raise my daughter myself. Deo doesn't like this idea any more than he approves of Lindy. It is his belief Lindy fills Arianna's head with visions of grandeur, and teaches the child of her importance. I wish he was correct, but Lindy does nothing of the sort. She mostly thrusts her tongue down the throat of one of my guards, and occasionally gives Ariana a good tongue lashing. My daughter was born knowing she is important.

Lindy, however, isn't important. She can't help me restore Arianna. If she found out, she would most likely gossip to anyone who'd listen.

"Your Majesty." Lindy makes a low curtsy when she catches sight of me.

"You may rise."

Lindy stands, but keeps her eyes lowered, as though she is interested in the marble floor. Unlike Deo, she is aware of her status and mine.

"How is my daughter?"

"Um ... well ..."

I keep my voice stern. "You don't know where she is, do you?"

"I ... I do. I mean, she was playing by the well, Your Majesty."

"You let the princess play next to a well unattended? How do you know she hasn't fallen in?"

Lindy is fidgeting with her hands, and shifting her weight from one foot to the other, her eyes not blinking. "I ... I'm most certain she has not!"

I almost feel guilty for what I'm putting her through. Almost. I mean, why *doesn't* she know what happened to Arianna? It is her job after all. "I think you have no idea where my daughter is. I think you have been spending too much extra time with one of the guards. George, I believe?"

I watch the flush rise from Lindy's arms to the roots of her dirty-blonde hair. "I ... well ... I was just looking for her."

"And why don't you know where she is?"

Lindy looks up from the marble floor, but she can't meet my eyes. Good. I'm not the only person who screwed up today. "I may have looked away for a moment."

I begin calculating in my head the length of time from when I accidentally turned Arianna to gold, to my conversation with Deo, and finally to successfully moving her to my dressing room. Lindy has looked away from my daughter for more than a mere moment. My guilt washes away, and is replaced by anger. I'm not toying with her any longer.

"I expect my daughter's nanny to be aware of her whereabouts at all times, otherwise why does she even need a nanny? Is this a good job? Are you not being compensated fairly for such an esteemed position as the nanny for the future queen of your country?"

"The pay is more than fair, Your—"

"Then I expect you to know where she is. Fortunately for you, Arianna is not lying broken at the bottom of a well. She came to see me, and she is sound asleep on the couch in my quarters."

"Oh, thank the gods!" Lindy's face relaxes. It occurs to me this is the perfect opportunity to keep her from looking for Arianna again.

"Don't be so thankful. I'm not pleased with you. Perhaps you need the week off without pay so you may remember your purpose here."

"Yes, Your Majesty." She bobs into a curtsy. "You won't touch me and turn me to gold, will you?"

I shudder. Does she think me the sort of king—no, man—who would render a cruel punishment? "Of course not."

She gives me a deeper curtsy, and I dismiss her. No one else should look for Arianna again until Lindy returns. There's Callista, but she pays little interest in our daughter unless Arianna is seated in court, and then it's only to admonish her. Motherhood doesn't suit the queen. I decide the answer lies with Silenus. He blessed me with this curse, and it stands to reason he is the one who would know how to fix it. I call for one of my manservants and request a message be delivered to him, hoping he will agree to pay me a visit.

Tired, I plop onto a bench. I'm grateful to be alone in my thoughts. I'm not allowed much alone time, though this has been one benefit of my curse. At first, no one could get enough of my new ability, but then I touched one of the guards and he froze into gold. Since then, my people have feared me and stayed away. I didn't miss the expression on Lindy's face.

My vision blurs as exhaustion tries to overtake me. I need to stay awake. I startle when I notice a frog hopping through the hall. How strange. Animals rarely if ever are seen inside my castle. Didn't Arianna mention something about pushing a frog into the well? I swear the amphibian is staring at me as though it is going to start to speak to me. Ridiculous. Frogs can't talk. I must be dreaming now. I need to wake before Silenus arrives.

Arianna, This Morning

"Let me cross the bridge, you big ugly troll!" I jump onto a marble bench waving my big stick sword.

"Go ahead and try to cross my bridge. I'll gobble you up." Frog hops toward the base of the bench, and sticks his long pink tongue at me.

"You don't want to eat me. You should wait for my brother as he is bigger and fatter than me." I walk across the bench as though it is a bridge and jump down. Running around, I pump out my chest, preparing to become the older brother.

"I want to eat a billy goat."

"You don't want to eat me. My big brother is coming, and he is much bigger than me. Let me cross the bridge and you can eat him."

"I know how this works. I let you cross, I'm still hungry, and your big brother comes and pushes me off the bridge. We are changing it up this time, billy goat. I'm eating you."

I hear Lindy calling me to breakfast. I love playing with Frog. He's my best friend now. I don't care anymore if he gives me my ball back. I don't like eating with him though. I kinda hope he doesn't hear Lindy.

"Princess. I believe it's time for breakfast. Will you pick me up?"

I roll my eyes, but I reach down for my friend. His skin isn't slimy like I had thought it would be. It's warm and papery. I don't mind touching him. He hops into my hand, and I slide him into my pocket. He squirms a bit until his face is popping out the top and he can watch where we are going.

I have a small table in my quarters where I eat my breakfast alone. I only eat dinner with my parents, and Lindy prefers to eat with the other staff. It's nice to have Frog sit with me, but I don't like the way he eats. He hops out of my pocket and sits on the edge of my plate. His large unblinking eyes stare at me, as his long pink tongue flickers out. The food sticks to his tongue as he pulls it back into his mouth. And he drools. Puddles of goo form on my plate.

Lindy is bustling around straightening out my room while we eat. It makes me feel like screaming. Why can't she wait until I'm outside playing? She doesn't pay much attention to Frog most of the time, but she looks over and wrinkles her nose this morning.

"Princess, what is on your plate?"

"It's Frog."

"We don't eat with animals. It's dirty."

"Frog is my friend."

Frog sits up straighter as though I scared him or something. If he had ears I think they'd be erect. "Friend?" he whispers.

"Yeah," I whisper back.

Frog disappears into Lindy's hand as she pulls him from my plate and throws him out the window. "Goodbye, disease-ridden nasty thing."

"But—" I jump from my seat and run to the sill. My hand reaches out as though I could catch him, but Frog has already landed. He is hopping away, not turning back. I think he's hurt because of the way he leans to the right. "He's my friend."

"Silly girl. You can't be friends with a frog."

My dark curls whip my cheek as I turn around, and I clench my fists. I want to punch my stupid nanny. I count to three like Baba taught me, tears stinging my eyes. I take a deep breath, imagining throwing her out the window.

"Now finish your breakfast. The king plans to spend his morning with you."

I can almost forget Frog when I hear Baba wants to spend time with me, but I'm worried my friend is hurt. Maybe Baba can help me find Frog. I gobble down the rest of my food, but it tastes terrible without my friend to share it.

Lindy pulls hard on my arm to hurry and change into my dress robes for the day. She's never nice to me, but it's worse when I have to get ready to see Mama or Baba. I'd be more helpful if she hadn't thrown my friend out the window.

"Now, remember, Arianna. You mustn't touch your father."

"Yes, Lindy." Sometimes I just want to punch her.

Baba enters my room, Dee-oh by his side. He is smiling, his arms ready for an embrace. "Baba!" I run to hug him. Lindy and Dee-oh both grab my shoulders.

"You can't touch him, Princess! I warned you," Lindy chastises me.

"It would be neat!" I say it before I think. I remember the way my ball clinked instead of bounced. Maybe it wouldn't be fun. Baba drops his arms and makes a sad face.

"Yes, we mustn't let this happen, Princess." Dee-oh's smile looks mean. I think he'd like it if I turned into a gold statue. He's not a nice man. I'm going to send him away when I become queen.

"I'd like to spend the morning with Arianna alone. You are dismissed," Baba says.

"Are you sure, Your Majesty? You may need assistance if you need to touch the princess. We wouldn't want any harm to fall upon her, and you can't even eat toast without mishap." Dee-oh grins like a hungry cat.

"I think I can manage."

"Very well, Your Majesty. We will leave you two alone." Dee-oh points Lindy toward the door and follows.

"Why can't you eat toast, Baba?"

"It turned into a big block of gold. Can you believe it? Even the butter was gold. Looked pretty, but it was hard to eat."

"Sounds yucky."

"Not as yucky as not being able to give you a big hug or tousle your hair. We'll make do though. Where's your golden ball?"

Uh oh. Frog hasn't given it back to me yet even though I have kept my half of the promise. Now he probably won't because of stupid Lindy. How could she be so mean?

"Umm." The marble floor looks neat. Not really, but I don't want to see Baba look sad.

"Arianna?"

"My friend Frog has it."

"Frog?"

"Yes."

"You're friends with a frog?"

"You told me to be nice to the frog, so I am. He has my ball."

"Mhm. Well, maybe Frog can let us have it and we can play?"

"No."

"Why not, Arianna?"

"Lindy threw Frog out the window."

Baba folds his arms across his chest. "Now this doesn't sound like something your nanny would do."

I can't hold back the tears. "She did. I think he's hurt." I need to find my best friend. Peering out the window, I think I see Frog in the garden near the well. Tears form in my eyes as I reach for a hug from Baba, forgetting the danger. At first, I like the feeling of Baba's strong fingers touching my shoulders, but then I feel icy cold water spread under my skin. My arms and legs feel stiff. I can't move. I try to cry out to Baba, but I can't breathe. Everything is gold colored. He touched me. I'm turning into gold. My tears are solid and cannot fall.

It happens fast.

"Arianna! No!" I can hear Baba yelling. "Stop!" I can't stop though. I want to tell Baba this. He places his hands on both my shoulders, and stares hard into my eyes. "Arianna. Speak to me."

I want to say I'm okay. All I can do is stand there.

"I'm so sorry, Arianna. I'm so so sorry. I promise. No more gold. I'll stop."

Okay, Baba.

"I can fix this. I don't know how, but I can fix this."

You can?

"Who am I kidding. I'm just a stupid boob. I can't even dress myself let alone fix this."

I don't think you're a boob, Baba. I wish I could tell you.

"Maybe I should get Deo."

No, Baba. Please don't get Dee-oh.

He wraps his arms around me and tries to pick me up. He can't do it. He throws his robe over my head. I hear Dee-oh come and they talk, but I can't hear from underneath. Baba takes the robe off of me after Dee-oh leaves, and he promises me he'll come right back. I'm afraid to be alone like this, but I can't beg him to stay. I hear Dee-oh return.

"Well, well, look at what we have here, Princess. I hoped the king would make a foolish wish and cause his downfall, but what are the chances it would cause yours too? Don't worry, dear child. You'll be gold forever, and I'll soon be king. You'll make a lovely ornament in my new garden." Dee-oh laughs.

I wish I could slam my foot onto his toe. I promise I will if Baba figures out how to fix me.

"I'm going to leave you, for now, though. I don't think it's quite time to reveal this most wondrous development."

Two Days Later ...

Silenus has finally arrived. I asked him to be discreet and so far he hasn't announced his arrival. I'm relieved, fearing he was going to choose to stay away. He comes to my private chambers, circumventing the majority of the people in the castle. A few guards are aware, and I am certain at least one of them will report back to Deo, but no one knows why he is present.

In his absence, I had forgotten Silenus' odd appearance. One might expect the friend and tutor of a great god would have ... I don't know ... presence? Silenus is short. I mean, I'm short, but he's miniscule. The top of his balding head comes to my mid chest. The rest of him is diminutive, from his hands to his feet, to his dark beady eyes. When he was here before, Silenus was jovial and pleasant to be around though not quite sober, but today his lips are in a tight drawn line hiding horse teeth, and he keeps his arms wrapped tight across his chest.

"I am grateful you've come, most venerable one. I am in a good bit of trouble, and I hope I can implore you for your assistance." I bow my head as I speak.

"No."

"But I haven't even explained—"

"I don't care."

"It's a matter of—"

"There is nothing you can say to convince me to help, sir. I did the kindness of gifting you with an amazing present, and you have been nothing but rude and condescending ever since. I have no desire to help you now or ever. I only came to stop the incessant messages begging me to come."

"But it's the gift you gave. It's been nothing but a curse."

Silenus' eyes burn. "Like I said, sir. Rude and condescending. Not so much as a thank you."

I feel my anger rising. How dare he accuse me? Ever since he gave me this bloody curse, my life has been worse than Hades. He thinks I should thank him? Why would I thank him for the misery he's put me through? No one has ever called me rude or condescending in my life. I want to ignore the thought in my head reminding me I should rein in my emotions for Arianna's benefit. I can claim I never thought it, right?

"Thank you, most venerable one," I choke. "Thank you for ruining my life. Get your horse-toothed face out of here and don't you ever return."

Silenus smiles, but there is no kindness there. "Deo will make a fine king."

He rises, and leaves without another word. I need to stop him and apologize if I ever want to save my daughter. I know I have lost my throne. Any chance for my little girl is trotting out the door, and the idea of stopping the arrogant ass makes me want to vomit. I'd often suspected Deo was trying to dethrone me; now it is confirmed. Silenus has been helping him. I'm a fool, but I won't be fooled twice. Silenus can free my daughter, but at what additional cost? Whatever it may be, it is too high, and I won't pay it. Sorry, Arianna, but there will have to be another way, my love.

I leave the private receiving room and return to where the princess is hidden. I've been fortunate no one has spotted her, but my time is running out. I've decided it is time to confess to my mistakes. I can't hide anymore. I allowed my fear of Deo and my own insecurities to get to me, letting him win. The people will know my weakness, but I know I never succumbed to being their puppet.

Arianna stands there, her arms outstretched waiting for a hug. Her frozen face is caught in a smile. She is the most beautiful creature I have ever seen, and I broke her. I approach, and I give her the hug she has been waiting for.

"Arianna, if you are still in there, I love you." I stroke my tears from her golden cheek. I wish life was like a fairy tale, and my tears would release Arianna from her prison.

"I can help."

I release my daughter and look around the room, but there is no one there.

"Always looking up for help. Never looking down. That's your problem."

The frog is perched on Arianna's foot. His eyes glide open and shut, and his long tongue flickers out, barely missing a fly.

"Did you? Did you speak?" I have lost my sanity.

"Well, there's no one else in the room except Arianna, and she can't answer at the moment. She's in there though. We don't have much time before she'll forget she was once human and becomes a statue."

I crouch down to face the frog head on. "And why would you help me?"

"I wouldn't. I'll help Arianna, though. She's been my friend. Do you have any friends, Your Majesty?"

I think of the people in my life. I don't like my wife. I should be able to trust my advisor more than anyone, and he has almost ruined me. Who else is there? I broke Arianna. "No one matters more to me than my daughter, but I think I need to surround myself with better people."

His head bobs up and down. I think it's meant as a nod. "Let's fix this mess then."

"But how?"

The frog stares at me without blinking. "You won't be able to turn anything into gold anymore."

"Thank the gods!"

"Go to the river. I need a bucket of water."

"Can't I just go to the well?"

"If you don't want it to work, sure thing."

"I've never been to the river alone."

"Well, maybe it's time for a first. I'd go, but I can't exactly carry a bucket in my current condition."

"Condition?"

"I don't know if you've noticed, but I'm a frog."

I find a bucket, which turns to gold upon my touch, slip out unseen, and head to the river. It feels strange not to be surrounded by people, like receiving guests with no robes on. The river bed is steep, and my heel slips through the squishy mud. Dipping the bucket into the brown water, I'm careful not to touch the water itself, lest it turn to gold and I'll have to start over. I return to Arianna and the frog.

"I have water and muddy feet."

"You can wash them. Step into the bucket."

"Are you kidding me? The water will turn into gold, and I'll be stuck in the bucket."

"Oh. What a tragedy. Fine. Don't then. Arianna makes a lovely statue."

I step into the bucket. The water tingles, but it remains brown.

"Wash your hands."

I dip my hands into the filthy water, and run the liquid up and down my arms. It burns to the touch and sizzles. After, my skin feels cool and refreshed.

"Now, pick me up."

"I can't! You'll—"

"The water of your river was touched by Poseidon himself as a gift to the water nymphs who live there, and it has healing properties which should have removed the curse. If it worked, I won't turn into gold. If I become gold, I can't help you anyway. You need to test it, and I don't matter."

I start to reach for the frog and stop. I can't risk it. I step out of the bucket. "No. You're not just a frog. You're Arianna's best friend." I pick up the bucket and pour the water over my daughter's head.

"Your Majesty, if that doesn't work she'll be gold forever!"

"If I don't do it, she'll be gold forever. Can't lose."

Nothing happens.

I sink to my knees. Frog leaps onto my lap as the tears sting my eyes. What kind of man am I? I'm always crying instead of solving my problems myself. Frog's leathery skin is soft and warm under my fingers as he tries to comfort me.

"Your Majesty. It worked. I'm not gold."

"Look at her. She's still solid."

"Give the water time to soak in."

I scoff. Gold isn't porous. It's not like a sponge. The water slides off the statue into a pool onto the floor. It's all she is now. Still, I'm not ready to give up. We sit and watch her as the sun sets outside. After a time, we both must fall asleep, because when I awake, a small warm breathing child is curled asleep in my arms. I pull my Arianna tighter into my embrace. Everything else will be all right.

The golden sun is brutal to my eyes. Fortunately, it is the only thing gold. I've decided it's my least favorite color. Arianna and the frog are bouncing the red ball back and forth, both giggling with joy. When she sees I am awake, the princess bounds to me, and throws her tiny body at me.

"Oh, Baba!"

"I'm so sorry."

"Why?"

"I failed you."

"You saved me."

"I never—"

"Baba. It was Dee-oh. He planned it all. I heard him when I was stuck."

"I wish I was surprised. I've never trusted him, and I promise I will banish him forever. Later. Not now. Now I just want to hug you."

I notice the frog staring at us both. "Your Majesties—"

"Thank you for helping Baba, Frog. I knew you would." Arianna releases me, bends down and kisses his warty skin.

I am blinded by a flash of light, and my stomach feels queasy, as though I have fallen off an eight-foot wall. When my vision clears, there is not one child but two. My daughter's lips are pressed to the forehead of a little boy not much older than she. He appears as startled as I feel.

"Who are you?" Arianna asks.

"I am Frog."

"Were you cursed by someone? How were you trapped?"

The boy grins. "I was born a frog. I wished to be a human boy when you kissed me. Silenus' gift was not sincere, and it proved to be more of a curse, but when your father transferred it to you, it became a true gift of love."

"I can grant wishes?" Arianna's eyes sparkle. "I'll only grant good ones. I promise. Maybe when I become a grown up I can find people who really need wishes to come true."

Arianna, Twenty Years Later ...

Fuggetyfudge.

Why won't she just make a wish already? My shoes are pinching my feet, and I'm hungry. This girl deserves an act of kindness. I've seen the way she takes care of sick and injured animals when she should be sleeping. Anyone else would be passed out after all of the cleaning. Maybe it's because they make her sleep on the hearth in the cinders.

I've been watching a while. More than once I've wanted to find a bucket of sludge and throw it at the old hags, but if the girl wants to, she never lets on. If I could just help her and move on, I would, but the gift my Baba gave me so many years ago doesn't work that way. She has to make a wish.

"Oh, I wish I could go to the ball."

Victory. I close my eyes and picture it. A ball gown of silver and slippers of pure gold fall out of the sky and land on the ground at her feet. My job here is done. She looks from the gift to me.

"Who are you?"

"I'm your fairy godmother."

THE END

Avery D. Cabot is a middle aged bachelor from Lowel, MA, who has never once considered marriage or children as they are both beneath him. His goal is to return fairytales to their original art form—dark, often horrific and gruesome, and certainly not children's stories. Avery lives alone in a one room apartment overlooking the Merrimack River because the isolation allows his creative genius to flourish. His mother hates everything he writes, saying his work is far too terrible for human eyes, but he snuck this story past her. He swears he's not a Mama's boy, but he wants to make her proud.

Born in the Sign

Contemporary Fiction
Water

Jeanne Felfe

Until now, Tom Giacano had never gone anywhere. Never done anything. It wasn't that he lacked the means to do so, he just never had, preferring instead to remain ensconced in his safe, predictable life.

Until it wasn't.

Predictable.

Nor safe.

Tom had planned Anne's surprise fifty-fifth birthday down to the minutest detail. All their friends attended and toasted her double nickel to much fanfare. One week later he dragged home after a soul-sucking day at the office, where too many people wanted too many things, to a nothingness that threatened to swallow him whole. She'd never said a word, never given a hint. He sat stone-faced at the kitchen island—which sported new multi-earth-toned granite Anne had insisted they needed and that he'd only made the final payment on recently—staring at the computer-typed note, re-reading it for the fourth time. *Christ, couldn't she have at least handwritten it?*

"Tom, the party was truly lovely. You went all out, and I thank you for that. I am sorrier than I can say, but I simply can't continue to pretend I still love you. Can't pretend I'm happy. I haven't been for some time. And I think if you're honest with yourself, neither are you. Somewhere along the path I lost myself, and I must go find her. I've only taken what is mine and what I could fit in the car, as well as a bit of money to help me get started in a new place. I want to be fair, and I hope you will be too. Don't try to call me. I won't answer. I must do this alone. I hope you find yourself, too. Anne."

Once the initial shock wore off, he realized she was right. He'd also lost himself along the road of thirty-five years of married life. When he said "I do," apparently he'd said "I don't" to all the dreams of his youth. Dreams, it seemed, he could no longer even recall. *Surely I had some?*

What had happened to that bright-eyed kid who dreamed of adventure, like the swashbuckling heroes of the movies he loved? Had he really allowed fifty-six years to slip by without even once stepping foot outside the mid-sized, landlocked area where he grew up? He hadn't even gone away for college, choosing instead to attend the University of Athens and live at home, where he met and married Anne, the only girl he'd ever dated.

Now he vowed to change all that, hoping in the process he could grow into who he truly wanted to be—whoever that turned out to be—and secretly dreaming Anne would see his progress and come back.

A few days after his wife's departure, Tom stopped by the break room for a coffee refill. His mind jumped from idea to idea, grasping at possible ways he might go about discovering his passion. Lost in thought, he startled at a voice behind him, having not heard anyone enter.

"So, Tom," Jonah began. "I heard about Anne. Tough break, man."

Tom ducked his head, not really wanting to discuss his personal life with the playboy of the team.

"Say, have you ever been sailing?" Jonah asked.

Tom shook his head. "No. I've thought about it, always wanted to, but just—"

"Oh man, you should! Last year on vacation I went to Casablanca." He pulled out his phone and began flipping through picture after picture. "I *lived* on this tall ship for two full weeks."

He shoved the phone at Tom's face, displaying a picture of an elegant vessel that reminded him of pirate ships he'd seen in movies as a child.

"Yeah, we learned how to sail that sucker and work as a team. And don't get me started on shore leave. Man, the babes at the Mazagan Beach Resort." Jonah flapped his free hand, fanning his face as if it were on fire. "Best trip of my life."

"Don't you need to know how to sail at least a little to do that?"

"Nah, man. You get some shots and a passport, then go on a two-week training sail. They've even got some that sail all the way around and past the Cape of Africa. You can go as far as your time and money will take you."

"Did you do that?" Tom asked over the rim of his coffee cup.

"What, train? Of course—"

"No," Tom said, interrupting what he knew would turn into a long, drawn-out explanation. "Did you sail around Africa?"

"Ah, nah, man. Just my two weeks along the coast of Morocco. I ain't got that kind of money ... or time."

"Yeah, no, me neither," Tom replied. But the wheels had started to turn. He flashed on a memory long forgotten. His dad had given him a remote control sailboat for his tenth birthday celebration week on Lake Lanier. He spent hours guiding it around the protected cove close to their cabin, pretending he was Captain Tommy, the fiercest pirate on the high seas.

When Tom asked his dad if they could rent one of sailboats being hawked by the vendors along the shore, his dad refused. Too dangerous, he'd said. So Tom had never done more than sit in a dingy watching his dad fish. Heck, he hadn't even fished—

he hated touching the slimy worms, hated killing them by skewering a hook through their bodies. He swore he could hear them scream. His dad had called him a sissy-boy on that trip, and Tom hadn't wanted to go again after that.

That memory slammed him like a stone wall. It was followed by the niggling memory of wanting to sail.

Tom refreshed his now cold coffee. "I need to get back to it before the boss comes looking for me."

Jonah called after Tom as he walked away. "Man, check out that sailing thing. It's the bomb."

Two days later, unable to shake Jonah's words, Tom researched sailing while behind his closed office door. He found he could learn to sail, albeit on a small vessel, on Lake Chapman, right there close to home. Not waiting to talk himself out of it, he dialed and made an appointment for Sunday. *I'm doing this, damn it!*

Tom returned home from that first outing sunburned and totally head-over-heels in love with sailing and filled with a life-energy unknown to him. The instructor at the lake suggested that if he really wanted to learn, he should head to Lake Lanier for a more intensive lesson on a larger vessel. After rubbing aloe vera on his toasted skin, Tom googled sailing schools and lodging on the big lake located about an hour from home, the same lake where his father had failed to teach him to fish. He made a reservation for the following Saturday at The Clipper, which seemed to have good online reviews. He also booked a room for the weekend in a little cabin camp right next door. It might have been the same place his family used to visit, but like most of his childhood memories, this one was stored in a tightly locked box in his brain.

Tom returned to Lake Lanier each weekend for three months, feeling a freedom that had evaded him until now. He felt light, almost airy, as if a great weight had been lifted off his shoulders. The excitement of the wind in his thinning gray hair and the spray on his skin ignited a fire deep within.

As he made the call that would forever upend his world, his hand shook, but not from fear.

After checking the balance in his 401K and confirming with HR that he did indeed meet the qualifying rules that would allow him to take an early retirement, he walked into his boss's office.

"Marshall? We need to talk."

"I was just going to call you, too," his boss said. As usual, he launched into his spiel without waiting to hear why Tom was there. "We've got a monster project coming in that's going to need your expertise."

Tom allowed his boss to prattle on for a few minutes, while second-guessing himself as to whether this was the right decision. Marshall outlined the details of the new project—yet another data tracking system for some Fortune 500 company Tom disdained. Knowing he'd be expected to manage it, Tom's

neck muscles tightened and began to ache, drawing his shoulders toward his ears, confirming that this, indeed, was his best move.

"We'll need to pull a team to—"

"Marshall," Tom interrupted, holding up a hand, unable to withhold any longer. "I can't take the project."

"What?"

"I won't be here."

"Won't be where?" his boss repeated, a frown arching across his forehead. "Did I forget about a vacation?" He paused while flipping through the paper calendar on his desk. "Wait ... don't tell me you're retiring. I can't lose you, too. You're my best Senior Program Manager."

Tom shrugged. "Sorry, boss. I'm retiring."

"Holy hell! You're the third one this month. How am I supposed to run a business if everyone keeps leaving?"

"I guess that's the downside of having a seasoned staff."

"Is it me? The money? If it's the money, I can talk to HR. See if we can get you a bump."

"It's not you and it's not the money. Since Anne left, I've been doing a lot of thinking. I'm still young and have a lot of life left to live ... things to do. I want to get started now while I'm able to enjoy them."

A heavy sigh sailed across the desk and landed like a perfectly tossed pebble. It felt great to be so well-thought of his boss would try to convince get him to stay.

"How long do I have you?"

"Two weeks."

"Two—Damn! You're serious." Marshall's tone indicated he understood the finality of Tom's decision. He shook his head and chuckled. "I predict you'll be bored and crawling back within two months. Whatever will do with all your spare time? You don't even golf."

"Wheels are already in motion for my first trip."

"Trip? Where you going?"

Tom grinned perhaps his first genuine smile in quite some time, he realized, other than when he was at the rudder. *Maybe Anne was right.* "To sail the seas." Even as he said it, fear blended with panic and excitement to the point he actually tingled.

Not thirty minutes after Tom walked out of his boss's office and settled into his own, Jonah poked his head through Tom's open doorway.

"You're retiring?" Jonah charged across the room and slapped him on the back a bit too hard. "Congratulations!"

The speed at which news traveled in this office never ceased to amaze Tom. "Thanks. Yep, time to do something for myself."

"So you're going to Morocco to sail, like I told you, eh?"

Tom thought about the chance chat that had set his sights on the horizon and felt gratitude. "Well, yes, I'm going sailing, but not to Morocco. I always wanted to visit Australia, so I decided to combine them into one journey. I'll spend nine days training on a tall ship off the coast of Sydney. Then we'll anchor in Tasmania, where we'll spend three days exploring. After that, who knows? Maybe I'll hitch a ride on a tall ship and never return."

"Holy wow, man! Way to rock it!" Jonah said as he strutted out the door.

For several hours Tom's colleagues paraded through his office one or two at a time expressing their congratulations. And something else. Was that envy he spotted in their eyes? In his entire life, he'd never been envied by anyone. He decided he kind of liked it.

Tom arrived at the Atlanta airport bright and early, ready for his first-ever flight. Since he'd never been anywhere, he had to request a rush for his passport, which arrived just in time. The journey across the Pacific to Australia would take just under twenty-four hours, including a brief stop in Los Angeles. He had a new set of headphones on hand so he could pass the time catching up on some in-flight movies.

At the two-hour mark during the flight out of LA, he paused *Crocodile Dundee*—cheesy, he knew, but he'd never seen it and figured to gain a little knowledge about his temporary home—and rose to stretch his legs. He ventured to an empty row and slid into the window seat. The view wasn't what he expected, although he hadn't really known *what* to expect. It was a cloudless day, but below, all he could see was what he assumed to be the undefined vastness of the ocean. Although he suspected it must surely be moving beneath him, it looked more like a vast stretch of blue-gray sand, reaching from horizon to horizon and covered in little dunes of murky green, black, and tree-bark brown. The fear of flying he'd been hauling since take-off, lifted, replaced with excitement. He felt lighter, calmer. A random line of lyrics floated into his head ... *born in the sign* ... He stopped abruptly and frowned when he realized he couldn't remember the words. *Something about water and sea animals? Who wrote that song anyway?* That song had been one of his favorites because he was a water sign. Now, it bothered him that he couldn't remember the words. He reminded himself that he didn't put much stock in astrology, but resolved to look it up once he had internet.

After returning to his seat, and snuggly strapping back in, he pulled one of the sailing books from the bag at his feet and continued the research he'd started pre-flight.

The screech of tires on runway jolted Tom from a fitful airplane sleep. He opened his eyes to the Sydney airport. After retrieving his bags, he stepped into the blinding sun and glanced around, hoping to find a taxi just waiting to whisk him to his destination. Luck was on his side and a bright orange one pulled up in front of him. A young man in shorts and flip-flops jumped out and loaded the bags into the trunk with barely more than a "G'day mate." *Or is that boot?* Tom thought, practicing his local lingo.

Tom climbed into the backseat and instructed, "Sydney Harbor Marriott, please."

Ready to begin this adventure, Tom scoured the skyline, amazed at the size of this ocean town, gawking as only a true tourist could. When the taxi neared the Sydney Harbor Bridge, he gasped at the majesty of the Sydney Opera House. The wings of the roof rose up like the billowing sails of a tall ship. Although he'd seen it in pictures, nothing had done it justice.

The cab driver pulled into the covered check-in area and parked. As Tom reached over the seat to pay, he caught a glimpse of a man unloading his bags from the trunk. Tom jumped out of the cab.

"Wait! Those are mine," he said, reaching for the bag sitting on the curb.

"No worries, mate. Got ya covered." When Tom hesitated, the crisply dressed man waved toward the sliding doors. "Go on, register."

Tom eyed him for a moment longer, then reluctantly went inside to the elegantly appointed counter. The reflection of a massive floral arrangement glistened in the black marble.

After escorting Tom to his room, the bellhop waited, hands laced below his belt. Tom slid a folded bill into the man's hand, damned proud of himself for having researched all aspects of this trip, down to the customary tip for every conceivable type of service.

Tom raced to the patio door like a little kid and flung it open, breathing in the damp, salty air. The sounds of the bustling city blended with those from the harbor, filling the air with a delightful cacophony. He lounged on the balcony for an hour before crawling into bed, exhausted from his flight.

The morning sun blazed in through open blinds awakening Tom at sunrise. He bolted out of bed so energized to finally be out on the water sailing he skipped breakfast.

At check-in on the dock, Tom's excitement bubbled out as he struck up a conversation with a tall, lanky man whose ebony skin shone under sun-bleached dreadlocks trailing down his back.

"Hi, I'm Tom."

The man took Tom's outstretched hand, and his powerful grip almost took Tom to his knees. "Agwe," was all he said through a full-toothed grin, exposing a set of perfectly aligned, brilliantly white teeth.

"What's Agwe?"

"My name, mon, my name. It means Spirit of the Sea." The man's thick Jamaican accent required all Tom's attention to comprehend.

"Well, then pleasure to meet you. Are you on this ship, too?"

A rolling barrel laugh burst from the man's throat. "Am I on it? Mon, it's me ship."

Tom lifted an eyebrow. Childhood images of pirates that had made their way into his living room via the solitary television his family shared, flitted through his mind. Now, he was intrigued. *Add an eyepatch and my captain could be one of them.* Interesting indeed.

"It is your first time?"

"Oh, I've been sailing for about a couple of months now. But only on a lake, never out in the ocean."

"Well ..." Agwe dragged the word out. "Pay attention, and you just might live to tell your children about taming the high seas." He laughed again and strode away, leaving Tom bug-eyed and slack-jawed.

Tom wiped sweaty palms on his shorts and approached the check-in table, his confidence a bit shaken.

A pretty young woman—not much more than a girl really, sporting a deep tan and pixyish dark hair with a greenish-blue streak down one side—sat at the table with a pile of forms. She flashed a brilliant smile and blinked eyes that matched the ocean. "Well, hey you."

Her familiar, deep southern accent threw Tom for a second, but then he smiled at her. "You're not from around here are you?"

"How'd you guess? No, I'm from Alabama. Came over here three years ago for a two-weeker like you're goin' on and ain't never gone home," she said, her voice filled with an airiness that reminded Tom of the breezes on Lake Lanier. "Agwe hired me on as a mate."

"We were practically neighbors then. Name's Tom Giacano, from Georgia."

"I'm Danie." She searched for his name on a list that covered less than a single page. "Found you!" She handed him a stack of papers.

"You gotta fill these out. You can go on into that room over yonder." She pointed behind her. "Grab yourself a coffee and pastry while you wait for Agwe. He'll be in shortly."

Tom took the forms and pen, dipping his head in acknowledgement. "Thank you kindly. So, you'll be on the boat?"

She giggled. "Well, first, it ain't a boat. It's a ship. And yes, I'll be out there with y'all."

How is this little slip of a girl going to be of much use trimming the sails?

Turning to walk to the room, Tom caught sight of a strawberry-blonde ponytail swinging like a pendulum above the most perfect backside he'd seen in years. At first, this thought shocked him, but then something in his brain shifted. *Haven't even looked at another woman in decades. Guess I can now.* He released a breath he didn't know he'd been holding.

He scanned his shipmates, counting seven men and three women, one the owner of that ponytail, equally as enjoyable to look at from this angle. He surmised he was the oldest by at least two decades, except for ponytail-lady. *She looks to be closer to my age.* Better late than never, he figured.

After grabbing a steaming hot cup of black coffee, he took a seat across from the pretty lady and flipped through the papers. When he reached one with "Limited Liability" in large, bold, red ink across the top he paused to read every word. His heart raced and pounded in his temples. "Not liable for any injury sustained while on Cool Change. If needed, you can be airlifted back to Sydney at your own expense."

In his line of work, preparedness was a natural as breathing, so he wasn't worried about the money. Travel insurance would cover the cost. No, the insides of his mouth went dry and his stomach quaked as an image of being flung over the bow assaulted his mind. *Maybe I should re-check my travel insurance.* He gulped his coffee, trying to wash down the fear of drowning, scalding his tongue in the process.

He glanced around the room, comparing himself to the rest of these would-be sailors. *Damn, I'm old. They must think I'm crazy.* He came close to standing up and leaving. *No! I've come this far, damn it. I will see this through.* His gaze drifted over to Ponytail as he thumbed the simple gold band on his left ring finger. He couldn't quite face taking it off. Not just yet.

"Okay, sailors! Listen up." Agwe's resonant voice bounced off the walls of the small room. Eleven sets of eager eyes turned in his direction.

"Today, we learn the lay of the ship, assign cabins and work details. Tomorrow, we sail into the Tasman Sea. Cool Change will be your home for two weeks. Anything over the thirty-three pounds you're allowed on board you can store at Billy Goat Locker—they give my passengers good rate." He pointed out the door, apparently to the dock. "When you return, all tanned and strong, you pick up. Questions?"

Six hands shot into the air. He noticed Ponytail's wasn't one of them. Tom waited also, thinking he'd let someone else ask all the stupid questions. *Maybe she's doing the same?*

"Do we sail at night?" one of the women ventured.

"Yes, we sail non-stop until we dock off Tasmania in nine days."

Tom watched as her eyes widened. *Guess I'm not the only one feeling apprehensive.* Maybe all were equally clueless and naïve.

"Anyone afraid of heights?" Agwe asked and two hands went up, one belonging to a rather rotund man who didn't look like he could climb anyway.

What on earth is a man like that doing sailing?

"Okay, no tower look-out for you. We cannot have you spinning out up there and falling into the ocean. Even if the sharks need to eat, too." His laughter was met with stone-cold silence.

Tom would swear Agwe winked at him before calling on another person.

"How do we use the bathroom?" That question came from a man-boy who appeared too young to shave.

"The head," was all Agwe said, leaving what that meant for another time. The ship master outlined some of what to expect in the daily life as a sailor.

Tom thought he was prepared. After all, he'd researched this, reading three books on the topic. He'd packed enough anti-motion sickness pills to last more than the full fifteen days. And "always prepared" was his motto, so what could go wrong? Prepared, that is, until Agwe covered details Tom hadn't considered—like the possibility of a tsunami. An image of a twenty-story-tall wave crashed through his mind and he felt seasick while still on dry land.

"You will learn that your time on the seas is a dance with the forces of nature. Learn that dance and you will change in ways you cannot possibly imagine. Ignore the dance, and the next two weeks will be nothing but drudgery, and perhaps even hell. The sea … she is always in motion, always in flux. One minute calm, the next a monster.

"Now, let us meet your crew." Agwe waved to the door and five men and one woman entered. "You've already met Danie, my First Mate. Second in command only to me." He jabbed his thumb into his chest and then proceeded to introduce the five men, who became a blur of bleached-out hair and brawny bodies.

"You will rotate through all of the work assignments, except you two landlubbers who do not like heights. You two will get extra kitchen duty, or perhaps latrine. We shall see." He winked at the larger man whose mouth had sagged open. "Just kidding. There is always something for everyone to do on board ship."

Agwe peered at his clipboard before continuing. "Let us go 'round. You mates will spend two weeks in close quarters, so is best to know one another before you got no choice. Tom—tell us who you are, where you are from, how long you been sailing, and what you would like to get out of this voyage."

Age before beauty I guess. Tom stood and looked around the room, rubbing his palms on his shorts, even though they were oddly dry. "Name's Tom Giacano, from Athens, Georgia. I recently retired from Project Management after thirty-two years." *Shit, this makes me sound even older.* "Uh, I ... Let's see ... sailing experience would be spending every weekend for the past three months on Lake Lanier on daysailers and catamarans. This is my first ocean voyage and I seek ... adventure?" His voice lifted on that last word indicating how unsure even he was of this. *I sound like an old idiot. Is it too late to get a refund?*

"Adventure you say." Agwe clapped his hands and roared. "Well, you certainly will have that here." He pointed at the manboy who'd asked about the bathroom. "You next."

As each trainee and crew member introduced themselves, Tom grew increasingly nervous. *That couple is planning to sail around the world after this. Even that fat guy knows more than I do. I'll probably slip off the deck and get eaten by a shark. Or tangle my neck in the halyard and strangle when no one's watching.* He again wiped his now sweaty palms on his pants.

Ponytail stood last. "Hi, I'm Suzette." She gave a little wave, quirked her mouth and leaned her head to one side, in a coquettish way. Tom was instantly transfixed by this elfish woman with pale eyes and an Irish accent that brought to mind images of rolling green hills. A bridge of freckles arched across her nose and cheeks. "I'm on holiday from Tanzania and this isn't my first voyage. I enjoy sailing with newbies. They remind me how much fun it is to learn new things."

Tom thought he noticed a kind of sadness behind those eyes that didn't match her upbeat voice. Perhaps he wasn't the only one fleeing a broken life.

While Danie stepped them through the list of supplies each trainee was required to bring on board, along with those things to leave behind, Burl—whose muscles bulged like knotty growths on a tree, much as his name suggested—walked among the trainees checking boat shoes, ensuring the rubber grips were sound. It seemed that everyone had read the pre-travel information and was properly equipped.

Danie continued, "You can bring your smartphone, but it's for emergencies and the occasional blog post of your trip. We've got a satellite uplink, but mostly you need your wits about you at all times. Too much screen-time is a dangerous distraction. We've never lost a sailor and we intend to keep it that way."

A girl, who looked to be the youngest—maybe thirteen—rolled her eyes and huffed out a breath, slumping back into her chair.

A muscled blond with chiseled features named Wall, or Brick, or something like that—Tom wasn't paying enough attention during introductions to know—stood next. "You mates ready for a tour?"

Tom scanned the hull as he and the other trainees followed the man up the plank and onto the deck. As soon as Tom's foot hit the wood, the gentle rock of the water underneath replaced his nervousness with excitement. *I'm really doing this.* He inhaled the sea air, holding the breath longer than needed.

Tom retched over the side of the ship for the third day in a row, unable to gain his sea legs, even with anti-nausea pills. He'd just finished wiping bile and seawater off his face, when Agwe joined him portside.

"Tom, my friend. I am not sure this sailing thing is working out so well for you."

"I'll get it. I just need ... to ..." Tom heaved again. *Maybe Agwe's right. This sign I was born under, this sign of water ... perhaps ... it's some other kind of water, not the sea.*

Suzette walked up, saw them, and turned in the other direction. She'd kept to herself the past three days, mostly doing her work in silence, observing.

"She is cute, no?" Agwe grinned and nodded toward where the woman disappeared out of Tom's sight.

Yes, she is. Tom thought it but didn't say it, preferring to keep those thoughts to himself. He didn't want to be crude.

"This ocean life, she ain't for everyone and as they say, 'the teacher will appear when the student is ready.' Perhaps your journey leads elsewhere."

When Tom stood, Agwe handed him two pieces of green cloth that looked like tiny sweatbands.

"But ... you are here now. Try this. These work sometimes better than anything else." Agwe slipped a band onto each of Tom's wrists and lined up a small protrusion over a soft gully between two bones. "When you feel liking barfing, press on one and then the other. If this does not fix you within the day, I am not sure anything will."

Agwe paused and sucked in the salty air, then patted Tom on the shoulder and walked away, leaving Tom pressing on the new buttons attached to his wrists.

An hour later, the heaving stopped and for the first time since setting sail, Tom looked at the water as something other than his enemy. He strolled to the front of the ship and found Suzette lounging with a book. While everyone else wore shorts and some even bikini tops, she dressed in a gauzy white material that covered almost every inch of skin and topped off her outfit with a tan wide-brimmed hat. Her pint-sized legs stretched out in the sun, the cloth flapping like the sails in the breeze. Not wanting to disturb her, he stood and looked out over seas that had finally calmed. Cool Change rocked gently, not moving in any direction. A lull, Agwe had told him.

"You better now?" Her lilting voice came from behind him.

Tom turned and held up his wrists. "These things are miracles. I think I'm finally ready to get down to this sailing business."

Moving toward the seat next to her, he asked, "Where you headed after this trip?"

She didn't answer, but instead quirked her mouth to one side, and held up her left hand, a tiny gold band glinting in the sun, and shrugged her shoulders. Tom hadn't seen the band during introductions and had been too busy heaving to notice before.

Warmth rode up from Tom's chest and onto his face. "I didn't mean ... uhm, yeah, I'm married, too. Just making conversation. Sorry." He turned to walk away, but she called out, stopping him.

"Wait." Relaxing her face, she smiled a broad, genuine smile that sent sparks of light dancing in her ice-blue eyes. "No, I'm sorry." She huffed out a heavy sigh and shook her head. "I'm just so used to men hitting on me I keep my defenses up." She waved to the seat.

He noticed that she hadn't answered his question so he let it drop. Maybe she just didn't like talking. They lounged like this until a wind kicked up. Agwe joined them on deck.

"Storm be a brewing, mates." Agwe pointed to the horizon, then nodded toward the seats. "Life vest time. If it gets bad, you'll go below deck and the crew will handle everything."

Tom looked where Agwe had indicated, but saw nothing but blue, not even a cloud. He did as he was told and strapped on a life jacket. In the short time that took, the wind had risen and dark clouds formed in the distance. A jagged strike of lightning broke the horizon, followed by a deep, ominous rumble of thunder. The crew came on deck, lowered and secured the mainsail, then each of the smaller sails. They clipped safety harnesses to their life vests to keep from being washed out to sea. Agwe had outlined this procedure during orientation, but Tom had seriously doubted such a thing would be needed. Now he gawked, frozen in place.

Burl yelled at him, "Get below deck. Now!"

He turned and realized that Suzette had already gone, apparently needing no convincing.

Tom gripped the step railing as the ship began to pitch. He lost his footing when it dipped, and he swung over the rail but didn't let go.

"Where the heck did that water come from?" The large land-lubber passenger, the one who was afraid of heights, huddled in one corner, gripping a rail bar. His eyes held a look of fear Tom didn't quite comprehend.

It's just a little storm, right? What am I missing? The thoughts had barely floated through his head when a rush of water sloshed over the coaming and through the open hatch, soaking him. Tom caught a mouthful of salty water and coughed.

"Hold on!" Agwe yelled from above.

Tom didn't need prompting. He wrapped an arm through a rail and braced as another deluge of water hit him full in the face. He came up gasping. *How did I think I could do this? I don't even like to swim.* The shrieking wind almost drowned out the whir of the bilge pump. For the next two hours, he fought to stay upright as the ship lurched and pitched and groaned. Then just as suddenly as it had begun, it stopped, the violent seas replaced with a rolling rocking motion. And silence except for the pump.

Agwe called down. "Everyone okay?"

Soaked passengers called back as they assessed the injuries: lumps on heads, one twisted ankle, cuts and scrapes. They'd been lucky. No one was dead. All were shaken. Tom longed for dry land.

I want to go home. Tom warred with himself while doing his required shipboard chores. It had been two days since the massive storm nearly capsized them a hundred miles out from Sydney. The ship had sustained some damage, but still limped toward Tasmania.

Water. That's all Tom could see. Water, now calm from horizon to horizon, flat. Not a single cloud broke the monotony of the crystal blue sky. A peaceful scene, but Tom was anything but peaceful on the inside.

I'm an idiot. I shouldn't have come. What was I thinking? These thoughts, and others, had hounded him since his near-drowning—at least in his mind—in the hull of this ship. He couldn't seem to break the almost mantra-like repetition.

"You've been awfully quiet." Suzette's musical voice startled him back to the present.

Tom turned and gave her a pained expression. He hated to admit his failure to this sprite. "Do you know that song about Brandy and his love and lady being the sea?" he asked her.

"Of course, *Brandy*, by Looking Glass. A song from *our* time. The youngsters on this ship probably wouldn't know it." Her gentle smile warmed his heart.

"I had actually convinced myself that I was meant to sign up for one of those cross-ocean voyages on a tall ship. That storm shook that crazy idea right out of me. Maybe my call to water, this sign under which I was born, isn't the sea. Although I can relate to that song, it's not me."

"I'm a water sign, too. I sail because it's so vastly different from my day-to-day life. Sailing is the one place where water is everywhere. So unlike my home in Tanzania."

Tom looked at her puzzled. He'd forgotten that part of her introduction. Now he wondered how this freckle-faced Irish girl had ended up in Africa.

"Being out here, battling the forces of nature, is a choice and a privilege, but it isn't for everyone. I certainly wouldn't want to be out here longer than two weeks," she added.

"I still love sailing, but right now all I want is dry land. Perhaps I'll stick to smaller bodies of water. And much smaller boats."

"Dry land, eh? You haven't seen dry land until you've been to the Serengeti in dry season. Perhaps you're right then about the sea not being for you." She looked out over the water, and Tom's gaze followed hers.

Tiny white caps now broke the surface as the wind lifted and billowed the sails.

"Don't give up on a dream so easily." Suzette turned back to him, the sun glistening off her moist eyes. "If not this water, there's something else. You just have to look and be ready."

Tom watched her turn away, the yellow gauze of her pants fluttering, wrapping around her delicate thighs. *What are you doing?* He brought himself up short at the idea that he was looking at her in this way. *You're married for Christ's sake. But am I? Really?* He gave his ring a bitter twist, pulled it off and stuffed it into his pants pocket.

Although plodding, the next few days brought them ever closer to the exotic-sounding island of Tasmania. Tom and Suzette shared several moments on deck and below. At least he thought they were moments. But his thoughts kept returning to the fact that she was married.

The night they dropped anchor off the shore of Tasmania, Tom stood at the railing watching moonlight flicker on the water. The sight, like tiny bits of jewels, was one he wanted to commit to memory. In case he never returned. As he breathed in the ocean air, he felt someone next to him and startled. Gasping, he grabbed the rail, tacky with dried sea spray.

"It's beautiful out here, isn't it? Magical almost."

When Tom realized Suzette was standing only a breath away, he paused and released a heavy sigh. "I sort of lied to you before. I told you I was married ... and I am ... or I was. She left me a few months back and I took up sailing."

Suzette laughed, and it was like warm honey pouring over his battered heart. "That's okay. I lied too." She flicked her eyes in his direction, catching his gaze in a playful stare.

"Wait. So neither of us is married?" It was his turn to laugh. *Of course I'm married. Aren't I?* He thought again. "Here I've been avoiding you because ..." He stopped at what he knew would sound ridiculous.

"Because ... what?"

Although Tom couldn't be entirely sure in the dim moonlight, he would swear she winked at him.

"Because I think you're one of the prettiest and most intriguing women I've ever met." There, he'd said it. His heart soared and then swooped into his belly as he waited for a response. *What the hell am I doing?* Feeling like an imbecile, he wanted to dive over the rail and disappear into the sea.

But then she smiled, deep dimples punctuating her pale cheeks. "Thanks. You're not half bad yourself."

Now his heart pounded, fluttering out a rhythm of possibilities. An electric silence pulsed between them. Tom wondered about her ring, but assumed if she wanted him to know she'd tell him, so he simply waited.

She finally broke the silence like the wind billowing the sails. "My husband died four years ago." She paused, her gaze returning to the sparkling ocean. "Four years. Nine months. Three weeks. And ten days ago."

"I'm ... so sorry."

She shook her head. "Don't be. I found out he wasn't the man I'd believed him to be. A whole closet full of secrets. Left me an insane amount of money I didn't even know he had."

She huffed out a heavy sigh before continuing. "I spent a year sitting around our cottage in Galway, wallowing and wondering about all the things I hadn't known about the man I'd married. Until I bored even myself. Fifty was too young to do nothing, so

I joined the Peace Corps and went to Tanzania. I remembered how much I'd loved the country and its people when we went on safari there several years ago. After six months, I returned to Ireland, sold the house and almost everything I owned and moved there permanently." She shrugged before continuing. "No kids, parents gone, nothing that would tie me to Galway."

"And here I thought *my* mid-life crisis was intense."

She moved closer and leaned her head on his shoulder. Tom lifted an arm and placed it around her waist, hesitantly, trying to not scare her off. Instead of pulling away, she nuzzled into the crook of his arm, before shifting and gazing up at him.

His body knew before his mind what he was going to do and he leaned in, kissing her softly, as if it was the most natural thing. He was alive. For the first time in a very long time, something beyond sailing exhilarated him and lifted him to a dizzying height.

They stayed entwined, lips exploring for what seemed like a long time. The sound of someone clearing their throat caused Tom to look up. Agwe was disappearing around the side of the cabin toward the hatch. Tom laughed and leaned back, staring into Suzette's eyes.

"What do you do for the Peace Corps?"

"I work with this amazing organization called Save the Rain."

Tom wrinkled his brow while a new idea about water tickled his brain, and asked, "How does one save the rain?"

"I use my engineering background to help villages gather water so school children don't have to spend so many hours each day doing it. It's challenging, but more rewarding than anything I've ever done."

Tom shook his head. "School children?"

"Tanzania is this amazing country, but it is incredibly poor. Many villages have no access to potable, running water. It's quite a sight to drive through rural areas and see people of all ages walking alongside the road carrying jerry cans. Instead of attending a full day of school, many children walk to and from distant gathering locations to help their families have enough clean water."

Tom's mind drifted back to his home in Georgia and long weekends spent watering his quarter-acre of green grass. Well, green if he watered it. If he didn't, it would scorch and turn brown. He was suddenly consumed with guilt over his wastefulness.

"I had no idea. I've really never been anywhere except home and," he said, waving his arm toward the rest of the ship, "and here."

"You should really get out more. There's a whole world of adventure a plane ride away."

"I always wanted to go to Africa when I was a kid. I'd watch Wild Kingdom, pretending to be one of the big cats chasing a hyena."

"The Maasai call the Serengeti 'land that goes on forever' or 'endless plain.' The land stretches for miles, broken only by scattered acacia trees. In dry season it looks like an undulating sea of tawny brown as the breeze flutters the tall prairie grasses. You could drive right past a lioness without ever seeing her because her color blends perfectly."

"Really? They're just roaming around loose?"

Suzette laughed. "It's not a zoo. People pay big money to go on camera safari to see the wildlife. I've been a few times, always a different park. But if I go to the Serengeti, it's always with my brother, Proseba."

"You have a brother in Africa?"

She laughed again. "Not my literal brother. He adopts everyone who safaris with him. You spend a lot of time together on safari and he makes it fun. I've been on the Serengeti three times now—twice to see the great migration of wildebeest and once during the dry season. The different seasons make it like going to two entirely unique places."

Tom listened, his mind painting a picture from her words.

"I would love to do that sometime," Tom said, wondering when that time might be. The idea of driving around amidst wild animals chilled him. "What kinds of animals can you see?"

"Many of the larger tour groups—those in buses, mostly— seek the Big Five—lions, leopards, rhinos, African elephant and the deadly Cape buffalo. Tour companies actually stole that phrase from African hunters. They refer to these as the five most dangerous animals to hunt on foot."

Tom looked at her thinking she must be trying to fool him. "Buffalo are that dangerous?"

"The first time I stayed in a mobile tent camp, I met a young Maasai warrior who was our guard. We weren't allowed to walk alone in camp after dark and the first night as he walked me to my tent, he shone his flashlight into some bushes far ahead. He said, 'Buffalo. Very dangerous.' When I asked him what he was most afraid of he waved his hand toward the hidden creature. 'Buffalo. Many hunter killed—more than all other animals.'

"I could hear snorting and foot stomping coming from the bush. He told me 'Maasai warrior not fear lion' and explained that lions were actually afraid of them, because they used to hunt the males with nothing but a single spear, returning with its head, in order to become a man."

"Wow. I had no idea." The night winds shifted and picked up, whipping the tethered sails above his head.

"What do they call a gazelle on the Serengeti?"

Tom looked at her, puzzled. "Uh, a hooved deer?" he replied, shrugging his shoulders.

"Cheetah Burger." Her laughter bounced off the night sky, delighting Tom.

She stifled a yawn and Tom said, "I guess it's getting late."

She took his hand and leaned in to kiss him. "Not *too* late."

Her intense gaze met his, leaving no doubt she wanted him to join her. He followed her to her stateroom and quietly closed the door behind him, leaving his former married self behind forever.

A blaring foghorn yanked Tom from a deep sleep and he awakened to find himself curled around Suzette's tiny frame. It felt right. Right in a way Anne never had. Sex between them had been perfunctory, when it happened at all. She had been his first.

His only. Never had he questioned whether he was missing any-thing. Now, he knew he'd been missing everything.

Suzette stirred and rolled toward him. "Guess that means it's time."

"We could ... uh ... call in sick."

"Are you kidding me?" She laughed and rose with seemingly no inhibition whatsoever, despite her fully exposed, alabaster skin. "It's Tasmania—you don't sleep through Tasmania!"

Tom, however, wrapped a sheet around himself, watching her every move, as she slid into blue gauze pants and shirt.

"Come on. We don't want to miss the transport."

"You go ahead. I'll be right there."

"Suit yourself," she said, and stepped out of the room.

Once she was gone, Tom dressed quickly. He peeked both ways outside her door before racing to the head. *Good, no one saw me.* This thought was immediately followed by, *who cares? I'm a grown man and if I want to sleep with a beautiful woman, no one has a right to say I can't.* He ran to his room and threw on clean clothes.

They spent the next three days wandering the island, often just the two of them, sneaking away from the others, exploring on their own, while exploring each other. A plan began to form in Tom's mind.

At the end of the third day, they walked back to the dock, arm in arm. Tom's entire body buzzed with the excitement of this new experience. Before he could reveal his plan to Suzette, she pulled him to her.

"I'm too old for games." Suzette paused and tilted her head, studying him. "Come back to Tanzania with me. Save the Rain can always use an experienced project manager." She paused again, hesitating. "Unless, you're in a hurry to get back home."

Tom creased his brows into a puzzled frown. "I could do that? Don't I need some kind of work visa or something?"

"You can stay in the country up to three months on a travel visa. Come with me and learn more. If you like it, you can work out the details. And by the way, we're all volunteers."

"That's not a problem."

"Then it's settled." She turned and climbed into the skiff that would take them back to the ship for the final eleven hour sail back to Sydney.

Settled? How can it be settled? Can I really simply not go home? Do other people do this kind of thing?

Tom cradled Suzette in his arms on the last night of their adventure. He watched her as she slept, seemingly perfectly comfortable sharing her bed with him. He'd been watching her since the moment he met her, but now he felt a keen connection, unlike anything he'd ever experienced. Although he'd known her less than two weeks, it seemed as if he might be willing to follow her anywhere.

The next morning, Tom and Suzette walked off Cool Change together, hand-in-hand. When he left home over two weeks earlier, he thought his call to water was about sailing. He knew now that he'd been wrong. He was certainly stronger, but the man who boarded Cool Change was not the same man who disembarked. It was hard to believe, but he'd needed Anne to push him out of his safe cocoon in order to find himself. And to find Suzette.

While his fellow trainees-now-sailors returned to their normal lives, for only the second time in his life, Tom didn't know exactly what awaited him. He was headed for parts unknown with a woman who already held his heart in her hands. He was, indeed, called to water, but that call turned out to be so much more than he could have imagined.

A joy filled his heart and he pulled Suzette into a bear hug. The teacher had indeed appeared when this student was ready. "Thank you for being right where I needed to find you."

Tom was now home in a way Georgia had never been. Home in his skin, home in his heart.

THE END

Jeanne Felfe is the author of *The Art of Healing - A Novel*—published in June 2016, which is being rereleased under the title *Bridge to Us* in early 2019. Since 2014, more than 20 of her short stories and essays have been published in a variety of publications. When not writing, she gives back to the writing community in many ways, including serving on the board of her local guild, Saturday Writers. She also spends her spring and summer writing by the pool or caring for her yard-full of tropical plants. She resides in St. Charles, MO with her fiancé and two dogs who believe they are tiny humans.

Jeannefelfe.com
https://www.facebook.com/author.JeanneFelfe/

Washed Clean

Magical Realism
Water

Ekta R. Garg

The city of Bhubaneswar, eastern state of Odisha, India, May 1990

O n the day he met Amit Jaisingh for the first time, Pundit Narayan Sharma didn't know about the windfall that would come his way.

He awoke to his mother and his wife screaming at one another. Usually they managed to keep their bickering to a minimum, in volume at least. But on this day his wife, Diya, had seemed to hit a limit.

The screaming match continued as he walked out the back door and went to the outhouse. During his morning ablutions, the pundit wished he wasn't considered a holy man so he could swear at his wife. He washed his hands, smoothed out his face to what he hoped looked like a serene expression, and returned to the main room in his home. As he entered the kitchen, Diya threw a pot on the floor where it skittered across the concrete and the clanging metal rang.

"*Om Nama Shivai, Om Nama Shivai,*" Pundit Sharma said, invoking the name of the god he preached and worshipped most often. "The sun hasn't even touched the earth yet, and you both have started already. You should start the day with the name of Shiva. It will bring you so much inner peace."

And peace inside the house, he added in his mind. He tried to ignore the irony that the god Shiva was often denoted as the Destroyer in Hindu mythology. The pundit's morning had certainly been fractured.

He made attempts to appease first his mother then his wife and failed with both. They each had a side to the story, each had their own opinions, and, like always, both of them were right to an extent. Of course, Pundit Sharma couldn't say that.

As their voices began increasing in volume again, he raised a hand in blessing and said a prayer aloud. At least that put a stop to the screaming. By the time he left for the temple, both women had retreated to separate corners of the small home they all shared.

"*Om Nama Shivai,*" Pundit Sharma continued to chant under his breath. Some days he wondered if Shiva really did hear his exhortations. Calling on the god's name didn't always make him

feel better, but in times like these he had no other outlet for his frustration.

Things got worse when he reached the temple. Several suppli-cants had arrived ahead of him, and he tried not to groan when he saw them waiting. Some stood with arms crossed; others crouched comfortably on their haunches. None of them looked like they would leave until they'd gotten answers for their press-ing questions.

He knew his *kismet* was one of service to the people of Bhuba-neswar. He'd been born into a family of pundits, and this was his lot in life. Sometimes, though, when he lay in the dark and stared at the ceiling of his humble home, Pundit Sharma wished he could leave everything, and every*one*, behind.

With a sage nod to the people waiting, the pundit entered the temple and went into the small room in the back set aside just for him. He washed his feet and then took a deep breath. Another day of service ... and longing for change.

He met with people who wanted his intercession on their big-gest challenges. A student offered fruits and money to Lord Shiva for good grades in his board exams. Parents picked up the yellow sapphire ring he'd commissioned for their daughter to wear in the hopes it would please the gods and increase the chances of finding her a suitable groom. Another set of parents wanted to schedule a *pooja*, hoping the formal prayer ceremony would help their son's wife conceive a child—a boy, preferably. By the time the Jaisingh family came to the priest, he wished, as

he did every morning, that he could join the line and find someone at the head of it to get advice on what to do with his wife and
mother.

"Namaste, Pundit-ji," a woman called as she stepped barefoot
into the temple. She used the free end of her bright pink cotton
sari to wipe the sweat from her face then reached for one of the
bells hanging from the ceiling of the temple and used its clapper
to strike it as a way to alert her arrival to Lord Shiva.

Pundit Sharma inclined his head to her in both blessing and
acknowledgment.

"Namaste, namaste."

She tugged along a small boy who tugged back in a way familiar to the pundit. Most children no longer wanted to spend time
in the *mandir*. So many of them preferred to stay home and play
in the alleys with their friends.

"My name is Shilpa Jaisingh," the woman said, ignoring the
child pulling at her hand. "We have just shifted from Kanpur,
and today is my husband's first day in the steel mill. I wanted to
do a small *pooja* for him."

"Of course."

The woman let go of the child's hand and opened the purse
hanging from a long strap off her shoulder. She took out some
rupees, an apple, and a handful of marigolds wrapped in thin
plastic. Cupping the items with two hands, she placed all of them
in the pundit's open palms.

Pundit Sharma turned and placed the fruit and flowers at the feet of the life-size statues of Shiva and his wife, Parvati. The rupees he slipped into the collection box to the side of the statues. As he folded his hands in prayer, he could hear the woman murmuring behind him.

Sweat beaded on his forehead, and he said an extra prayer for a break in the blistering heat. The air bulged with the promise of the start of the monsoon season, which brought mosquitoes and malaria, but at least the heat would abate by a degree or two.

After his prayers, he pulled a plain stainless steel plate from under a table covered in a white cloth. The plate had a high rim for religious offerings, and in it he placed the apple the woman had given him as well as some of the marigolds. He handed the woman the plate, signifying Lord Shiva's blessings to her, and half bowed. She wiped her face yet again, took the plate, closed her eyes in a final prayer, and touched the plate to her forehead. With a smile at him, she turned to her left.

"*Chalo*, Amit, let's ... Amit? Amit!"

The boy had scampered off the minute his mother let go of his hand, and he began running around the open-air temple. People who had come to the *mandir* for quiet introspection frowned as he ran with his arms held wide like an airplane. It didn't help that he made airplane sounds to go with it.

"*Beta*," Pundit Sharma called, fighting the urge to scream at the boy, "no running, please! You've come to God's house, na? You must be respectful."

"I want to go home!" the boy called back, still doing airplane glides. "I want to go play with Sameer and Gopesh."

The pundit looked back at the mother who smiled in embarrassment then darted after her son. After five or six steps, she caught up to him and dragged him back in front of the pundit. With a good shake of his arm, she commanded him to stay put.

Some of the temple goers voiced their displeasure.

"Why can't you control your son?"

"Oh, Madam! This isn't your garden. Please tell your son to be quiet!"

The woman turned back and apologized to them. Pundit Sharma saw an opportunity to make himself look good. He bent at the waist and put his hand on the boy's shoulder.

"Amit, *beta*, you've come to the temple to pray, right? Why don't you ask Lord Shiva for something?"

The boy stared at him with a furrowed brow, his gangly arms folded tight against his chest. "I want to play with my friends."

The pundit smiled on the outside, but inside he seethed. His wife kept pestering him that they had no children of their own yet—as if *he* had anything to do with it—and on days like this he said an extra prayer of thanks to Shiva that they didn't. He didn't think he could stand the screams of children on top of the ones from his wife and mother.

"*Chalo*, go, it's okay," Pundit Sharma said, waving his hand in a gentle manner toward the entrance of the *mandir*. "Once the monsoon season starts, it will be difficult for you to enjoy with your friends."

The boy rolled his eyes. "The *barsaat* will be very late this year. I'll have plenty of time to play. Mummy, *please!* I want to go!"

Pundit Sharma turned toward Mrs. Jaisingh with an indulgent smile. "Children are so smart these days, na? So knowledgeable."

Mrs. Jaisingh, however, didn't return the smile. She stared at her son, who had gone back to acting like an airplane, then turned back to Pundit Sharma. In that second before her smile came back, he saw worry.

The pundit appraised the boy a second time. He looked like all the other urchins who ran through the streets after school. His legs, two brown sticks poking from the bottom of his shorts, pumped harder as he kept running.

"Uh, Amit?" Mrs. Jaisingh called out after a few moments. "Come, *beta*, let's go. Pundit-ji, thank you so much for performing the *pooja*."

Once again Pundit Sharma raised a palm in blessing, but the woman's reaction bothered him. Most mothers wouldn't have given their children's words a second thought. What had caused Mrs. Jaisingh's anxiety?

An elderly man approached the priest, distracting him from his thoughts. The pundit went on with the rest of his day, blessing people, listening to their tragedies or excitements, offering a few words of encouragement. By the end of the day he had even booked a wedding where he would perform the main ceremony.

"Any date is fine as long as it isn't during the *barsaat*," the mother of the prospective groom said with a laugh. "I don't want my new daughter-in-law's dowry to wash away in the rains! My brother is in America, and he said after the start of the new year is best for him and his family to travel, but you tell me, Pundit-ji, what is the most auspicious date?"

The priest sat with the astrological charts of both the groom and bride in front of him, looking for compatibility and clues to favorable dates for the wedding. The mother's words about the weather made him think again of Amit, of the child's self-assured declaration that the monsoon would get delayed this year. Could the boy be right?

"Pundit-ji?"

The pundit shook himself out of his reverie. "Yes, not in the monsoons, of course. I see two good dates in November and one in February of next year. The one in February is the best."

"Ah, the weather will be so nice," the woman agreed. "Yes, *chalo*, we'll fix the date for February. How much, Pundit-ji?"

He quoted a sum for the service of finding the date and reassured the mother he would keep it open for her family. The sun had almost set by then, and while technically the *mandir* stayed open 24 hours for anyone to come whenever the mood struck, the pundit usually went home around this time. He put the lock on the money box and carried it into the back room to keep it safe; the salty odor of his own perspiration made him hurry.

"Please, Shiva, let the boy be wrong," the pundit murmured, "and let the rains come. I don't know how much more of this heat I can stand."

Despite his devotion to the gods, Pundit Sharma's plea went unanswered. Long past the typical start of the monsoon season in

June, people found themselves looking up at the sky. The atmosphere seemed ready to burst like an overripe guava, but still the rains refused to appear.

The pundit spent time almost every week visiting first one family and then another where someone had died because of the heat. Laborers in the steel mill keeled over right at their posts, and farmers from surrounding regions visited the famous "City of Temples" to beg for the pundit's intercession. Their crops needed the rain, and their families needed the money.

As the weeks wore on, Pundit Sharma's prayer ceremonies both in the temple and in people's houses became elaborate. He used fancier flowers, which cost the families more, and spent longer preaching about Shiva's benevolence. He pointed to Shiva's son, Ganesha, the remover of obstacles. The pundit preached patience and forbearance, and people bowed their heads in acquiescence.

He couldn't stop thinking about the Jaisingh family, particularly about Amit. How had the boy known about the monsoon? Had he told anyone else? And most important of all, could Pundit Sharma find a way to turn this to his advantage?

The pundit kept an eye out for Mrs. Jaisingh, hoping she would stop in the temple on her way to the market or as she walked Amit to school. Hadn't she come to ask for a *pooja* for her husband's job success? Maybe the prayer the pundit performed had worked, and she would return to thank him.

Several weeks went by, but Mrs. Jaisingh didn't return. The rains did, however, and they brought with them cooler temperatures, insects, and disease. Once again the pundit remained busy. Depending on what the family wanted funerals could often bring more money than weddings, and the pundit took on as many of both as he could.

It gave him a chance to earn extra money and stay away from home.

Nearly a year to the day after Amit and his mother first came to the temple, the two returned. Although the boy had grown taller, he seemed as gangly as a young goat, and he still wandered around the *mandir*. Thankfully, however, he didn't fly like an airplane this time.

"Mrs. Jaisingh!" Pundit Sharma called. "It's been quite some time. I hope you all have settled well in Bhubaneswar."

Mrs. Jaisingh nodded, although she looked distracted. She murmured a nondescript greeting and handed the pundit marigolds and a coconut as well as cash. Pundit Sharma tried not to stare too hard at the wad of notes.

"My husband is very ill," she said in a soft voice, stepping toward the pundit. "Can you please pray for his good health?"

Pundit Sharma blinked once or twice. "Yes, of course. What happened, Mrs. Jaisingh? What has made him so sick?"

"He caught malaria at the end of the last rains."

The worry lines made her brow furrow deeper. Pundit Sharma raised a palm in a gesture meant to soothe her anxiety.

"Don't worry, everything will be fine," he said. He pushed the money into the box, turned, and made the offering to Shiva and

Parvati. As he whispered a prayer, he could hear Mrs. Jaisingh's fervent pleas behind him.

The pundit gathered some flowers and a couple of pieces of fruit and put them in a plate. Then he picked up a small gold-plated chalice with a narrow mouth and poured some of its water into a similar looking vessel made of stainless steel. He handed the whole offering to Mrs. Jaisingh.

"Here is some *ganga-jal*," he said in a reverent voice. "Tell him to drink this holy water from the Ganges, and it should give him strength."

Mrs. Jaisingh's lower lip trembled as she accepted the plate. Pundit Sharma raised a hand in blessing and glanced at Amit. The boy hung back with a scowl on his face.

"Come, Amit, *beta*," Pundit Sharma called. "Come take blessings from Shiva-ji."

Amit didn't say anything. He just grimaced, as if in pain, and turned away. The pundit watched as Amit trotted down the few steps, put on his leather sandals, and crossed his arms, waiting for his mother.

"Forgive him, Pundit-ji," Mrs. Jaisingh said. "Between his father's health and his own ..."

"Is Amit also sick?"

She shook her head. "Just a pain in his stomach. He gets them sometimes when the rains ... I mean, he says that the weather ..."

Pundit Sharma's curiosity needled him to ask, but he couldn't, not when Mrs. Jaisingh had other things on her mind.

"It's all right," he said. "Just take the *ganga-jal* home to Mr. Jaisingh, and if I can serve your family in any other way, let me know."

It was as if he'd spoken a wish into existence. A week later, Mrs. Jaisingh's sister came to the mandir. Mr. Jaisingh no longer remained in this world, she said, and Mrs. Jaisingh had requested that Pundit Sharma come to the Jaisingh home to perform the last rites.

The monsoons arrived that year with a ferocity demanding respect. It was as if Lord Shiva himself wanted to annihilate anyone's false notions that they controlled their own lives. Nature and the gods alone knew what the state of the world would be on any given day, and anyone who questioned that truth found themselves floundering in the floodwaters.

Pundit Sharma watched in awe as sheets of rain made visibility difficult and moving around even tougher. For two days he couldn't even walk from his home to the *mandir*, and that's when he knew Shiva must have been testing him. His neighbors had to deal with the realities of the rain. He had to deal with his wife and mother.

The latest source of conflict came from children—or the lack of them, rather. His mother had started putting serious pressure on the pundit and his wife to reproduce. His wife cried and stated that they could only reproduce if her husband stayed home. The pundit declared that if Shiva and the other gods willed it, then they would be blessed with children.

In fact, Pundit Sharma had spent a lot of time thinking about children and one child in particular. When 40 days had passed—the prescribed time for continuous mourning after the death of a loved one—he returned to the Jaisingh home. As he entered the brick wall surrounding the verandah outside the main entrance, he glanced heavenward and thanked the gods for a short break in the rains.

Maybe it's an omen, he thought as he swung open the metal gate. *Maybe it's destiny that the Jaisinghs came to Bhubaneswar. Amit can help the people of our city so much.*

His own financial gain was a given, of course.

The pundit crossed the small verandah and rang the bell. A single long ring, like a bicycle bell, sounded deep in the house. After a moment, he rang again. A young girl, the Jaisinghs' servant, came to the door.

"Is Mrs. Jaisingh in?" Pundit Sharma asked.

"Yes, she's here." The girl opened the door all the way and gestured inside.

The pundit crossed the threshold and went to his left into the drawing room. The servant girl darted ahead and into the kitchen. Pundit Sharma perched on the edge of the formal sofa, overstuffed enough to discourage people from lingering for more than a cup of tea. The girl came back with a single glass of water on a tray and murmured she would bring out the tea soon.

Mrs. Jaisingh came in then, and the pundit noted her correct attire of all white. Her sari, devoid of color, indicated that she had entered widowhood. Plain steel bangles and small studs in her ears replaced her gold jewelry. Most telling was the lack of *sindoor* in the part of her hair. Only married women applied the red powder, and Mrs. Jaisingh no longer had any right to it.

Pundit Sharma sprang to his feet, prompted by the sofa.

"Mrs. Jaisingh, how are you?" he asked in a deferential tone.

She pressed her palms together in greeting. "Namaste, Pundit-ji. *Bas*, fine, thank you. We have the support of our family. My parents have gone to the market, and my sister has gone home for a few days to see her husband and children. She'll return at the end of the week."

"And you have the blessings of Lord Shiva as well. If I may serve your family in any way ..."

She gestured for him to sit again. The servant girl came back with the tea and placed it and freshly fried *pakoras* on the austere coffee table. She held out her tray for the pundit's glass, which he placed in the center.

"Please, Pundit-ji," Mrs. Jaisingh said, opening a palm to the table, "have something."

Pundit Sharma tried not to show his eagerness in putting the batter-dipped onions and chutney in his plate. Funerals might mean more money, but they also demanded the blandest food. An end to the formal mourning period also meant a return to tastier edibles.

"If you know of any families who need tuitions, I am happy to oblige," Mrs. Jaisingh said. "I can teach them in maths. I also know some simple stitching and can fix sari blouses, petticoats, pants, those sorts of things."

"*Zaroor*, absolutely," the pundit said. "How is Amit?"

Mrs. Jaisingh's eyes took on a faraway look. "Amit ... He wants to know where his papa has gone, why he had to go. He wants to know why his stomach hurts when ..."

The pundit's pulse picked up speed. "When it rains?"

She shook her head. "Not quite but almost. If you ask me the truth, Pundit-ji, we came to Bhubaneswar because we hoped all the temples would give Amit's soul some peace. Since he was a young boy, his health has seemed tied to the monsoons. When the rains don't come, or when they get delayed, he knows it will happen because he says ... he says his body tingles. Like he's about to get an electric shock. When the rains come early or too heavily, he gets severe pain, especially in his stomach."

"Hmm," the pundit said, for lack of a better response.

"Shifting one's home is so difficult," Mrs. Jaisingh went on in a quiet voice, "but Mr. Jaisingh wanted the best for Amit. He thought living in such a holy city would help him. We didn't know we would come here and ..."

Tears appeared, and she used the edge of her sari to wipe her face. The pundit busied himself with the tea, embarrassed by this sudden show of emotion from the widow. True, he had seen her cry and wail in grief during the days of mourning, but at those times other people always surrounded them. Here, in the quiet of the drawing room with no one but a servant hovering nearby, the woman's sorrow seemed too close.

"On top of everything, Amit seems to be having trouble in school," Mrs. Jaisingh said after bringing her tears under control. "He keeps saying he misses his old friends, his old school, that his teachers in Kanpur were better."

"But he has friends here," the pundit said.

Mrs. Jaisingh nodded and reached for her own tea cup. "Friends, yes, but one can't spend the whole day with friends only, na? Education is important. We keep telling Amit he must concentrate on his studies. He can't let his education go by, but he doesn't listen. I just don't know what to do ..."

Her hand began to tremble, causing the tea cup to rattle against the saucer. She brought the cup to her lips and took a tentative sip, then put both cup and saucer down. Drawing her hands into her lap, she folded them in a tight squeeze.

Pundit Sharma watched all this and knew the right moment had arrived.

"Maybe he should find something where he can serve others," he said in a voice as soft as the one Mrs. Jaisingh had used. "If Amit focused on service, he would forget everything else. It could change his life."

"But what can he do? He's not even ten years old."

"If you like, he can help me in the mandir. He can sweep the steps, help the elderly, fetch garlands from the shop for anyone who wants to buy them. I can teach him about the holy texts, and he will be serving the gods and the people."

Mrs. Jaisingh sniffled. "And you think he will be happy there?"

To cover his eagerness, Pundit Sharma took a moment to put down his own tea cup and reached for one of the snacks. "There is no greater service man can do than for his fellow man. When the soul is troubled, the *mandir* is the place to find peace. I find my own inner peace there every day."

After considering it for several moments, Mrs. Jaisingh finally nodded. "Yes, I think you're right. I think Amit should learn to serve others. Maybe, by doing so, he'll become more himself again."

The pundit hid his satisfaction by pressing his palms together, both a sign of greeting as well as supplication.

"Whatever you wish."

And so Amit began going to the temple every day after school.

For the first month, he did nothing but sulk in a corner. Pundit Sharma greeted him with a pleasant attitude and asked throughout the afternoon whether Amit needed anything. The boy just crossed his arms tighter and shook his head in anger.

When his second month in the mandir started, Amit walked in and headed toward his customary spot. Pundit Sharma put his hand on the boy's shoulder and stopped him. Amit scowled.

"I need your help today," the pundit said in a soft voice.

Amit glared back but couldn't reject him outright, and Pundit Sharma was pleased the boy still remembered the basics of *sanskar*. Even if their culture had become more permissive with time, at least youngsters still knew their place. Yes, Amit's attitude could have been more respectful, but they would work on that.

That day Pundit Sharma put Amit to work sweeping the steps, as he'd promised Mrs. Jaisingh. He also made Amit go to the foot of those steps and keep people's shoes straight, matching pairs and making sure no one from the street stole a worshipper's sandals. Pundit Sharma could tell Amit liked that job by the watchfulness of the boy's gaze and his eagerness to ask those coming down the stairs if they had, indeed, claimed the right pair of shoes.

In the weeks that followed, the pundit gave the boy other tasks: going to the flower shop to order the fresh-flower garlands for the statues of the gods, asking people who entered the mandir whether they needed any special *poojas* performed, and counting the money in the money box. Under his careful supervision, that is. One couldn't be too careful, even with children.

Several months passed, and the seasons changed. So did Amit's attitude, albeit one slow day at a time. On some days he came to the mandir with a zeal for his work. On other days, he dragged his feet across the floor and snapped at the pundit. Pundit Sharma wanted nothing more than to grab Amit by the shoulders and give him a tight slap. Instead he bided his time until the next monsoon season.

It was Amit, in fact, who alerted the pundit to the coming rains. He arrived at the temple clutching his stomach. Pundit Sharma put his hand on the boy's shoulder, surprised at how tall Amit had grown in the last year.

"What's wrong, *beta*?" he asked.

Amit grimaced. "I have a lot of pain in my belly. I think ..."

"Are you sick? Do you need some *nimbu-paani*? The lime water may soothe your pain."

Amit shook his head. "No, no, it won't help." He grimaced again. "I think ... I think the *barsaat* will come early this year. But it won't be ..." He exhaled in a loud breath, and his face relaxed a little. "It won't be as bad as the rain last year."

Pundit Sharma nodded in a practiced manner, although he wanted to jump for joy. The opportunity he'd spent nearly a year cultivating had come to fruition at last. He insisted Amit go to the stall across from the mandir and buy some *nimbu-paani* anyway. Amit obeyed, although the expression on his face said he knew the lime water would do him no good.

A farmer entered the mandir just as Amit left.

"Om Nama Shivai," Pundit Sharma said in greeting. "*Kaise ho?* How are you?"

The man tipped his head from side to side, the universal Indian gesture for "so-so."

"I want to pray for my crops this year, Pundit-ji," the farmer said, handing the priest some money and a coconut. "Last year they were all washed away, and my family struggled to eat. I just hope the rains this year don't last as long."

Pundit Sharma kept his movements slow, deliberate, as he deposited the money and placed the coconut at Lord Shiva's feet.

"The rains will come early, I'm afraid," he said, "but they will not destroy everything as they did last year. Have trust in Shiva and Ganesha, and they will guide you."

The farmer chuckled. "So, Pundit-ji, now you can see the future? Have you become a *jyotish?*"

The priest handed the man a stainless steel plate with some flowers and fruit as well as a few sweets.

"I see what Lord Shiva shows me," he said, "and I share what I know in service of the people of Bhubaneswar."

The farmer murmured a quick prayer and then thanked the pundit. Amit came back looking a little less in pain. Pundit Sharma put the boy to work circulating with a tray full of sweets throughout the worshippers who came that day.

"Any occasion, Pundit-ji?" Amit asked.

"Just the desire to make this a good day for all," the pundit said.

The rains came, as Amit promised, and they didn't storm the land as they had the year before. The farmer returned and praised the pundit in loud exhortations for his correct predictions. Pundit Sharma ducked his head and shied away from the praise and wonderment of those in the *mandir* that day. News of the farmer's claims, compounded by the priest's modesty, spread fast. Soon people came to the temple to find out how the weather would treat them from week to week.

The answers to those questions were easy. Pundit Sharma asked Amit every week what he thought the next week would be like and then turned around and wrapped those predictions in enough ambivalence to escape any serious consequences should the boy's predictions not land true. After five months, Pundit Sharma dropped the ambivalence. Amit was never wrong.

Other questions, naturally, tripped right along with questions about the weather.

"Pundit-ji, will my daughter-in-law have a boy?"

"Pundit Sharma, will the government's new scheme to privatize companies really help us?"

"Pundit-ji, when will the riots end?"

The priest did his best to reassure people about personal matters and national ones alike, and his certainty about the weather made up for his inability to make accurate predictions about other issues. Early on he did try to consult Amit about the people's non-weather questions, but Amit just stared at him with a blank look before frowning.

He didn't say anything, however, until two years later. It was the year 1994, and Amit had recently turned 13. The boy no longer looked like the gangly youngster who had crossed the threshold of the temple four years earlier. He'd grown as tall as the pundit.

Unbeknownst to Pundit Sharma, the boy had developed a sharp eye as well.

In the middle of the monsoon season that year—a fairly normal one, by Bhubaneswar's standards—Amit came to the mandir with determination on his face. Pundit Sharma sensed right away that Amit had something on his mind. He asked the boy about it, but Amit refused to answer.

"I'll talk to you before I leave today," he said when Pundit Sharma pressed him for the third or fourth time.

As the pundit performed religious ceremonies all day, he analyzed Amit's request. Were the boy and Mrs. Jaisingh going to move? It would make sense; a widow had limited options for a livelihood. It helped that she was young and had a son; both could work to earn enough money to keep the family alive. But ultimately widows moved back in with family members to live out their days as pitied members of the household.

That wasn't a prediction; it was the way of life in India.

At some point in the early afternoon, though, Pundit Sharma knew speculating would get him nowhere. Better to wait until Amit told him point blank what he wanted. If nothing else, being a priest taught a man to be patient when life threw challenges his way.

As the rays of the setting sun streaked across the sky, the pundit prepared to leave for the evening. He sent Amit to the mandir steps to make sure no one had left their slippers behind, and he took the money box into the back room. After straightening up a few things and one last look around, Pundit Sharma nodded in satisfaction. Everything was as it should be.

Just then, Amit came back from his task at the temple's steps.

"Pundit-ji, I would like to talk to you," he said.

Pundit Sharma's pulse picked up speed again. "Of course. What is it, *beta?*"

"I have been helping here at the mandir for two years now, and I've learned a lot about serving people. Mummy says she's seen a great deal of change in me, and that's because of my time here in the temple."

The priest turned around in piety and looked at the huge statues of Shiva and Parvati. "It's God's grace that you've become such a sensible young man."

"Being sensible doesn't help run a household," Amit said, and he crossed his arms. "Mummy wants me to study in a good college abroad. For that we need money, and she says maybe I should stop coming to the mandir and find some paying work."

Steady, Pundit Sharma counseled himself. *Don't say anything that would make him leave.*

"I think it's commendable that you're thinking about your future," the priest said, "but what of all the people here who you would leave behind? The ones who come and ask only for you when they come to do their *pooja*? Surely you would miss them."

Amit nodded. "Yes, I would, but I also have to be responsible. After all, Pundit-ji, you're the one who does the bulk of the work here. I'm simply a helper. It's not as if you're unable to run the temple without me."

Pundit Sharma's mind raced. He thought of the gold jewelry he'd bought his wife and the three new saris he'd gifted his mother in the previous year on Diwali. Although the Festival of Lights was still a few months away, he'd already begun scouting out gift ideas for this year. His income had increased dramatically in a short period of time, thanks to all the extra ceremonies he was able to convince people they needed because of the weather. If Amit left, how would he continue taking in that income? How would he be able to buy the good-quality leather sandals for himself and the best fruits and vegetables of the day instead of waiting on donations of shoes and coming one request short of begging for food?

Amit's ability had confounded him. In the last two years, he'd asked several questions to try to pry out of the boy the secret to his knowledge. No amount of rewording the same questions or patience in asking them repeatedly, however, yielded the results the pundit needed. If Amit left, everything would go back to as it was before. He wouldn't be able to continue with plans of the new home he wanted to build.

They would go back to blaming him for everything wrong in the house.

"Pundit-ji?"

"I think it's time, then, that the mandir offer you some sort of compensation," the pundit said, hating the words even as they came out of his mouth. He didn't want to give Amit a cut of his profit, but if Amit wasn't there he would have no profit at all. "How about 50 rupees a month?"

Amit's eyes went wide in shock. "Fifty rupees? Really?"

"Yes, of course," Pundit Sharma said, doing what he could to appear as serene as the dusk around them. "As I said, you're becoming a sensible young man, and it's good for you to learn responsibility."

After a few moments, Amit nodded and a smile of satisfaction crossed his face. "Fifty rupees per month, then. I think that will be a good amount for me to continue helping here. I'm sure I wouldn't get more than that anywhere else, at least not yet. And if my mother ever needs more …?"

And so it had come to this. Both of them knew it was outright blackmail, though neither of them would name it so brashly. Pundit Sharma balled one hand into a fist to resist the urge to slap Amit.

"The mandir is here to serve all who have needs of any kind," the priest said. "It is here for you and your mother in every capacity."

Amit nodded again and bid him farewell. The pundit replied with his customary evening blessing, but as he watched Amit leave he wondered whether the boy had managed to trap him into a long-term exchange or whether he really just had his mother's welfare in mind.

In the years that followed, the mandir's coffers became so full that Pundit Sharma had the Shiva and Parvati statues repainted twice. The painstaking work cost more than the pundit previously made in a whole year. Thanks to Amit, however, the priest could spend the money in a week and still not see the bottom of the money box.

Pundit Sharma's wife went from being known as a mousy, homely woman to one of the best-dressed in their whole colony. Her eyes gleamed at all the compliments she received, especially when she made sure to present a beggar with more than enough alms. A couple of the neighbors complained that she donated too much—the beggars would get used to their own level of affluence, and then how would they remember their place in society?

His mother began holding kitty parties, inviting friends from all over the city to attend the monthly women's social gatherings so they could exchange recipes and gossip of their respective households. When those friends pressed her as to why the pundit and his wife had no children yet, she would sigh in a dramatic fashion. Her son was busy serving the people, she would say, and the gods saw fit for Pundit Sharma to spend his life in service for now.

Plans for that new house did take shape, and Pundit Sharma visited an affluent colony in Bhubaneswar to inspect one of the last available plots there. Moving to the new neighborhood meant he could no longer walk to the mandir every day, but he would compensate for that by buying a top-of-the-line scooter. He considered a car for a short time, but his wife argued successfully against it. They didn't want to flaunt their new wealth in front of others; a pundit, after all, was expected to project piety, even in his chosen mode of transportation.

He made sure to pay Amit the 50 rupees on the first of every month—after all, everyone had bills to pay, and it would be in bad form to give the money late. He also managed to ignore the scowl that had begun to appear on Amit's face during the exchange. The pundit didn't have time for a child's tantrums; he had to worry about making sure he secured the best gardener for his new lawn.

It took more than two years for his new home to become a reality; even an abundance of money couldn't loosen the inertia so common among the labor class that built residences.

On that day in late 1997, when the time came for the *greh pravesh* service at his new home to bless it and ensure the gods would protect it, Pundit Sharma cracked the coconut on the front steps and looked as pleased as a chilled glass of *lassi* as everyone clapped. His eyes swept over the new neighbors and some of the old ones. He nodded genially to many of the worshippers who attended the mandir regularly and Amit. Except Amit wasn't smiling.

Pundit Sharma's own smile faded, and he went through the words of the blessing of the *greh pravesh* a little faster than he should have. He and his wife followed his mother inside the home, and friends and extended family came after them as everyone trooped to the kitchen. Pundit Sharma consulted his watch and then announced the auspicious moment for lighting the gas stove for the first time. Everyone clapped again, but this time the priest looked around and found Amit boring his eyes into him.

"*Chalo*, come, everyone, enjoy some snacks and some *lassi*," he announced, and servants began moving through the guests with trays of the sweet yogurt drink that would take the edge off the heat.

Amit stepped forward and grabbed the priest's elbow. "Pundit-ji, we need to talk."

"Yes, yes, *beta*, of course," the priest said, shaking off Amit's hand. "Later this week when you come—"

"No, now."

The pundit looked Amit straight in the eye and saw the anger there.

"*Beta*, would you like some *lassi*?"

Both the priest and Amit turned in the direction of Diya Sharma.

"No, thank you, Auntie," Amit said. "I need to go soon. I just wanted to talk to Pundit-ji for a few moments."

"Have something to eat at least," the priest's wife said with a kind smile. "Pundit-ji tells me all the time how much you serve the people of the temple and how grateful he is to you."

"Really?" Amit said.

"Come, Amit, let me see you out," the pundit said, a swath of anger covering him. He put one arm around Amit and clamped down on his shoulder. They began a swift walk through the house and around the party attendees.

As soon as they reached outside, Amit broke free of the priest. "How dare you, Pundit-ji? You've built yourself this palace, you buy yourself new clothes every week, the statues in the mandir get new paint and new clothing, and all you give me is a paltry fifty rupees a month?!"

"Amit, listen to me," Pundit Sharma began.

"No, *you* listen to *me*," Amit said, holding up an accusatory finger. "Either you start giving me more money, or I'll tell everyone in there you're a fraud! The only reason you've made all that money is because of what I tell you about the monsoons. You're a fraud and a cheat! I know how you overcharge people for weddings. And funerals? You should be ashamed for making your profit off someone's death!"

The pundit seethed. How dare this boy accuse him of fraud? After all he had done to make sure Mrs. Jaisingh would get an extra income. He had given Amit a purpose and allowed him to be a part of a place that would teach him invaluable lessons about life and service.

Under the fury, however, lay fear, which only served to make him angrier.

"You ungrateful boy," the pundit said in a low voice to avoid attracting attention. "Do you have any idea what you're saying?"

Amit's eyes flashed with anger. "Only the truth, Pundit-ji."

"The truth?" the pundit scoffed. "We make our truth based on what we want that truth to be, Amit. If you haven't learned that by now working in the temple, you've learned nothing."

"Then I want my truth to be more money," Amit said. "Pay me three hundred rupees a month, or I will stop helping you."

Pundit Sharma sucked in a sharp breath. "Are you crazy? You're not worth three hundred rupees a month! You're barely worth the fifty I give you!"

"Fine!" Amit said with a sneer. "Don't give me the fifty. Don't give me anything. I'm not coming back to the mandir at all! You want to make your truth a reality, Pundit-ji? All of this ..." He waved his arms around to indicate the house and the elaborate landscaping. "This is your truth now, so you can find a way to fund it yourself!"

Before the priest could utter another word, Amit whirled on his heel and stomped away.

It took Pundit Sharma two months to believe that Amit wouldn't come back.

For the first week, every time he heard footsteps his attention snapped to the source. Temple goers would ask for Amit, and the pundit made excuses: he was busy with exams; his mother wasn't well; he had gone to visit his grandparents. After a few weeks, people stopped asking. The priest, however, didn't stop waiting for the boy.

In those two months people kept coming to Pundit Sharma for answers about their personal lives and, yes, the weather. He muddled along with their questions about their immediate concerns—births and marriages and college placements—and he made up answers about the seasons. For a time the latter worked; he and Amit had talked through enough of the rains in advance that the pundit could offer realistic advice. The longer Amit didn't show up, however, the more vague the pundit's answers became.

Mandir attendees began to notice the discrepancy, but it didn't become truly obvious until the following year. It had been eight years since Pundit Sharma first met Amit and six years since the boy had started coming to the mandir. It shocked the priest how much of a habit it had become for him to see Amit around the temple.

The following year was a bad one for Pundit Sharma. People still came to him for religious ceremonies to bless their homes, their cars, and their children, but they stopped asking the pundit their questions about the *barsaat*. It was clear to them, residents whispered, that the pundit had lost whatever divine connection he had with the gods and the rain.

That last thought took root faster than the pundit could blink, and slowly the requests for run-of-the-mill ceremonies slowed down too. If the pundit had lost his most important connection with the gods on something that ruled their lives every year, what guarantee was there that the ceremonies he performed would please Shiva, Parvati, Ganesha, and the rest of the heavenly host? No, better to seek out another pundit, someone who hadn't lost that holy link.

Once again Pundit Sharma had to pay attention to his mother and wife complaining. The size of the house had increased and with it the size of the arguments inside it. Now, in addition to what to have for their meals, they argued about the right to the servants. They fought about who had the right to the drawing room for their social events. When the flood of money slowed to a stream and then a trickle, they fought about who had first right to the few rupees coming in.

For the first time in his life, Pundit Sharma found himself in debt, heavily so. He owed money on the house and the scooter. The servants started complaining about not getting paid, and they began leaving one by one. His wife voiced her displeasure at having to do the dishes again. If she was the wife of such a prominent pundit in the area, why should she wash the kitchen utensils like a common person?

Pundit Sharma didn't know how to tell his wife about the way the money had begun to dry up, about how much he had used Amit to bring in that income, about the boy's mysterious talent. Explaining things to her wouldn't have done any good anyway. She still screamed at his mother and complained to him every night.

"How is it possible for you to serve the people in the city and not take care of your own wife? We don't even have any children! Is there something wrong with you?"

There were many things wrong, although the pundit doubted it had to do with his virility. No, his problems stemmed from a teenage boy who had forsaken his duty and obligation. Despite spending considerable time trying to find a clever solution, Pundit Sharma could find none. He knew only one person could restore his fortune.

The start of monsoon season, Bhubaneswar, 1999

Once again Pundit Sharma found himself outside the Jaisingh home, although it looked radically different this time. Laborers hauled cartons from inside the house to a tempo waiting outside, and the priest skirted around the large truck as he made his way toward the front gate. He held the gate open for a pair of wizened old men with suitcases balanced on their heads then ducked inside before he could be delayed any further.

"Who do you want to see?" a young male servant asked in an unfriendly voice.

"Uh, Mrs. Jaisingh ... is she in?" the pundit replied, looking in amazement at the empty drawing room. The formal sofas had disappeared, presumably inside the tempo.

"Satish, I'll handle this."

Pundit Sharma turned toward Amit's voice and did a double-take. The boy had grown to nearly six feet tall, and his brawny frame seemed to fill the space around them as he put his hands on his hips and scowled. The male servant, Satish, scurried to the interior portion of the house.

"What do you want, Pundit?" Amit asked in a cold voice.

The priest managed to keep from gaping. The boy's insolence had grown into downright disrespect. Since when did he deem it appropriate to drop the honorific "ji" from the names of elders?

"Are you going someplace?" Pundit Sharma asked. If Amit couldn't speak with respect, then the priest had no compunction to answer anything.

"My mother is moving back to Kanpur to be with my *maasi*, and I'm going abroad for my studies."

"Abroad?" the pundit repeated, astonished. "But ... what about the mandir and the people of Bhubaneswar?"

"You mean, what about your easy cash?" Amit said. "It's gone. In fact, I recommend you find someplace to go yourself, Pundit. This monsoon season ..."

"What?" Pundit Sharma said, unable to hide his eagerness at getting a scrap of information from Amit. It had been too long since they had worked together. Too long since the coffers at the temple had filled more than halfway.

Amit scoffed. "Leave it. I'm not telling you anything anymore."

"Amit, please. I ... I need your help."

It grated on the pundit's nerves to admit it. He was a grown man, and he had to beg a child for his assistance. Never mind what he'd done for the boy and how the boy should feel obligated on his own.

The boy stared at him long and hard, and Pundit Sharma realized it was unfair of him to call Amit a boy anymore—even if he did it in his own mind. The gangly limbs had disappeared, and the experience of life made Amit's eyes see things a little more clearly. Perhaps Pundit Sharma had not done well by him after all.

Amit narrowed those eyes of his and took a step toward Pundit Sharma. The priest wanted to take a step back. He didn't like the proximity between him and this boy who, he realized now, was much younger and stronger than him.

"All I can say is that whatever happens, *if* something happens, you're deserving of all of it. Now get out of my house."

Without bothering to see whether he complied, Amit turned and went into another room.

Pundit Sharma let go of the breath he didn't realize he held. He wanted to call Amit back, but a sixth sense told him he shouldn't bother. Like it or not, his association with Amit had ended.

It was a shame too, that that particular sixth sense was the only one the pundit had. In October of that year, a super cyclone hit the state of Odisha. The winds blew with such force in the city that they destroyed most meteorological instruments and power lines; for 24 hours the residents had no contact with the outside world. By the time the storm finished ravaging the various coastal towns and islands, more than 1.5 million homes had sustained damage.

One of those homes belonged to Pundit Narayan Sharma. He had gone to the temple that morning, as usual, and began a special *pooja* in the hopes the religious ceremony would appease the gods and bring peace to the weather. The torrential downpour prevented him from going home, and by the time he could leave the mandir and make his way back to his upscale neighborhood half of his house had disappeared. His mother and wife, too, could not be found. As the days wore on, the pundit began to accept bit by bit that they wouldn't return.

As he picked his way through the soggy remains of what was once his home, he kept swallowing hard. His throat burned, although he didn't know whether it was from regret or something else. Shame, perhaps? But why? He had made all the right choices, had always put his service to the people first. Why should he feel ashamed?

Not knowing what else to do, Pundit Sharma returned to the temple. The weather had stabilized somewhat, and he assumed people would return with offerings of gratitude that they had survived and requests for prayers for the dead. He sat on the lower portion of the dais in front of the statues of Shiva and Parvati and waited.

Some passersby glanced at him; most of them didn't bother turning his direction. He called out to one or two, but somehow his voice didn't reach them or their attention remained elsewhere. Pundit Sharma turned towards the statues behind him.

"Om Nama Shivai, Om Nama Shivai," he murmured.

The words remained just that: words. He gained no solace from them, no comfort. That night he slept on the cot in the small back room and came out the next morning, a little clearer than the previous day, with dwindled hope.

By the end of the week, the burning in his throat remained constant. He swept the temple steps himself, purchased flower garlands on his own, and stopped in small stalls alongside the edge of the road for the simplest of meals. The residents of Bhubaneswar often moved at a brisk pace in their daily routines, but Pundit Sharma got the distinct impression that people ignored him. Averted gazes and shoulders tilted away from him in abrupt movements told him all he needed to know.

He wanted to mourn what he had lost but didn't know how. The only consolation he could offer himself was that he would no longer wake up to the screams and tantrums of two women and that he finally achieved the change he had craved nearly a decade earlier.

THE END

With an MSJ in magazine publishing from Northwestern University, Ekta has written and edited about everything from healthcare to home improvement to Hindi films. She began her career in 2005. In 2011 she became a freelance editor for other writers' short stories, novels, and nonfiction projects like memoirs and self-help books. Ekta also manages The Write Edge and its three extension blogs of her weekly short fiction, her book reviews, and her parenting adventures. When not writing and editing Ekta spends time with friends (the ones other people can see) and counts her blessings, which include a loving husband and two beautiful daughters who astound her on a regular basis.

http://thewriteedge.wordpress.com

The Smokehouse on Pigtail Alley

Contemporary Fiction
Fire

Tammy Lough

I slam the gear shift into park and watch the black hearse grind and bump down a narrow rock path. It'll take a while to get where the gravedigger's got Grannie's burying spot all dug up. Shit. Been meaning to get up here for a visit, but life got in the way. Patsy got a job at the laundromat steaming shirts or some shit, so she couldn't ride along. Maybe she'll keep her trashy mouth shut long enough to make a hundred or so dollars 'afore getting fired. That old lady of mine, hell's fire, I reckon she's every bit of thirty-one now. She done got fed up with eve-rybody's crap a long time ago and don't take no duff no more. You got somebody needing an honest ass-kickin'? Call my Patsy. She'll git-r-done.

I slump down in my seat so nobody sees me. I ain't getting outta this truck and hauling my ass through the rain and mud to see Grannie's casket get buried. No way, no how. She ain't in there anyways. Wonder if she's a ghost? I get a little uptight thinking about it, so I stop. I don't need no heebie-jeebies.

I hear tapping on my shotgun seat ridin' window, and I'll be damned if it ain't Aunt Mabel getting all geared up to bang on it again. Shit. Shit. Shit. I wave my hand to tell her just go on with-out me, but she plants herself right outside my door. She ain't going nowhere. After banging harder and throwing me a chicken-fat arm wave to come on out, I roll my eyes and slam my fist on the steering wheel. Piss.

I light a ciggie and pull up the door handle. They's all gonna look over cause metal against rusted metal grunts and groans 'til it lets out a screeching squeal, and yup, they's all looking like they ain't got nothing else to do but get in my business. I cough real loud and spit a big ole loogie. Show 'em I don't give a shit, go on and look all ya want. Gotta take the last drag of my ciggie. Damn, tastes harsh, cause I'm sucking on the filter. I shove my hands in my pockets and here comes Aunt Mabel. I'll be damned if she don't grab my arm and shove her hand through my right chicken wing. She says she'll hang on, so iffin she takes to sliding on the slick grass, she won't get herself a mud bath. Hell if she won't. She ain't dragging my ass down with her. I'll push her off, that's

what I'll do. Her ass starts going in a mud hole, that bitch is on her own. She jabbers 'bout how am I, and what've I been doing with my time? I feel like saying, I lay 'round smoking weed all day, then asking if she wants t'buy a reefer.

I drive near two hours and park my old beater pickup in Grannie's driveway, right off Pigtail Alley. I get what I call the thunder heartbeats. They pound up against my chest and make me feel all dizzy and shit. No, I ain't got no business being here, but that ain't nobody's business. If somebody from the cemetery shows up and asks what I'm doing, I'll tell 'em to kiss my ever-lovin' ass.

Didn't figure the old house would be in such poor shape. I tilt my head up toward the windshield to get a good look at the roof. A fair bit of wood shingles is still hanging, but most is missing altogether. The clapboard siding might make good firewood, I reckon, but looks like somebody made off with the windows and doors. They probably got a pretty penny for the crystal door knobs. Them things, they was ancient.

I flick my cigarette butt out the window and light up another. No more cheap ciggies after today. *No sir, no way.* Me and my old lady, Patsy, we'll be smoking those fancy ciggies and buying 'em by the case. I holler as loud as my nicotine-tarred lungs will allow. "Whew, hot damn!"

The quarter bottle a'whiskey propped tween the legs of my Goodwill-bought 505s calls my name. I answer with a long swig, and damn if that shit don't burn good. "Fire in the hole!" I try to take a deep breath and get to coughing and hacking 'til my head feels like it's gonna explode. *That's sick. What if my head really did explode? Freakin' awesome that's what.* I laugh 'til it hurts, then cough some more. Stretching to the passenger floorboard, I snatch up my inhaler and suck a deep hit, then toss it back.

If you ask me, burying Grannie was more like planting a tree than laying somebody to rest. But, if I hadn't driven over to her place now, later'd be too late. If what's in her attic is what I think it is, this dude's gonna be rich. I lift the bottle for a swig and salute the label. "Thanks, honey," I say to the bottle. *Thanks, like it hears me or somethin'. That's messed up.*

The clouds all gray and threatening most of the day open up and now it's pouring like a bitch on the windshield. From what I remember, it usually *is* wet and nasty for a planting. I jerk the handle to open the rusted-out truck door and the wind yanks on the heaviness of metal, swinging it wide. It bounces back a time or two, making all that damn racket 'afore stopping. I look down to see the gravel's turned into a soggy milk bath. Should dry up pretty quick with all the wind behind it. Wind, hell. More like a damn tornada blowing in all ways, including sideways. I slam the door shut and square myself back into the seat. Shit, it didn't close. I slam it again. Time for another ciggie.

The couple hours it took to get here from the planting, my mind played movie reel memories of weekends at Grannie's. Days spent throwing washers, and playing hide 'n seek, Ante Over the washhouse, and eating sugar cookies chased down with strawberry soda-pop 'til we felt like puking. Sometimes, we did. All the boy cousins, we'd swim in the crick all day, peel our clothes off and toss 'em up onto the cattails and shit. Maybe we'd tie on a bobber and throw in a cane pole or two. One of us boys would get a wild hair up our ass and open the chicken coop. Those chickens, they'd run through the yard squawking like we was killing 'em. Then, Grannie, she'd squawk like she was gonna kill us. What a hoot. We'd coax the girl cousins up to the loft in the barn and plead with 'em to show us their titties. *Hell yeah!*

Nighttime, all us kids raced for spots on the two iron beds in the big bedroom. Some of us lay vertical like normal, others at the foot, horizontal-like. We didn't care, we was too tired to fuss. The grown-ups, they played 500 'til all hours of the night, their voices louder as the clock ticked later. Bursts of laughter, cards slamming the table, and Grannie's unmistakable cackle jarred me awake then soothed me back to sleep.

A hot ash falls off my ciggie and lands right atop my index finger. I shake it hard to stop it from blistering, but I'm wasting my time. Blister's already coming on, and it burns like a sumbitch.

I remember that spring day back in 1990 like yesterday. Cousin Robbie showed up with his car full of art tubes. Tubes like the kind you put paintings in to keep 'em from gettin' crudded up, wrinkled, and shit. Robbie came inside and flashed me a look akin to what the hell are you doing here? Like I didn't belong as much as he did. Grannie, she started hustling around and asking if he wanted some eats. No, he had a guy along to help unload some stuff and couldn't stay. Said he needed to store some things in her attic, and without even asking walked straight toward her bedroom. His friend, I think maybe Joe or Jack or some shit, followed him, carrying a wooden ladder under his left armpit. He propped the ladder where Robbie pointed, up against the north wall in Grannie's bedroom and right under a nearly invisible panel in the ceiling. If you didn't know it was there, you'd never see it. Gramps tore the real opening out soon after he and Grannie married and moved into the place. "Shit fire and save matches," he'd say when one of his buddies hired out help. "Do it yourself, and make folks wonder how the living hell you pulled it off."

Robbie climbed the rungs 'til he could lift the panel above his head and scoot it to the side. He climbed back down and propped the ladder into the opening. Hell, I bet they carried thirty or so of them white art tubes up there. A few of 'em was longer than my truck and others not no bigger than my forearm. Soon as they was done, Robbie kissed Grannie goodbye on her wrinkly cheek. 'Afore I could say, see ya later tater-tot, they was long gone. Soon after, the relatives bought Grannie a one-way ticket to a nursing home up in Drake. Seems like yesterday, but it's been pert near twenty years ago.

Grannie got her heart attack a few days back, and poof, no more Grannie. Robbie, he's been in prison for involuntary manslaughter and cousin Faye-Dawn said he's getting out soon. All I know is whatever he put in Grannie's attic, he'll be coming back for. *'Xcept it ain't gonna be here, asshole.*

It's still raining fierce, but I gotta get moving. Told Patsy I'd be back by dark, plus, I'm getting horny. I pull the ladder outta the bed of my truck and head up the cracked sidewalk. Feels kinda weird walking right into Grannie's old place, but heck, there ain't no door. The faded paper hangin' in shreds down the walls looks like somebody threw pitchers of Grannie's sweet tea at 'em. There'd been a metal table under the window where Grannie kept plates of cookies and slices of homemade pie. I 'member running a fingernail down a black, crusty, muck-filled table seam, then sticking it in cousin Nan's mouth. Damn, she got pissed. Gramps used to shave his poked-out whiskers by looking in a mirror he'd hung on the wall. I'd sit and watch him shave. He'd tease me. "Darryl, you're fixing to be next." When I'd stop paying attention, he'd pounce like a lion with shaving cream on his finger and plant it on my nose. It smelled like spearmint and him.

I take a quick look in the front room where we played hide the button for hours. "You're cold, gettin' warmer, hot, you're on fire!" The floor grate taking up space in the living room used to scare the hell out of me. Made of iron or some sort of metal, them grates hurt bad when we'd be playing and run over the top of 'em with our bare feet. It brought heat up through pipes that ran to the green, paint-chipped propane tank we'd hide behind when our mom's called bedtime.

I hoof it back out to the truck, grab a flashlight, and return to Grannie's room. Climbing the ladder, I steady my midsection against the rungs while lifting the panel. With back and forth jiggling, I scoot the panel to the side and out of the way. It only takes me a minute to climb down, reposition the ladder, and get back up there. I flip the flashlight to high beam and holy Jehoshaphat if there ain't fly and bug encrusted cobwebs hanging all over the damn place. Looks like they's been blown in for a Halloween party. There's probably a zillion creepy spiders holed up in here. I light a ciggie, take a deep breath, and blow smoke all around me. *Like that's gonna help, dumbass.*

The ridges on the flashlight make creases in my sweaty, shaking hand. I ease my grip and shine the beam across the attic. *Whoa, Robbie dude, you made a butt load of trips to Grannie's now, didn't ya?* Art tubes, maybe sixty to a hundred of 'em are stacked up nice and neat along the west wall. I walk over and grab the smallest tube, pop open the lid, and tilt it 'til a rolled-up painting drops into my cupped hand. I flatten it out and guesstimate the size at about twenty-eight by twenty-six inches. I ain't claiming to know much about fancy artwork, but this ain't no run of the mill starving artist bullshit. The signature, I've heard his name 'afore, Johannes Vermeer. He called this picture, *The Concert.* The next three I open are autographed by Rembrandt, a few by Degas, Monet, and some dude named Flinck.

My hands shake as I pace the floor waiting for Patsy to answer her damn cell phone. I tell her what I found, and she says to hang on a minute. I know what she's doing, firing up the internet. I hear a gasp and Patsy starts jawing about an art heist from some museum in Boston, the Isabella Stewart Museum. Next, she's screaming like a banshee and telling me about a five-million-dollar reward for finding this shit. I light a ciggie and take a deep drag. My shoulders shake while I cough. The harder I hack, the more my eyes bulge. I reach my hand into the pocket of my 505s and remember I left my inhaler in the truck. Through the hacking, I manage to tell Patsy I'll call her back.

Making my way to the ladder, I see sprays of blood when I cough. My breaths are getting short and choppy. I tell myself not

to panic. *Keep your cool, Darryl my man, keep it together.* I gulp a bit of air and pinch my ciggie tighter between my lips as I grab the ladder. My right leg swings for the rung so I can back myself down. I scream like a schoolgirl when my left-hand settles aside a black, hairy-bellied spider with wide fangs poking outta its head. He reared up to lunge at my face.

Next, I'm falling in what seems like weird slow motion. I musta hit six or seven ladder rungs as I death-plunge to the floor. When I hit, I hit hard, right on my damn head then to the flat of my back. Bam! I try to move and my head lifts but nothing else. I feel a sharp, searing pain zap up and down my back like an alcohol-soaked razor blade sliced my spinal cord all to hell.

Smoke? I smell smoke and 'member my lit ciggie. I hear a sound akin to bacon frying and realize it's the crackling of a fire. I watch the flames lash upward like dragon tongues licking the walls toward the attic. I can't move. I can't move nothing but my danged head, and I don't see nothing but thick gray-black smoke. I blink 'til my eyes are slits, but it don't do a damn thing to ease the burning pain under my lids and inside my nose. Tears and snot snake down the sides of my cheeks, pool in my ears, then trail down the back of my neck. I don't want to die. I don't want to die in a damn fire. Shit.

I need a ciggie.

THE END

Tammy Lough is a multi-published award-winning author. Her memberships include Saturday Writers, Missouri Writers Guild, and Romance Writers of America. She writes a monthly column for the Saturday Writers newsletter: "On the Back Page with Tammy." She is also the Romance columnist and Curriculum Director for Gabriela Pereira's DIYMFA.com Tammy has two amazing sons and three cherished grandchildren.

Visit her at www.TammyLough.com

Cottonwood

Grit Lit
Fire

Daniel Mitchell

He sat alone, far from the lights of town, away from anything he knew, anyone he'd loved, and watched the fire. It was fascinating. Pine logs that used to be a tree, that used to be home for any number of birds and insects, a source of winter food for all the neighborhood squirrels, shade in the summer and shelter in the winter for the last hundred years. A whole world really. Slowly, without mercy, the flames ate it all. In the end, there would be nothing left of their world but ashes blowing into darkness.

He wasn't sure how long he'd been there. Days and nights didn't mean much anymore. He measured time in cases of beer and gallons of whiskey. Last time he'd passed a town he bought five cases of Busch and four half gallons of Jack Daniels. The ice and food had mostly gone a while ago, but he didn't get hungry as much these days anyway. The creek behind his truck came straight down the Rockies from snowmelt somewhere above 13,000 feet, and it kept everything colder than any ice chest. Build a little dam of rock in an eddy, drop in the cans and bottles, and you had your own wet bar with no need to tip. No dress code. No small talk. Just the dullness, the darkness, and the flames.

Finding a way to sleep, a way to get through another night without thinking, was his only real need, but even that was deserting him.

For two full days he'd just sat and stared at the fire. Remembering her.

It was one of those fall days that sometimes graces Oklahoma between late September and early November, what the old folks called Indian Summer. Most of the leaves were still on the trees in a madman's quilt of colors. A cool breeze flowed down from the northeast, and dandelion clouds chased each other across the sky. Joseph gave the four-wheeler its head and slid around the curves on gravel and red clay all the way to Dougherty, only letting up when he came in sight of Jan's Country Store. He knew from experience she was likely to refuse him service for a week if he threw gravel in her parking lot. Jan seemed convinced all men were disobedient boys, desperately in need of a good switching. She wasted no opportunity to take them down a notch or three.

"Afternoon, Miss Jan."

"I ain't been a Miss in forty years and you know it," she said.

"Miss Jan, you can't be much more than fresh out of high school with such a lovely smile and figure."

She glared, but there was no real heat in her eyes. Joseph suspected she enjoyed these visits as much as he did.

"They fired you yet?"

"No, ma'am. They tried, but the place dang near shuts down every time I take a pee break. Just can't make it without me."

"Boy, you're more full of it than my daddy's back pasture."

"Why thank you, Miss Jan. That's what my momma always used to say too."

"She sounds like a smart woman. Shame she dropped you on your head so much. You want something or did you just come in to ruin my day?"

"I came to raid your beer supply and bask in the glory of your presence."

"Get on with it then, and get going. I got better things to do than listen to your lips flap."

"Yes, ma'am." Joseph grabbed a case of Busch from the cooler and a bag of Doritos from the shelf. Then he took his time looking around as if he'd forgotten something, mostly to irritate Jan. When he finally walked up to the counter he read her faded t-shirt that said, "Protected by Smith and Wesson" across ample, low-slung breasts.

"You eyeballing something?" she asked.

"Just admiring that shirt and pondering the loveliness it hides."

"Boy, don't make me call the dog."

She meant it too. Not that Prince Albert was much of a dog. Joseph glanced to where the mostly toothless basset hound lay stinking in the corner. By the time it got up he could probably be long gone, but he really wanted the beer, and knew Jan would take her time ringing it up, making him stand there while Prince Albert slobbered all over his leg in senile fury.

He was outside, using bungee cords to secure the beer and chips in the ice chest on the back rack of his Honda, when he heard the light crunch of gravel under boots and heard a voice as smooth as a spider web on your neck.

"Nice four-wheeler."

He looked up into eyes dark as a new moon and lost all rational thought. He realized his mouth had been hanging open for some seconds after she laughed and walked inside, brushing him with a swaying hip as she passed.

He glanced to the gas pumps and saw she had arrived on a new Honda Foreman with chrome rims and Mud Gator tires. It was glossy black and exactly the one he'd have bought, if he hadn't been too cheap to buy new.

She came back out, and Joseph took a quick glance at her left hand. When he saw no ring, his left knee buckled slightly. Midnight hair was tied back in a long tail over blue flannel and dark skin. Her high cheekbones left little doubt about her Native

blood. Everything about her was beauty and grace. A faintest scent of wild flowers and cedar lingered in her wake.

"That's a nice ride. If you ever want to go riding by the river, I'd be happy to keep you company or whatever," Joseph said so fast even he could barely make out the words.

She smiled, and he swore he could hear music someplace.

"I'll tell you what," she said. "You pack a picnic on that thing, and I'll meet you in the pines above your place tomorrow at noon."

"Done," he said. "Wait, what's your name?" She just started up her four-wheeler, smiled like a new dawn, and drove away. *And how do you know where I live?*

He dropped his keys twice trying to start his Honda. He blushed when he caught Jan smirking at him from the door.

"Who was that?" he asked.

"Boy, I believe you're about to find out," she said. "Yes, indeed."

Joseph traced the delicate lines where calf met ankle with his fingertips. He took in each tiny detail. The lines of muscle and ligament at the back of her knee, the gentle swell of thigh, and the flawless, dusky skin. They lay in a tangle of limbs; she was a snuggler. He'd always liked that feeling of euphoria that came with a new girl, but unlike the others, with Talia it never wore off. He'd made it three months before asking her to marry him. They were watching the sunset from high on a cliff across the river from his cabin. She smiled but didn't speak, letting the kiss answer for her. When she finally let go, he almost fell off the rock slab he had put there for a loveseat. Laughing as she pulled him back up, her deep brown eyes saying everything she never did.

Two weeks later they were married in that same clearing by a black-haired preacher who never stopped smiling. Her Choctaw family had insisted on a traditional ceremony. Joseph, Talia, and the preacher stood at the end of a circle of her relatives. The men wore colorful shirts of silk, velvet, or soft cotton with diamond designs down the sleeves and across their chests and backs. Most of the older men wore flat-brimmed black hats, and all had bright ribbons at their sides, hanging down the legs of dark pants. The women wore blue, red, or pink cotton dresses. White aprons with hand-stitched diamond borders matched their dresses.

Joseph and Talia joined hands as a single blanket was draped around their shoulders. The preacher lectured them on their duties to each other and quoted from the Bible in both Choctaw and English. The small crowd let out whoops as he pronounced them husband and wife. Her relatives sang a song in their native tongue as Talia led him in the stomp dance she'd tried to teach him. Joseph danced almost as well as he flew, however, and stumbled twice, to the great mirth of her relatives.

Sonny and Dirty Joe, the only hands from the quarry Joseph considered true friends, stood out in pale contrast to the crowd. Their clothes were far less colorful, but their smiles were just as big. Joseph's parents never responded to the invitation Talia made him send. He hadn't seen either of them in years. Other than brief phone calls when somebody died, they rarely spoke. In their eyes, Talia would never be more than an Indian anyway. Both were at least a quarter Indian themselves, like most Oklahomans, but they would never admit it. They didn't deserve to know her.

Back at the cabin, food of all kinds loaded down tables in the yard. Dark-eyed relatives sang and danced around the bonfire. A whole line of cousins played handmade drums and flutes. The music and singing in English, Choctaw, and Chickasaw went on long after Talia led him into the flower-strewn cabin. Everyone cheered as she closed and firmly locked the door. In the bedroom she untied her blue and white silk dress. It fell away in the candlelit shadows. He remembered vividly how she had left her white moccasins on.

Six months later, tracing every inch of her long, brown legs, he pulled away the sheet to see more of her and finally noticed the increasing swell of her stomach. His breath caught and he looked to her face, realizing she was awake and watching him.

Before he could ask, she said, "We'll name him Joseph, like his father."

Maybe God liked him after all.

He was running the old DC 10 dozer, scraping up a pile of blue diamond gypsum for Big Frank to grab with the track hoe when he got the call. He glanced at the caller ID and was surprised to see it was Talia's father. Bill had never called him before. Not once. Joseph got a slimy feeling down deep and shut down the dozer.

"Hello?"

"Joseph, you should come home now. Talia needs you."

"What's wrong? Is it the baby?" he asked, but the line was already dead. Bill never wasted time with words when silence would do. Joseph fired the dozer back up and pushed it as fast as it could go to the lot up the mountain, cursing it for more speed. He used the CB to call Sonny on the way and say he had to leave. He killed the engine before jumping down by his truck as sirens began to echo through the hills.

He slid to a stop in the driveway behind two county cop cars and ran inside. Bill stopped him in the living room.

"You should wait here," he said. "It's not good for you to see her this way."

"What are you talking about, Bill? What happened to my Talia? She's supposed to be at the doctor today!"

"Looks like she came home and interrupted them. TV is gone. Some other stuff. Even cut the copper pipes off your water heater. Big money for copper now."

Joseph tried to push past, but Bill held him without strain, deceptively strong with his long arms and big belly. "They shot her, Joseph. In the face. In the belly. Ambulance is coming, but it will be too late I think. They're always too late."

"Let me see my woman, Bill." Something in Joseph's face convinced him. Bill nodded and stepped back.

She lay on the kitchen floor. The two deputies were there, one holding a sodden red dishrag to her forehead, the other doing the same for the wound on her stomach. One of them was talking, motioning him back, but Joseph couldn't hear him. He couldn't really see anything either but the shallow movement of her rapid breathing and the way her long, black hair spread in the red pool around her head, like the Devil's halo.

There was a butcher knife by her hand. Even eight months pregnant she'd tried to chase them off. Talia feared no one, so they shot her over some copper pipe and a flat screen. He knelt beside her, his jeans soaking up her life, and watched as her breathing slowed. Became ragged. At the last her eyes opened. The left pupil was dilated, the right a pinprick, but she smiled at him. He struggled to speak, but she shook her head slightly and with her final exhale whispered, "Live," saying everything with that one word. He could only nod and watch her light fade.

When the paramedics finally arrived and tried to take her, Joseph picked up the knife and told them to get out. One of the deputies shot him with a taser. Bill tried to stop them, so they tased him too.

Four days later Joseph, Talia's father, and her brothers filled in her grave at the local cemetery themselves. Talia wasn't in it though. Late that night her relatives gathered to lay her to rest in the same clearing where they had first kissed, where he had asked her to marry him, and where they had taken their vows. It wasn't legal, and it wasn't even his land, but no one ever came here, not even the cows. As they piled rocks on the grave to keep the scavengers out, Joseph planted a small dogwood tree above her head for a marker. Come spring she could feed the first flowers of the year, and maybe in some small way she wouldn't really be gone.

Most of them stayed with him until dawn, singing hymns in Choctaw and English, then drifted away in twos and threes.

"Sometimes we can't understand things in this life," Bill said when all the others were gone, "but you will see her in the next one. Remember your promise. Live. For her and for your son. Live."

He sat on the bench he had built for her as Bill walked away. He thought about her promise. Her curse. Mostly he thought about little Joseph, the son he'd never meet, murdered before his first breath.

The cops were little help. The only evidence they found were some tire tracks in the yard. They matched the tread pattern to an all-terrain Kumo truck tire. Joseph had the same tires on his truck. Half the trucks in the state did. The cabin was too far out in the woods for any witnesses. A week after the funeral, the sheriff called to apologize for their impotence and the taser. Without something to go on, there was nothing more he could do. Joseph had heard the stories about this sheriff and his deputies. Everyone had.

Talia's brothers were asking around, but so far there had been little to go on. Jan had run off some shoplifting meth-heads the morning of the murder, but her security cameras hadn't worked in years. The only information she could give was their ragged T-shirts were hanging off skeletal shoulders, they had meth-mouth and shaved heads, and had taken off in a white Ford pickup. It wasn't much, but Talia's family spread the word anyway. If they were found, no one would call the police.

When Joseph showed up at work the following Monday, Sonny called him into the office.

"Are you sure you're ready for this, son? You look like you haven't slept in a week, and, no offense, but you smell like a hobo threw up on you. You haven't used a vacation day in two years. The good Lord knows you have it coming. I've got a little hunting cabin up in Utah near Flaming Gorge. Take that old Jeep of yours and stay as long as you like. I'll square it with the company and keep an eye on your place. Your job will be waiting when you get back."

Joseph spent the night drinking the last of his beer and woke up on the floor of the nursery. Talia and her cousins had spent weeks painting and decorating, then changing their minds and doing it all over again. They'd finally settled on baby blue with a yellow sunrise on the wall. He vaguely remembered falling asleep staring at the tiny dream catcher on the north wall above the crib. It was supposed to catch nightmares and keep them at bay. There was a larger version in his bedroom. Neither had worked.

Maybe Sonny was right. Another night here and he might do something stupid. He knew he'd never be at peace in that house again. He loaded up the Jeep with camping gear, Sonny's map, and his old .357. On the way out the door, he reached up on top of the grandfather clock and pulled down a pack of Marlboros and the Zippo lighter Talia thought he'd thrown away months ago. He lit a stale cigarette and the curtains, then gently closed the door.

THE END

Seduced by the book mobile at an early age, Daniel Mitchell grew up in a family composed equally of soldiers, outdoorsmen, and teachers. He worked a variety of jobs from life guard stands to loading docks, once managed the Oklahoma Shakespearean Festival, and spent some time in the oilfield building pipelines and perfecting the art of properly chosen expletives. For the last few decades he's been a public school teacher of English and Science in Oklahoma and Alaska. Happily married and the father of two children as shockingly attractive and intelligent as their mother, he holds a BA in English, an MFA in Fiction, and is currently working on the release of his first novel, A Portion for Foxes.

One World

Urban Fantasy
Water

Artio Murphy

Gravel crunched into her soft skin as she fell again onto the hard ground. Tears pricked her eyes from the unfamiliar pain and the bright sun. Allowing a sob to shake her, she gritted her teeth and forced herself back up onto shaky legs. Hearing a metal machine approach, she made sure to stay far to the side so it could drive by her. What she did not expect was for the "car"—her brain supplied—to stop several feet in front of her and the human inside to get out.

"Are you all right? Do you need some help?"

Her hand fluttered around her neck before settling with the other arm across her stomach. "I'm fine. Thank you."

The person in front of her didn't look convinced. "You're shivering something fierce. And your lips are blue. Did something happen? Do you need to see a doctor?"

"Yes, something happened, but I'm—I'm fine." Her heartbeat quickened as she kept her steady pace, moving to go around the human and his metal contraption. She tripped over her feet and landed, once again, on her knees and hands.

"You need help. Please, may I help you?"

She stared up at the person, a male human, if she recalled correctly, and bit her lip as she considered his offer. Reaching a decision, she nodded.

"That means I'll have to touch you, are you fine with that?"

"Yes. Thank you. Sorry to be a bother."

The person helped her regain her feet and drew one of her arms across his shoulders. He placed an arm around her waist. "Not a bother at all. Let's get you warmed up. Do you want to go to Urgent Care?"

"No. I don't need medical attention. I just need to warm up, is all."

∾ ∾ ∾

Her hammering heart calmed as water from the showerhead pounded over her. *Heated water; weird.* A smile curled her lips as she allowed water to pool in her cupped hands. "Ailbe. Ailbe, can you hear me?"

The water rippled. "Meara, about time. Are you hurt? You had us worried."

"I'm fine, Ailbe. The transition was rougher than I expected, and it took me a bit to be able to stand on my own."

"Where are you now?"

"In a human's home. He's offered me shelter and food until I can adjust."

Low chuckling echoed from the water. "Remember, Meara, do not get attached to the humans."

"I know. I am here to observe and learn why they are destroying us. That's all."

A knock on the door caused Meara to jump, dropping the water in her hands. *Did he hear me? Did he hear Ailbe? None of the humans are to know what I am.*

"Did you find the towels?"

Meara leaned out of the shower. "I did, thanks."

"Good. When you're finished, I have some clothes you can borrow. They're in the bedroom, on the bed."

"All right."

"Umm ... I'm going to run out for some food. I shouldn't be long. Do you need anything else?"

Meara wrinkled her forehead. "I think I'm good."

Footsteps grew quieter. A sigh escaped Meara as she returned to standing under the showerhead. She felt a ticklish sensation along her neck and, reaching up, she grinned.

Meara perched by the window, watching the raindrops race down the glass. Her gaze shifted to the human when the door opened and he entered, large cardboard boxes balanced on one arm.

"You're back."

He laughed. "I am. I live here, and I have food. You hungry?"

"Yes." Meara stood and followed him to the living room. "I'm Meara, by the way."

He held out his hand. "Connor. Pleased to meet ya."

She looked at the hand, head cocked to the side. *I remember something about this in the human basics class I took.* She looked up to see amusement dancing in his eyes. *Oh, that's right. It's a handshake.* She took his hand and held on, trusting Connor to end it when appropriate. The grasp broke as he bent to set the boxes on the table.

Meara smiled and sat, pulling the too-long sleeves of the sweater to rest above her elbows. "Thank you for the clothes and the help."

"Of course. Any decent person would have." He lifted the box lids to reveal two circles with various stuff piled on top. "Pizza."

Meara accepted a slice of the veggie. She tried to keep her face neutral as she tasted it. *What is this gooey stuff on it? And what kind of vegetables are these? Is this what all human food is like? I hope not, this is awful.*

"Mind if I ask where you're from?" Connor's voice pulled Meara from her thoughts.

Meara shook her head. "Not at all. I'm from Savannah, Georgia."

Connor cocked his head. "Really? You don't sound like you're from the south."

"Oh, that's, uh, 'cause I didn't grow up there. I've only been there two years or so."

He flashed her a wide smile, grabbing a slice of pepperoni. "Ah, that makes sense. So what are you doing all the way up here in Maine, then?"

"Kinda vacation. Kinda research. What kind of pizza is that?"

"This?" Connor picked off a pepperoni, raising an eyebrow, and held it out to her. She crinkled her nose at the shiny drop of liquid hanging on the bottom of it. "It's a pepperoni. It's greasy, but it tastes amazing."

Meara accepted the pepperoni. "But what is it?"

"Meat."

"Oh. I've never seen meat look like this." Meara popped it in her mouth. Her eyes widened as she let the pepperoni sit on her tongue. *What is this flavor? It's ... hot?*

Connor laughed at Meara's reaction. "This is a sliced roll of meat, called sausage, made of pork and beef. Then it's seasoned with paprika, mostly."

She chewed and swallowed, enjoying the flavor, but grimacing at the greasy feeling in her mouth. "It's interesting."

"So, you're here for research? Nice. For school or work?"

"School."

He nodded, taking a large bite of the pizza. "Whatcha researching?"

"Human impacts on ocean life. And possible ways to lessen it."

"You must be planning to go to the marine institute then. I have some friends who work over there. I can introduce you if you want, might make it a bit easier."

"Thank you, it would." Meara nodded, feeling her cheeks heat up. She studied the pizza slice in her hand.

"Do you not like it?"

"Oh, no, it's good. Guess I don't have much of an appetite." She accepted the napkin Connor handed her and set the pizza down on that. *I wonder if there's anything I won't lie about on this mission. Well, I am here to research, that's not technically a lie, right?*

"Okay. You have anywhere to stay while you are here?"

Meara shook her head. "Umm. No. And this may sound weird, but I don't have any money."

Connor quirked an eyebrow at that. "Okay, that seems like a story for another time though. Stay with me, don't worry about the money for now. If this is going to be long term, I'll help you get a part-time job."

"Is this what happens to the fish caught with giant nets?" Meara's forehead pushed against the cold glass of the giant window, eyes taking in the familiar underwater scene.

Connor glanced at her, a small grin on his lips. "Not typically. Those fish are killed and sold as food. Most of these guys were born here or in other aquariums."

Meara focused on a group of nurse sharks on the other side of the tank and ran around to get closer to them. "Why do places like this exist?"

"Well, it's difficult for most people to see what lives under the water, so aquariums and zoos with tanks like these are a good way for people to see what else lives on our planet."

"Do you know everything that lives under the water?"

Connor shook his head. "Nope, we're still exploring and discovering new things all the time."

Meara nodded, tearing herself away from the sharks to look at the displays in the middle of the room. A school group swarmed in, and she moved closer to Connor, grabbing his arm. He gave her a reassuring smile.

"It's fine, just school kids. The friend we're meeting today is doing a presentation for them, and then we'll talk to her afterward."

Meara nodded, chewing on the fingernails of one hand. Connor tugged her hand away from her lips. "There's no need to be anxious."

"Is that what I'm feeling?"

"Probably. Let's go over to the touch pool until she's done."

Meara let Connor lead her across the room to a long table with water running through it. He pointed out the different animals hiding in it.

"Hey, Connor, thanks for stopping by, man." A woman in a dark blue shirt and khakis walked over to them. She hugged Connor and smiled at Meara.

"Meara, this is Thea."

Meara stared for a moment at Thea's outstretched hand before remembering to shake it.

"Connor tells me you're here on a research trip."

Meara nodded, biting her lips. "Yeah, I am. For school."

"Which school?"

Meara froze, eyes growing wide. Connor noticed uncertainty cross her eyes as she glanced between them.

Thea smirked, eyes glancing around the room. "I thought so from the story Connor told me of how you two met. All right, you two, come with me. We can do a little behind-the-scenes adventure."

Connor held Meara's hand as they followed Thea over to the tank with the nurse sharks. "Let's wait here. It's almost feeding time for the sharks, and the dive crew should be by shortly."

"Wouldn't we see better in front of the tank?" Meara asked, pointing to where they could see people standing in line.

"Perhaps, but if the sharks are cooperative they can bring one or two over and you can help feed and touch them from here."

Meara beamed, turning her attention to the water before them.

Connor leaned in toward Thea. "What do you think?"

Thea watched Meara as she paced around the edge of the tank. "I think you're right."

"So what do we do?" Connor tensed as he caught movement out of the corner of his eye and turned to see the dive crew getting ready.

Thea waved to them. "We help her. She either doesn't remember what she came to the land for, or she's not aggressive like the last few were."

Connor nodded, scratching at his chin. Meara's laughter distracted them, and they both smiled at the group of sharks in front of her.

"If that doesn't prove it, I don't know what would. You know the sharks only act like that with their kind."

Connor glanced to the dive crew as they finished suiting up. "Are they cool with it?"

"Hmm. As far as I know. None of them have said anything to me. Can you keep housing her?"

"Not a problem."

A few weeks later, Meara once again stood in the shower, cupping her hands.

"Ailbe?"

"Meara! Have you learned anything yet?"

Meara sighed, slouching. "Nothing new or that we didn't already suspect. Plastic is everywhere, and it's in everything. Even their clothing and the cleaning products they use for their bodies. They use it to eat, to store everything, even other plastic bits. They have toys made of it. It's just ... it's everywhere, Ailbe. There's no end to it. They decorate with it, for Lir's sake!"

"That is troubling indeed. How does so much of it end up in the oceans?"

"I'm not sure yet." Meara sucked on her lower lip.

"You aren't? You've been there for three weeks."

Meara nodded, though she knew Ailbe could not see her. "I know. I got sick. And I've had troubles adjusting. Oh, and I have a job at the marine institute, which takes up quite a bit of time, though it's also proving informative."

"I see. You know the sickness does not bode well for you turning back."

"I know. We'll deal with that later."

"Connor?"

Connor grunted and grabbed his bookmark from the arm of the couch, eyes flitting across the pages. Reaching a good stopping point, he marked his place and set the book down, smiling at Meara. "Yes?"

"Umm ... I was wondering if I could ask you some weird questions." She fiddled with her hair.

"Sure but I'd like to ask a question in return."

Meara nodded and perched on the opposite end of the couch, pulling a blanket over her chilled legs. "Umm ... what are the different bins in the kitchen for?"

"Really?" Connor blinked as Meara blushed and nodded again, keeping her eyes downcast. "There's a recycle bin, a trash bin, and a compost bin."

Meara furrowed her brow. "Recycle is when things are reused?"

"Essentially."

"What is compost?"

Connor pointed to some orange peels on the coffee table. "It's food and a few other objects that can be broken down naturally and used as fertilizer in lawns and gardens. It's a great way of getting rid of items without contributing to landfills."

"Landfills are giant areas of trash?"

Connor nodded.

"You have a small garden out back."

"And some flowers out front, yeah. I use the compost bin in the kitchen to take the scraps and whatnot from inside to the larger compost bin outside. I have to turn it tomorrow, if you want to see it."

Meara gave a small smile. "I would like that. So, then what goes in the trash that ends up at the landfill?"

"Everything else. Meat and the things that aren't recyclable." Connor scooted closer to Meara and leaned forward, propping an elbow on a knee.

"If everything has a place to go after being used, how come there's still litter that ends up killing animals in the water?" Meara lifted her gaze to Connor as he showed a sad smile.

"Because not everyone composts and recycles. And not everyone cares. Some people will toss their trash wherever they happen to be, and then wind and water and animals move it around. It's a large problem."

"Oh. Okay. Thank you, Connor." Meara stood to leave but stopped when Connor gently touched her arm.

"I have a question for you, remember? Think you can answer it now?"

Meara sat and pulled at the hem of her shirt. "Oh, I'm sorry, I forgot. Of course."

"Why do mermaids keep leaving the ocean to come to land?"

Meara's heart stopped, and she felt the blood drain from her face.

How can he know? There's no way he could have guessed, I must have done something weird to give it away.

"I—I don't know what you mean." She clenched her hands into fists to stop them shaking.

Connor smiled. "I think you do."

"How did you know?"

He chuckled. "I actually suspected it when I helped you on the side of the road. The way you react to everyday things and the questions you ask betray you."

"What are you going to do to me?" Her voice was just above a whisper. *Is he going to lock me up? Isn't that what humans do? Before they start cutting apart the so-called mystery in front of them?*

"Do *to* you? I'm not going to do anything. I want to help you."

"Why would you want to do that?"

Connor placed a hand on Meara's. "Because I want to improve the world for everything that inhabits it."

Meara slouched low in the bubbling, heated water, relishing the gentle feel of ripples in and around her gills. *It's so nice to be completely surrounded by water, even if the heat and bubbles are odd. This would be so dangerous in the ocean.* A faint chuckle registered enough to cause her to open her eyes and see Connor's face lit up with joy. A grin tugged at her lips, and she tilted her head so she could talk while hiding her gills.

"Is something amusing?"

Connor shook his head. "No, I'm happy to see you finally relaxed. I was wondering if you would ever feel comfortable here."

"Oh." *He wants me to feel comfortable? I guess that makes sense with everything he has said so far. Does he want me to consider this place home?*

"Would you like a drink?"

She crinkled her nose. "None of that vile alcoholic stuff."

"No worries. I have some sparkling mineral water I think you will enjoy."

Meara nodded, sitting up to accept the glass. She felt Connor's eyes on her and glanced at him.

His mouth hung open, staring at her neck. "Meara, are those your gills?"

She slapped a hand over the side of her neck, nodding, feeling her face heat up. *He's going to get freaked out and kick me out. Just because he knows I'm a mermaid doesn't mean I can relax and allow slip-ups like this to happen.*

"Umm ... do you mind if I join you?"

Meara pulled in a slow breath, lowering her hands. "Sure, you can get in."

Slowly entering the hot tub, Connor sat opposite Meara.

"You don't need to hide them."

"I don't want to scare you. I know from some of my schooling how humans can get when things are different and scary."

"You had training on humans?"

"I suppose you could call it that. We don't have a lot of information on your kind, but they told me what they could."

Connor squeezed her hands. "Yeah, humans struggle at times at accepting what's different from them. I don't find your gills scary or freaky at all."

"Really?"

"They're a part of you. You're a mermaid. Why would they be anything other than normal?"

Meara shook her head. "You are one of the strangest humans I have ever met."

"I'm one of the only humans you've ever met."

They laughed as Meara splashed some water at him.

"But how am I strange?"

"You don't judge me for being a mermaid, you care about the wrongs your kind has committed, and you work to correct them. You care more about others than money or possessions."

Connor tipped his head side to side, pondering her words. "I suppose I am, particularly when the ugly side of humanity is the dominant one at times."

"The ugly side of humanity?"

"Yeah. Humans are incredible. We carry so much potential, and that potential is realized time and time again in different ways. A lot of it is bad, horrendous, even. But a lot of it is good and amazing as well."

Meara realized their hands were still entangled between them. "How so?" She didn't want to pull hers back.

"Let me show you. We both have Thursday off. I'll take you to some museums and some of the not-for-profits around here."

"Okay."

Meara shook so hard she felt like she was about to fall apart as she walked behind Connor. He opened a path for her down the crowded sidewalk. *Some of these humans are so dirty. Why do the men keep looking at me like that? I don't like that at all.* She pulled the large jacket around her, trying to find some measure of comfort. Keeping her eyes down, focused on Connor's shoes, she shrunk in on herself until a splash of color on the grey ground caught her eye. *Oh, what was that?*

"Connor."

Connor stopped and turned around. "Yeah? Are you all right, am I going too fast? I'm sorry."

"No, it's not that. I thought I saw something on the ground over here." Meara walked back a few paces, looking at the ground in front of the stores. *Oh, there it is, that blue.* She bounced and pointed. "There, what's that?"

"That's one of my favorites, it moves every few months." He led her over to the wall so they could crouch out of the way of pedestrian traffic. He pointed to the different parts as he talked. "This black hole here isn't a hole, that's chalk. This is in the traditional shape of a cartoon mouse hole. Here's the door, and a welcome mat, which is probably what caught your eyes. And here is the mouse's head as he peers around the corner."

"So cute! That's adorable." Meara beamed at Connor, who chuckled.

"It is. I know it can be difficult but try to keep your eyes open for more. There's lots of art in the downtown area. Artists will find different spots to create various art pieces."

Meara widened her eyes. *That is incredible.*

Meara ended up holding onto Connor's arm as they walked to the museum. She would tug on it if she saw something she wanted to look at closer.

"This is hilarious." Meara laughed at the spray-painted word **RESISTANCE** with an arrow pointing to some live dandelions growing in the cracks of the concrete.

They spent five minutes staring at one wall in an alley.

"What are those animals?" Meara didn't recognize any on the wall they looked at.

Connor pointed to each one. "Passenger pigeon. Thylacine, or Tasmanian tiger. I'm not sure what rhino species that is, but I know the ones still alive are also in danger of extinction. Umm ... some sort of tiger, not sure which one, they're like the rhinos. We have tigers, but they are endangered. Oh, that bird there is a great auk. Not sure about the rest."

"But, what are they doing behind this cloaked person hugging a ... polar bear?"

"Yeah, that's a polar bear. And the cloaked figure is Death. A lot of times in human culture, especially here in America, we refer to him as the Grim Reaper. All those animals behind him that you asked about? They're all extinct. Not a single one of them lives on the planet anymore."

Meara's heart plummeted, and her eyes and sinuses burned with sudden tears. *This is a list of the destruction caused by humanity.*

"Some street art, and art in general, is fun and happy and amusing. Some make a statement, like this one. I imagine the artist here is making a plea for humanity to open its eyes and its heart to stop Death in its rampage."

Meara held open her hand, full of different colored beads. *This is so much fun! I would have never thought a museum could be interactive.* She studied the sign in front of her.

She walked over to the first painting, one of sunflowers arranged in a bouquet sitting in a yellow pot, Connor following behind with his own handful of beads. A tube containing dozens of beads sat next to the painting, and museum visitors were invited to put the beads they held into the tube to reflect how they felt when they looked at the art. Pink beads indicating happiness filled this tube, with the occasional dark blue bead for thoughtfulness mixed in. *It seems most people felt happy at this.* Her gaze focused on the picture. *I know these flowers.* She dropped a pink bead into the tube, smiling at the name of the artist on the pot.

"What about it makes you happy?" Connor dropped his own bead, dark blue, into the tube.

Meara cocked her head to the side. "I like sunflowers and the color yellow. They make me happy. And seeing the clear brushstrokes, the love and care that must have gone into the creation of this painting, is astounding."

Connor nodded. "That makes sense."

"Umm ... is that wrong?"

"No. Art makes us feel how we feel. That's part of the beauty of it."

"So, umm ... why did you put in dark blue?"

Connor's smile didn't quite reach his eyes. "Because I know the history of the artist, and seeing his work always makes me thoughtful. This particular piece does make me happy as well, but mostly thoughtful. About his life, about my life, about what the world would be like if he had never existed, or never painted."

Meara studied the painting more. "I see."

The morning passed with them placing beads next to all sorts of exhibits. A sculpture of a heart with stitches and pins received a dark blue from both Connor and Meara. A table of shaking grass received a light blue for sadness. By the time lunch came around, Meara had run out of pink and dark blue beads, while Connor still had an even amount of each color.

"What do you think of humans now?" Connor slid a tray onto the small table.

Meara ate a fry as she thought. "I see what you mean, I really do. I came here knowing some of the atrocities of humankind, but none of the good. Seeing the beauty you can create in the art museum, how you love and preserve the past, how many of you love and care and fight for animals, it's incredible. You are truly a species of potential. And your greatest strength as a species is your compassion."

"How did you get that?" Connor bit into a burger.

"That's what all the art said. I know we only saw a small part of it, but even the darkest pieces that called out the horrors of the past are steeped in a plea for compassion and empathy. Why else would you hold on to the past in so many ways, particularly the tragedies of it? To teach compassion and empathy and how to be better than those before you. When the hate and evils of mankind appear, why are the museums destroyed and an attempt at erasing history made? So that compassion fades and there is nothing to teach it, nothing to learn from. Why would any of you care about the animals who cannot do anything for you? Compassion, love, and hope." Meara's voice stayed steady, and she felt the truthfulness of her words resonate to her core.

Once again, she needed to report in, but still had none of the extra information Ailbe and the council wanted. Pulling in a deep breath, trying to relax the ball of nerves in her throat, she held her hand over the still water of the hot tub, then touched it with her hand.

"Meara?" Ailbe sounded tense.

Meara nodded as a picture of Ailbe and the Council appeared. "Hello, Ailbe. How are things there?"

"Not well. One of the humans' oil rigs has started leaking again."

Meara grimaced. Oil was impossible to clean off anything. "How bad is it?"

"Bad. Evacuations of merfolk are happening now. We are sure it will be a lot worse. We also saw most of the humans leaving the rig. A hurricane is coming this way."

"Where is everyone evacuating to?"

"Evacuating? Who's evacuating?" Connor slid the screen door closed behind him. Meara shook her head. *No, Connor, Ailbe can't know that you know.*

A picture of Ailbe and the council appeared on the water. "Meara, is that a human?"

Meara grimaced, and hung her head. "Yes, Ailbe. This is Connor. He's been kind enough to house me."

Ailbe's eyes narrowed. "And what does he take as payment?"

Meara's cheeks heated, and she waved her hands in front of her. "Nothing, it's not like that. He's not like that. But he does know about us, he wants to help."

"Nonsense. Humans are not so altruistic."

A rare burst of anger flared through Meara. "Of course they are. How else do you think they have survived for so long? What could you possibly know about them having never lived among them or observed them with your own eyes? You base all your decisions and opinions about humans on stories that are centuries old and speaks to only a small part of humanity."

Ailbe scowled. "You argue their goodness while in such a heated state? This state of anger is unusual for you. Clearly they have had a negative impact on you."

"If anything, they have only been a positive influence on me. I have seen such beautiful things which evokes a wide range of emotions, including the negative. Anger has as much use as any other feeling."

"You do not know what you are talking about."

Meara's hand gripped the edge of the hot tub. "No, Ailbe. You are wrong. On so much. Like this mission. There is no way to stop humans. They are trying among themselves to reduce their consumption of many things, including oil and plastics. And though the movement for that grows, progress is slow."

"Meara, what in Lir's name are you saying? We can't give up this mission. We can't roll over and accept this way of life."

"Do you even realize how many humans there are in this world? How widespread their population is? They don't have a collective weakness. This is not simply a matter of intimidating them until they stop using a material that is ingrained into every aspect of their everyday lives."

"Then what do you suggest we do?"

Connor grabbed his phone, typing furiously. "Ailbe, do you have a way to show us the damage done by the oil?"

Meara tried to glimpse at the phone screen. "Connor, what are you doing?"

"Messaging a few friends who might be able to help. Ailbe?"

Ailbe cleared her throat. "I do. How did you figure out that was the issue?"

He flashed a smile. "You mentioned plastics, oil, and evacuation. The only thing that made sense to me was a spill. There's nothing in the media yet of a spill. I don't suppose you can tell me where this is happening?"

"No, absolutely not. Out of the question." Ailbe scowled.

Connor doesn't seem bothered by Ailbe's demeanor. Meara watched as he pulled up the camera function of his phone.

"All right, that's fine. If you can show us the damage, though, I can take pictures and post them. Draw some attention to the repercussions of oil spills in the ocean."

They saw Ailbe shrug her shoulders before the scene on the water changed.

Meara gasped. "This is from the ocean floor looking up. I recognize this area, it's a common recreation area for Atlanta. If you see the light trickling through, it's brown and murky. That'll be because of the oil."

"Any of it fall to the ocean floor yet?" Connor tapped the shutter button on his phone rapidly as the scene changed to show lines of merfolk swimming out of the coral city.

Ailbe's voice echoed through without the picture changing. "No, it hasn't been long enough for that yet. We noticed this spill three days ago and immediately started relocation plans. It can take a few weeks for enough of the microscopic life to die off to cause it to form. If we're lucky, the humans will find this soon and stop it before that can happen. Our city in the Gulf can never be restored from the spill in 2010—it's covered in too much oil sediment."

"Ailbe, what about the other creatures?" Meara leaned over the edge of the hot tub.

"We have a good number of specimens for colonies to keep them going. After nearly losing the bristle worms and amphipods in the Gulf, we've made sure to keep a collection of the small creatures ready to move."

Meara let out a relieved sigh. "Oh, good."

Meara waved at the small girl walking away from the touch station with her parents. She pulled out her hair band and ran her fingers through her hair as Thea strode over to her.

"You're doing great. How are you liking the job?" Thea fixed the position of the hand sanitizer bottle.

Meara returned the broad smile. "I'm loving it, actually. I have to focus a lot to keep my hands looking like a human's, but the kids are great. I love their curiosity about their world."

"Glad you are enjoying it. It's time for your break, I'll take over for you."

"Thanks! This is a fifteen-minute one, right?"

"Yeah, but there's a talk about to start over in the Sandy Shores area I think you'll be interested in. It's about twenty minutes. Go, learn, ask questions. Come back after." Thea waved Meara off as a small school group approached the touch table.

The presenter held up a plastic bag and a plastic bottle. "So who has been paying attention? Can anyone tell me why plastics are a problem?"

A bunch of kids sitting on the floor raised their hands. The presenter motioned to one of the boys on the left to answer.

"They are used once and then thrown away. 'Cept they don't stay thrown away. They escape and end up in rivers and oceans, killing things."

"That's right, good job. When I'm done, be sure to go see Millie over there and she'll give you a prize." He set the items down and picked up a knotted pile of plastic twine. "What about this?"

A child on the right side answered this time. "Birds can think its nesting material or food. Sometimes they feed it to their babies."

The presenter nodded. "You get a prize too. And that wraps up our talk on plastics. Hopefully you learned something today. There are a lot of ways to reduce plastic usage in everyday life. It only takes a little effort until it becomes habit. My assistants and I will be hanging around for a while to answer any questions you might have, and thank you for visiting our aquarium."

Meara wandered closer to the presenter. She waited for the crowd around him to clear a bit. Finally, he turned to her and offered a hand. "You must be the new girl. I'm Alan."

"Hi, Alan. Meara. Great presentation. I enjoyed it." She shook his hand. *Finally have this greeting habit down.*

"Thanks. Thea mentioned you were doing research. On plastics and its impacts on ocean life, is that right?"

Meara nodded.

"Here, I have some photos I can show you of the more gruesome effects. I don't pull them out if there are a lot of kids. Parents tend not to like it too much." He led her over to a small table that held the props he had used. He handed her some pictures.

She flipped through, grimacing. Stopping at the last one, she felt her breath leave her as she stared at a seahorse, floating in crystal blue water, tail wrapped around a pink cotton swab. *I know this picture. I was behind the photographer. This is why I volunteered for this mission.*

Alan peeked at what picture she had stopped on. "That's a newer one, from just a few months ago. It's getting a lot of shares and likes on social media."

Meara set the pictures down. *I don't understand. How can anyone look at photos like this and not care?* "Why is it so hard for ... people ... to stop doing this?"

Alan released an exasperated sigh and dragged a hand over his face. "I ask myself that a lot. A large part of it is convenience. A lot of it is people don't realize how much trash escapes the confines of garbage bags and landfills. And they don't make the connection between their personal actions and items washing up half a world away. It makes it easy for them to disassociate from the whole issue."

"Can we do anything about that?"

Alan pursed his lips. "Perhaps. I've had the thought that if we can trap the trash as it leaves the rivers and streams, it would draw everything closer to home for people. If we could trap it before then it would be even better."

"So why don't you do that?"

"We don't have enough people to do something like that manually, every day, for, say, the next month. I don't know of a good way to trap it without impacting the ecosystem even more, so I do what I can here with education."

Meara tapped her lip then raised her eyebrows. *That's it. That's the plan.* "What if you had help?"

"What do you mean?"

"What if there were creatures in the oceans who could help you collect and catalogue where it was all coming from?"

Alan stared at her. "What, like mermaids? Nessie?" He chuckled.

Meara gave him an innocent grin.

She leaned over the edge of the hot tub with Connor. She drew in a calming breath and nodded. Touching the water with a finger, she called out to Ailbe.

"Meara? Is that you?"

Meara smiled. "Yes."

"Is something wrong? Are you in trouble?" Ailbe's voice pitched with worry.

"No, Ailbe, I'm fine. Umm ... I have an idea to run past you."

"It had better be a good idea, Meara. I have enough to deal with down here with the evacuations and all that."

Meara drummed her fingers on the hot tub. "I have found there are a lot of humans who want to help, but most of them have no idea how. At the same time, there are more who don't recognize how bad things are in the oceans."

"So?"

"So, what if we reveal ourselves to the humans and offered to help them?" Meara bit her lower lip.

Silence rang in their ears for so long, Meara thought the connection had been lost.

"Ailbe?"

A sigh. "Do you have any idea what would happen to us if we reveal ourselves to the humans?"

"I know the risks, but this is worth it. Having another species on the planet almost like them in every way would be good for the humans, I'm sure of it."

"Why do you say that?"

Meara leaned closer to the water. "Because in their hearts, at the very depth of their beings, the vast majority of them are good, compassionate, and caring."

"How do you know they won't call us a hoax and ignore us like they've done others?"

Meara glanced at Connor who nodded and smiled. "Because there are some of them who already know about mermaids, and they've agreed to vouch for us. If we do a live broadcast on their social media sites, we can pull this off."

"What does that mean, human?"

"Ah, sorry. Much like how we are speaking now, humans have the abilities to capture conversations like this and share it with each other."

"Can things not be faked with this method?"

"They can, but I think we can prove the reality here."

"What would that be?" Ailbe furrowed her brow.

Meara took a breath. "I will transform on the live feed, on land, where they can see everything."

Connor clasped a hand on Meara's shoulder. "You sure about this?"

Meara licked her lips, twirling a strand of brown hair around a finger as she contemplated the aquarium tank in front of her. "Yes. This will help. I'm sure of it."

"All right. Thea is out ready to go live on social media. We have some news stations out there as well."

"Thank you for helping with all of this over the last month. How did you ever get the head of the aquarium to agree?"

Connor laughed. "I have my ways. And between you and me, the head of the aquarium? Also a mermaid."

What, I wonder why they haven't introduced themselves?

Connor's walkie buzzed, and he held it up to his ear to hear it better. He nodded and pressed the button that would allow him to talk. "Copy. Sending her in now." Connor gave an encouraging smile. "It's your time to shine, Meara."

Without thinking, not allowing herself a moment of hesitation, Meara dove into the tank. *Stay human, stay human. A little longer.* She waved to Thea, who gave a thumbs up. Meara bowed, then allowed herself to transform.

Thinking on what she had seen of transformations in human movies, she supposed it was rather disappointing. There was no glowing light, no swirling water. One moment, she appeared as an ordinary human. The next, she relaxed into her natural state. Gills fluttered open along the sides of her neck, the webbing on her hands grew. Her legs melded together as fish scales grew to create her tail. Her eyes grew more bulbous, and her nose flattened, with the nostrils thinning.

When the transformation finished, she looked out to find everyone, except Thea, with their mouths hanging open. She waved to the gathering and smiled. *It feels so good to be myself again, even if it's for a short time.*

The internet exploded as everyone rushed to watch the video of the transformation again and again. Skeptics tried to disprove it, politicians denounced it, and scientists worked to figure out how such creatures could exist, while religions around the world labeled merfolk as either demons or angels.

Meara laughed at the initial reactions of humans. Some were accepting and immediately set out to find out all they could about Meara and why she revealed herself.

"My people need help, as do the animals of this planet, whether they occupy land, air, or sea," Meara found herself repeating in all the interviews she gave afterwards. "I was too scared to speak before the transformation, but feeling like myself again, I found courage."

Just as it seemed nothing significant would come of her reveal, and it was almost forgotten and overshadowed by the next meme, other merfolk began to speak out. First it started with others who had been living as humans, including the head of the aquarium. Then merfolk began appearing at beaches all over the globe, some walking out of the water on legs, others lounging on rocks or the sand in their natural forms with water tanks secured around the gills on their necks.

"That reveal didn't seem all that hard," Connor commented one night after he, Meara, and Thea all watched the news together. "Humanity appears to have accepted your species' existence. Hopefully things will stay cordial between our species."

Six months later, Meara found herself as a spokesperson at a conference with other merfolk and several humans.

"What do merfolk want?" inquired a reporter.

Meara cleared her throat and was given a nod to speak by the moderator. *Breathe, Meara. You deserve to have your voice heard, breathe.* "We want to live in safety and peace with humanity. Our environment, our homes, are in worse and worse shape because of the decisions humans make every day. All we ask is for some consideration."

"This has been a consistent message since you first revealed yourself. Care to elaborate?"

Meara shifted in her seat. "In the last several decades we noticed an increase in trash floating among the currents. Now it rains down on our towns daily, and that's not accounting for the oil spills. We have had to abandon entire cities due to those." Meara stopped herself as she felt sadness threaten to choke her. *Deep breath, focus. Stay calm.* "We know that changing an entire way of life can be a difficult and daunting task. That's why we offer our help in cleaning up rivers and oceans, and in cultivating algae safely to use as one replacement for oil."

"Since you can clearly take human shape and live as humans, why should we do anything to help you stay in your homes in the oceans?"

All the merfolk looked shocked at the question. *Even after all these months, they still surprise me with how utterly uncaring and unsympathetic some of them can be.* Finally, Meara found words to speak. "Because it's our home, and who doesn't want to keep their home?"

Connor held Meara close in a tight hug. "I'm sorry to see you leave, though I'm glad you get to go home."

"I'll be back to visit."

Connor sniffled and let her go, nodding. Thea swooped in for a hug. "Good luck in your new job. You're gonna be great."

Meara smiled. "Thanks, both of you, for helping me, and teaching me, and caring for me, and everything. We can make a real difference now, right? I'll head the cleanup efforts on my end, organize teams to trap and catalogue any new trash that finds its way into the water systems, and keep a tally on fish populations."

"Right," Connor said as he and Thea both smiled and waved.

Meara climbed over some rocks to stand above the ocean. She breathed in the salt-kissed air with a grin. *Home. I am finally going home.* She looked back one last time to see her two best friends watching her before she dove into the cold water, transforming back into a mermaid.

THE END

Artio Murphy lives in colorful Colorado with her husband. She actively hikes all year round, and most enjoys the moments where there is a bit of magic to nature and the world. When not writing or hiking, she is either working her part-time barista job, or practicing her martial arts training. She has one children's book published, and two poems in an anthology under a different name. She is currently working on her first novel, a fairy tale fantasy due out in 2019. She is most active on social media through Instagram, where she can be followed @artiomurphy.

In The Hiss of the Dark Surf

Slipstream
Water and Earth

Joseph Y. Roberts

Melinda Banks beached the lead Zodiac on Motu Wairua, the abrasive black sand carving a multitude of fine scratches into the inflatable boat's hull. Her two companions scanned the palms crowding the high tide line as the second Zodiac skidded onshore.

"I'll check the tree line," said Hunter Marx. As he hopped from the skiff, the volcanic sand crunched beneath his boots. He crept toward the dense, tropical flora, right hand on the holstered pistol on his belt.

"Oo, the big man makes his play." Trevor Sumner smirked.

Hunter shot him a scowl and continued his advance on the trees.

Melinda pulled a walkie-talkie off her belt and keyed it to hail the chartered boat anchored offshore. "We made it okay. See you in a month. Over."

"Veddy good," said the captain, his thick Kiwi accent crackling from the talkie. "Good luck. Don't let the ghosts get ya," he added in a cheery tone.

Melinda keyed the mic again. "Ha ha. Funny. Just don't miss the pick-up date, okay?"

"No worries. Cheers."

"Sure," Trevor grumbled. "No worries, he says. He's not the one who agreed to be stranded on an island with only the Zodiacs to get us around. Except they can't. Not to any other land anyway." He pantomimed dusting off his hands and crossed his arms. "Yup. Nothing to worry about."

Melinda exhaled loudly as she stepped onto the beach. "Quit bitchin'. We've got satphones. We can yell for help."

Trevor kicked at the sand. "Which would take days to get here."

"Augh! You're impossible." She shook her head and followed Hunter. His crouched posture and darting movements raised her concern. "A bit early for alert mode, isn't it?"

Hunter kept his gaze on the copse of trees. "Just doing my job." He tilted his head from side to side, shifting his view. "Besides, shouldn't you be directing the unloading?"

She shrugged. "Not necessarily my job. It's not like the others don't know what to do."

"True. I guess you're the wilderness survival expert, not the micro-manage-all-things expert." Hunter squatted and ran his fingers along the grass at his feet, picking at the occasional stray stone.

Best you think that. Melinda cocked her head. "What're you looking for?"

He stood and brushed his hand off on the seat of his pants. "Nothing ... there's nothing," he muttered.

"What?"

Hunter turned and strode toward the beach. "S'okay. C'mon, we got boats to unload."

Melinda paused and surveyed her five teammates, sent to learn why the previous year's team had vanished. They placed various cartons and plastic tubs beside the skiffs, backlit by the sunlight sparkling off the deep, vibrant blue of the Pacific. Trevor darted among them, tapping and swiping on his tablet. *Checking the inventory.* Her lips pulled into a crooked smile in bemusement.

What a motley crew we are. Two scientists, a technician, a combat vet security expert, a native guide, and me to help them stay alive. Yeah, this is going to be fun.

Wiremu Kakakura, the Maori guide assigned to them by the New Zealand government, did most of the heavy lifting until

Hunter joined him. *The strongest backs, I guess, but it doesn't feel right somehow.*

She trotted to them. "Hey, let me help."

⌇ ⌇ ⌇

After unpacking the Zodiacs and dragging them onto the grass beneath the palms beyond the high tide's reach, the team pitched a temporary camp atop a bluff overlooking Landing Beach, as they elected to name it. The six sat in a circle about their camp-fire and noshed on vacuum-packed rations. A warm breeze wafted the palm fronds above them. The sun set, and the sky exploded into a shining canopy of stars.

Trevor gaped at the celestial display. "Wow. There's no black. It's all stars."

Dr. Conrad Van Lauer, the Dutch archaeologist, chuckled warmly. "Never been away from city lights before?"

Trevor shook his head, eyes locked on the sky. "No. My first time. Amaze balls!"

A ripple of laughter ran among his companions. Melinda grinned. "Newbies." She nudged Trevor in the ribs and pointed over the bluff edge. "Check out down there."

In the direction she indicated the surf tumbled on the shore, shining with a blue-green glow like a neon sign. Trevor's jaw dropped. "What the ..." He jabbed a finger at the sight. "How long has *that* been going on?"

Melinda smiled. "Since it got dark. You were too busy gawking at the sky."

Trevor's eyes grew wide, and his voice dropped to a whisper. "But what is it?"

Dr. Irdina Binti Ishak, the Malay geologist, sought to calm him. "Relax. It's only bioluminescence of the plankton agitated by the surf. It's natural and common."

Melinda leaned closer to Trevor. "Think of it as the aurora of the sea. These are what you see when you leave your comfy video studio."

Trevor gulped from his water bottle. "Yeah, I'm definitely outside my comfort zone."

Hunter chimed in. "You like it?"

Trevor swallowed. "I'll let you know." His brows twitched, and he blinked. "Say ... what did the boat captain mean about 'don't let the ghosts get ya?'"

Conrad stuffed his empty rations package into the garbage duffel bag. "Just a joke. But I think our guide could expand on that."

All eyes locked on Wiremu. He paused in licking his spoon, startled at suddenly being the center of attention.

"What? Oh, you want me to talk now. All right then ..."

He set his meal down and gazed into the fire. "My people's full name for this island means 'land where only the spirits walk.' It's shortened to *Motu Wairua*, which means 'Spirit Island' in Maori. My people never settled this island because they believed the gods reserved it for themselves." A wicked grin split his face. "We're technically breaking a taboo. That's what the captain meant." He grasped his plate and resumed dining.

"What?" exclaimed Trevor. "And Dr. Gresham's team disappeared here? Why wasn't this mentioned in our briefing?"

Wiremu shrugged. "It's just a stupid island myth. I don't believe it, and it's *my* culture. Why should you, fanboy?"

Doubt rippled across Trevor's face with a curl of his lip and a furrowed brow. "Uh, I guess not. It's just creepy."

"Never told campfire ghost stories?" said Melinda.

He shook his head.

She gave him a pitying, sisterly grin. "You poor, deprived boy."

Hunter tapped his spoon on the side of his enameled coffee mug. "Okay, we should discuss our plan of action for tomorrow."

"Who made you boss?" asked Trevor.

The veteran glared at him, and Trevor shrank. "I withdraw the question."

Hunter cleared his throat. "Since we have some of the GPS data from Gresham's team, I propose we locate their campsite, investigate it, then plant our base camp somewhere nearby. I'm assuming they already selected the best spot for a long-term camp." His eyes swept the team. "Does this sound doable?"

A murmur of assent rippled through the party. Trevor frowned. "Yeah. Sure, I guess." Hunter nailed him with another glare.

Melinda's gaze darted between both men, weighing their attitudes. *I'm going to have to referee these two at some point. That's just great.*

She stood and walked to the bluff edge, seeking a moment of zen. She drank in the dancing glow of the waves as they washed ashore, retreating with a hiss in the sand. The moment absorbed her.

~ ~ ~

The next morning, the team pressed inland in search of the first team's camp. They pushed through lush ferns enshrouding the forest of palms, following Melinda as she tracked their location by the GPS on her satphone, comparing it with the record on Trevor's tablet. She pressed through a thinning in the undergrowth and stopped short. "Looks like we're here."

Her five teammates gathered around her to stand at the edge of a clearing about thirty meters across beneath an oval-shaped break in the forest canopy.

"What happened here?" asked Trevor in a hushed tone.

Near the center of the clearing, seven dome tents in various states of decay stood in a circle. The tent farthest from them bore the worst signs: its nylon fabric hung in thin shreds from its six arched struts, fluttering in the breeze like pennants in a Mayday festival. The other tents remained intact, with few tears, their fabric only thinned by the weather.

Trevor pointed at the damage with a trembling finger. "Did something with claws do that?"

Melinda shook her head. "No. It's what I expected."

"Yes. It's been a year since the last expedition season," added Irdina.

Hunter strode toward the derelict campsite. "We need more clues."

"There the big man goes again," said Trevor.

Melinda poked Trevor's forearm. "Shush, you. He's right. Let's go."

The team spread out through the camp, eyes scanning every detail. At the center of the tent circle they found a folding table with four plastic camping chairs. Four meters away lay a ring of scorched stones suggesting a long-disused fire pit. A solar charging station sat on the table, its USB cables splayed about it like the tentacles of an exhausted octopus. One of these ran into a port on a laptop, accumulated dirt defining water rings on its closed lid. Frowning, Trevor examined the weather-worn device. "At last, something I understand."

"Then you'll love this," said Irdina, emerging from a tent with another laptop in hand. She carried it to the technician.

Trevor beamed. "Cool beans! One that hasn't been rained on." He snatched it from Irdina's grasp.

"Patience, young man," scolded Irdina.

He flipped open the lid and jabbed the power button. "Erm. And as I expected. Battery's dead." He closed the top, slipped off his backpack, and placed the device inside. "Once we set up our camp, I'll plug it into our charger. Then there'll be answers."

"What about this one?" Melinda waved toward the rain-stained laptop.

"That'll take my elite skills to rehab. Might still not work. But I'll try," said Trevor. He unplugged it from the equally weather-worn solar charger and slipped it inside his backpack to join its cohort. He patted the backpack. "Dude's had a tough ride."

Hunter addressed the team. "Okay, looks like we have what we need from here. Let's search the surrounding area for a site for our base camp." He clapped. "C'mon. Burnin' daylight."

Trevor whispered to Melinda, "Again. Who made him boss?"

She patted his shoulder. "Just roll with it for now. Okay?"

He grunted with a scowl. "If you say so. But this alpha male trip is wearing thin."

"I know, but it's his job."

Trevor's brows shot up. "What? To be a dick?"

She tugged hard at his t-shirt sleeve. "I'll smack him down if he gets to be too much of a testosterone case. Now let's go."

He sighed. "Well, okay. Suppose I don't have much of a choice."

"Right now, you don't. C'mon, mush."

"Mush?"

She shrugged and followed the others, thinking of their youngest team member, easily ten years her junior. "Kids."

⮾ ⮾ ⮾

They found a smaller clearing three kilometers farther west. A narrow creek ran through it toward the western side of the island. Melinda nodded her approval. "That water supply will make our stay more comfortable and sustainable. This is the place."

"I agree. It's also defensible," added Hunter.

She shot him a side-eye glance. "Sure. If that's important."

"It is. C'mon, team. We've got a lot of gear to hoof."

Melinda raised an eyebrow. *What is he not saying? Still in alert mode. Why?* She made a mental note and moved on.

They spent the remainder of the day relocating their temporary camp to its permanent place. Like the first team, they erected their dome tents in a circle to share the light of a central fire. Trevor set up a folding work table two meters from the fire pit and assembled a solar charging station at its center. He plugged in the laptop Irdina found at the first camp to charge. After sunset, they relaxed and enjoyed rations pan-warmed over the fire.

Hunter finished his meal and wiped his mouth with his thumb. "I think now would be a good time for us to compare notes about what we found in Dr. Gresham's camp."

Trevor raised his hand. "I'll keep the minutes."

"Don't be a smart-ass. This is serious," growled Hunter.

Trevor glared at him.

"It's not like it's a crime scene," said Conrad.

Hunter gave him a level gaze. "Are we sure about that, Doctor? Contact was lost with Gresham's team with no explanation, no apparent reason. Reported they'd made a great find, then silence." He rubbed his hands together. "And what we found at the camp was ... *inconsistent.*"

"Inconsistent? How so?" said Irdina.

"I noticed sleeping bags in the tents but no other personal effects," said Conrad.

Hunter pointed to him and smiled. "Good. Exactly the observation I'd hope for from a trained eye."

"I found a satphone," added Wiremu.

Trevor shook his head. "They had a lot more devices than a charger, two laptops, and a satphone. I know, I read their gear inventory. Where's the rest?"

Melinda tended the fire with a stick, shifting the burning wood. "Hunter's right. It doesn't add up. If they abandoned camp suddenly, there'd be more things lying around. But no, just a few items left in place. It's like it was only half-abandoned. But why do that? It doesn't make sense."

Hunter stroked his chin. "Maybe ... they were ambushed and their attackers only took what they wanted and left the rest."

"Attacked! By who?" said Trevor, alarmed.

"Pirates, perhaps?"

Trevor snorted. "Pirates. I don't think Captain Jack Sparrow sails these waters."

"No, it's possible," said Conrad. "Tough times have driven some to revive piracy. Remember Somalia."

Wiremu nodded. "Yeah. Sadly I know some blokes who've taken to boarding and robbing tourist boats. Easy prey."

Melinda turned to Hunter. "So that's why you're on high alert?"

He nodded. "Yeah. It's not unwarranted."

Trevor tapped at lines of text on his laptop screen. "Well, speaking of inconsistent and unwarranted, maybe one of you can explain something else weird I spotted in the records."

"We can try. Tell us," said Irdina.

"Why was the last expedition led by Dr. Gresham, a nuclear engineer? To an uninhabited island with no technology? Makes no sense to me."

Conrad shrugged. "Well, like us, they were employed by the Diogenes Foundation for *Interdisciplinary* Inquiry. Clearly, they felt his expertise was needed."

Trevor threw his arms wide. "For inter-*what* inquiry?"

Hunter stood. "I think it's time you saw this." He walked to his tent and returned with his laptop. He resumed his seat, called up a video, and turned the screen for everyone to see.

In the frame, a satellite view of the earth played before them. The outlines of Australia and New Zealand were unmistakable. In the ocean east of these land masses a searing, white blaze of light flashed. Compared to the scale of the coastlines, it had been huge—larger than the island beneath it. Their jaws dropped.

"What the hell was *that?*" exclaimed Wiremu.

"A meteor?" offered Irdina.

Hunter shook his head. "The experts have ruled that out. The spectrum is wrong."

"Volcanic eruption?" said Conrad.

Irdina shook her head. "The two volcanoes that formed this island haven't erupted in recorded history. They're extinct."

Wiremu nodded. "Yeah. My people say the gods keep the volcanoes asleep so the spirits can live here in peace."

Trevor held up his palms and shrugged. "So what *was* it?"

Hunter stopped the video app and closed his laptop. "You all agreed to an unknown mission, but I think it's time to tell you that's what Gresham's team was sent to find out. He was tapped to lead because it was suspected the flash might be a covert nuclear test."

Melinda cocked her head, brows knitted in concern. "By whom?"

"Any rogue nation attempting to hide a nuclear weapons program by not testing in their own backyard. Plausible deniability."

Trevor scratched his head. "So now it's up to us to find out?"

Hunter stood and walked to his tent. "No. Diogenes wants us to learn why Gresham's team vanished and to resume their work on the 'Big Find.'"

"Big Find?" asked Conrad, brow raised.

"That's where you come in, Doctor." Hunter nodded at the archaeologist. "Gresham's last report said they'd found evidence of habitation on this island where no one was believed to have ever settled."

Conrad scoffed. "What evidence?"

"*Ruins.* With your digs at Nan Midol and on Easter Island, you know early Polynesian culture. This is your bread and butter."

Trevor leaned back and crossed his arms. "And why wasn't *this* mentioned in our briefing? And why were you the only one read in?"

Hunter shrugged and shook his head. "As to the first question, you didn't have a need-to-know. As to the second, as the security expert, I did. The chance of pirates is not unlikely."

Trevor snapped out of his slouch and scowled. "That's bull, and you know it."

"Maybe, but that's life, Junior. Get used to it," said Hunter with his hands spread.

"Grr." Trevor stood and stormed off to his tent.

Wearied by the two men's verbal sparring, Melinda heaved a sigh. *God, I wish we were still at the beach. I could use some neon blue surf zen right now.*

❦   ❦   ❦

Melinda's eyes shot open, awakened by cries of, "Who's out there? What do you want with me?"

That's Wiremu!

She rolled from her sleeping bag to a crouch and unzipped the tent flap. Clambering out on all-fours, she found the clearing dimly lit by the waxing crescent moon and the dying embers of the campfire. The surrounding trees stood like ashen specters encircling them with malicious intent.

Wiremu shouted toward the forest as Hunter scrambled to his side. The security man played the beam of his Maglite across the trees, casting ghastly moving shadows. Melinda stood and joined the two men at the camp's center.

The remaining tent flaps unzipped in near unison. Trevor and the scientists poked their heads out like prairie dogs. Trevor spoke in a groggy slur. "Waz happening?"

Hunter looked at Wiremu. "I'm wondering the same thing."

Melinda snapped, "What happened to the fire?"

Wiremu flashed a sheepish look, barely visible in the wan lighting, and rubbed the back of his neck. "I was on watch, and I dozed off. I missed tending the fire."

"Fine, but what were you shouting about?" asked Hunter.

Wiremu darted his eyes at the forest and he leaned close to them. "I ..." He licked his lips and ran his hand through his hair. "... heard someone ..."

"Yes, and?" said Melinda.

Wiremu's face grew pale as beads of sweat started from his forehead. He whispered with a hoarse voice, "... call *my name.*"

"What's he saying?" called Conrad, sticking only his head out of the tent flap.

"That he heard someone call his name from the forest," said Melinda.

"Ach! Must've had a dream. Good night, *again.*" Conrad drew his head back into his tent and zipped the flap closed.

Grumbling, Trevor and Irdina did the same.

"But I did hear my name. We are not alone here."

"Relax. This isn't the military, so you're not in trouble for sleeping on watch," said Hunter.

"I'm not worried about that."

"I know you're not. But all's quiet out there now, so we can stand down."

Melinda tapped Wiremu's forearm. "You're tired. I'll relieve you on watch. Why don't you go to bed?"

"Okay. I'll try to sleep." He walked off to his tent and turned in.

She frowned and squatted beside the dying fire to rekindle it. Hunter sat next to her.

"So, what do you think?" he asked.

She shrugged. "Probably just a dream. A dozing mind is an unreliable thing." As the flames rose and brightened, she locked gazes with him. "How 'bout you? Was it pirates?"

Hunter shook his head. "Nah. If it had been, we'd been awakened by gunfire, not Wiremu screaming at demons."

Melinda gawked at him. "Demons? That's a bit harsh."

"Sorry. Figure of speech." He stood and fumbled with his watch. "I'm turning in. Alarm set. I'll relieve you in four hours."

"Nighty night."

She glanced at the moon and noted its position. *That'll be about dawn.* She sighed and prodded the fire with a stick, shifting the wood. Satisfied, Melinda stared into the blackness of the forest. *Take it easy. There's nothing there that wasn't there in the daylight. It's just wilderness jitters.*

She gazed at the stars blazing in the canopy gap above her. *At least I hope so.*

⌇ ⌇ ⌇

The rays of the morning sun angled through the trees, dispelling the prior night's tension. Melinda stuffed empty ration packages into the trash as Conrad, Irdina, and Trevor sat around the folding table fussing over laptops.

The two scientists consulted topographic maps to estimate the location of the ancient settlement the first team found. Frustration strained their voices and rang clear in Melinda's ears. She frowned in concern.

Hunter and Wiremu gathered firewood at the clearing's edge. A load of small logs cradled in his arms, Wiremu strolled beside her on his way to the firewood pile. "So, I bet everybody thinks I'm crazy, right?"

She cinched the bag closed. "No one's said a thing. I think they've all put it behind them."

He threw the logs on the pile. "Ignore the wild raving of the savage, huh?"

"No, it's not like that. You just had a dream."

He shot her a scowl as he strode past to seek more wood. "Nice try. I've heard it all before." He paused and locked eyes. "It wasn't a drea—"

"Woot! I did it!" hollered Trevor. He shot to his feet and broke into a spastic victory dance.

"What's wrong with you?" barked Conrad, clutching his own shirtfront in alarm.

Irdina touched his hand. "Easy, Conrad. It's just youthful exuberance."

"Could've given me a heart attack." He puffed several times and his shoulders relaxed. His gaze fell on Irdina's hand upon his, and he smiled. She returned one of her own.

Melinda, Hunter, and Wiremu rushed to join them.

Trevor leaned on the table and beamed at the archaeologist. "You're in luck, Doc! I just cracked the password on this baby, and it's Dr. Ishiro's laptop."

Conrad gaped in anticipation. "You mean …?"

Trevor slapped a palm on the tabletop. "Yes! The first team's archaeologist." He spun the computer around to face Conrad. "And here's his notes on the Big Find."

"Great job, son!" He slid the laptop closer to himself and Irdina. "There's the coordinates of the site."

Trevor straightened and puffed his chest. "Told ya I was elite."

Irdina squinted at the screen. "That's about eight kilometers to the northeast. Farther up the same stream running through our clearing."

Hunter gazed to the northeast and rubbed his chin. His fingers raised an audible scratch as they ran across his wiry scruff. "Eight klicks … That's about a two-and-a-half-hour march at a moderate pace." He nodded. "Doable. We can be out and back within the day."

Conrad stood, his expression brightening. "We're going today?" he said in the tone of a child who had been told he was going to Disneyland.

Hunter turned and smiled at him. "Sure. Why not? It's what we're here for."

"I'll get my excavation gear," said Conrad, rushing off to his tent.

Melinda chuckled at his exuberance. "Okay. Everybody be sure to drink your fill from the stream as we hike, using your Mini Sawyers. We want to stay well-hydrated."

‿ ‿ ‿

The team pushed upstream along the creek into the island's interior. The watercourse carved a natural break in the dense foliage for their path. The forest canopy closed over their heads, casting dancing, gloomy shadows on them as a gentle breeze hissed through the branches.

Melinda found her own senses pricking to high alert. *It's getting hard to see. Don't wanna misstep here.*

After three hours and two rest stops, they broke through the undergrowth into another clearing. They spread out and took in the sight.

The far side of the clearing rose into higher ground. At its base squatted stout walls of interlocked dark gray stone.

"They look like Lincoln Logs made of rock," said Trevor.

"Yes ..." whispered Conrad. "Much like the construction of Nan Midol." He turned to Irdina. "Would you say that's basalt?"

The geologist stepped to the nearest wall and ran her hand across its surface. "Yes. Definitely. This would be a stone easily quarried on this island."

"Gresham and Ishiro were right. There's no doubt this was a settlement of some sort." Conrad stood in an opening that formed an inward angled trapezoid. "But I've not seen arch-like construction like this in any Polynesian site. These builders had a similar culture but are some sort of offshoot." He removed his ball cap and ran his hand through his gray-streaked, blond hair, sending droplets of sweat flying. "Or, rather, perhaps a progenitor culture ..."

Melinda touched his arm. "What do we do now, Doctor?"

He blinked and gave his head a small shake. "Oh, yes. My apologies, lost in thought." The archaeologist took a knee, unslung his backpack in front of him, and unpacked his laptop, a digital camera, and other gear. "Yes, now you all get to partake in an excavation." Conrad smiled at them and chuckled. "You are all my undergraduate assistants."

Hunter checked his watch. "Well, we can do five hours today before we have to head back to make it home before sunset."

Conrad nodded. "That's an excellent start. This will have to be done over the course of many days, anyway."

Eyes bright like a newborn, Conrad snapped a photo of the trapezoid archway.

☙ ☙ ☙

After a day's work and the hike back to camp, the team sat about the fire, eating dinner rations as the sun sank below the horizon.

Conrad summed up his findings to his companions between mouthfuls of vacuum-packed stroganoff. "No sign of any kind of writing. So that makes them unlike the Easter Island culture. The builders of Nan Midol also had no written—"

Wiremu threw his meal to the ground and stalked off to his tent, disappearing inside.

"Did I say something wrong?" asked Conrad.

"Don't know. I'll find out," said Melinda as she walked to Wiremu's tent. She knelt beside it and called to him. "Are you all right? Is something wrong?"

"No. Yes," said the Maori. "You can open the flap."

She unzipped the fly and let it drop open. Inside, Wiremu sat at the far side of the tent, hugging his knees drawn up tight to his body. He panted in tight gasps, face ashen.

Melinda's jaw fell aghast. "What's wrong? Are you sick?"

Voice weak and trembling, he croaked, "It called my name again."

"I didn't hear anything."

He pulled his legs tighter and rested his forehead on his knees. "Of course, you didn't."

"Why do you say that?"

"Because it was a spirit, and only I would hear it."

"Why only you?"

He raised his head and locked gazes with her. "I'm not a traditionalist or a revivalist. I don't wear the *Ta Moko*. But I did grow up with our legends. A spirit calling my name means ..." He dropped his head onto his knees again.

"What does it mean?"

His reply came, muffled by his arms and legs blocking his face. "That it wants me to join it. That I will soon ... *die*."

Conrad stepped beside Melinda. "You can't believe that, my friend. You're a modern man. That's no different than the European tale that an owl hooting outside your bedroom window means one's going to die. It has no correlation. You're safe."

"I knew you wouldn't understand." Wiremu lunged forward and zipped his tent closed.

"Wiremu?"

"Go away."

Melinda scowled at the archaeologist. "Thanks, Doctor. I was talking him down."

"No, you weren't," Wiremu snapped back. "Go away."

Conrad shrugged. "You heard the man. We're done here."

"No thanks to you." She stormed back to the fire.

As the two approached the group, Irdina frowned at Conrad. "I heard what you said to Wiremu. You were rude. I thought archaeologists were supposed to study and respect others. How did we come to get landed with the broken one?"

Conrad grinned. "Good fortune, I suppose."

Irdina's scowl deepened and she shook her head.

Hunter bolted to his feet, darted several meters away, and played the beam of his Maglite into the forest. "Who's there? Come out!"

"Someone call *your* name now?" said Melinda.

"No. I saw motion back in there. A dark shape wobbling side to side."

"Dude, it's night. You can't see dick," called Trevor.

"I saw its outline in the starlight."

Conrad scratched the side of his neck and quipped. "I'm beginning to wonder if there's something in that stream water."

"Are you sure?" said Melinda.

"Yeah, I've seen it before," said Hunter.

"What? When?"

"When we first landed on the beach. I saw the same motion beyond the trees. I thought someone was spying on us." He lowered the Maglite and looked at her. "That's what I jumped out of the Zodiac to check. Could've been a survivor of Gresham's team."

She folded her arms. "I knew it. You *were* looking for something."

"I'll remember I can't pull anything over on you." He slipped the Maglite back into its belt holster.

"So, what do we do about this?"

He exhaled loudly. "No idea. Don't know what we're dealing with. But I think Wiremu's right."

She followed him back to the others. "About what?"

"We're not alone on this island."

⌒ ⌒ ⌒

The next day, they resumed Conrad's dig at the enigmatic ruins. He came no closer to identifying their builders. Shortly before their lunch break, Irdina called out, "Conrad, come here. I've found something."

The team rushed to her side. Conrad knelt beside her as she brushed at an object partially buried at the base of a wall. "Let me see," he said.

Melinda stood on her toes to peer over his shoulder. A smoky black cylinder, lying on its side, half protruded out of the dirt. Irdina swept more of the object clear with her camel-hair brush.

Conrad set a ruler beside the object and snapped several pictures to document its size and its location in the dig site. With his own brush, he joined Irdina in freeing the object from the soil. In time, he held it aloft in his fingers.

Clearly an artificial creation not from nature, the object had a perfectly cylindrical shape about seven centimeters in diameter, fifteen centimeters tall, with a small chip missing from one end.

In a voice hushed with awe, Conrad whispered, "Our first artifact."

"What is it?" said Wiremu.

"I don't know, but isn't it wonderful?"

"In my opinion, it's obsidian," said Irdina.

Conrad worked his jaw side to side, contemplating the observation. "Yes ... though it's not the typical color. I had hoped there would be an inscription on it."

"Can I see that?" asked Trevor.

"Only if you promise to be *very* careful with it."

With a straight face, he replied, "I promise."

Conrad passed the precious find to Trevor, who took it as if it were a Fabergé egg. He turned it over in his hands, blinking. An eyebrow twitched, and he lifted it to his right eye, peering through it at the sun. His jaw sagged. "Wow," he whispered. He handed it back to Conrad.

"Well. What did you see?"

"I ... want to run some tests on it back in camp."

Conrad gazed at him sideways as he slid the cylinder into a pouch. "What kind of tests?"

Trevor held up a hand. "Strictly non-intrusive, I promise."

Conrad nodded. "Very well. You've aroused my curiosity."

∽ ∽ ∽

The remainder of the workday turned up no further surprises. After packing the cylinder away, the team hiked back to their camp.

Near the halfway point, Trevor cried, "Hey! What's that?" He pointed off the trail, into the gloomy depths of the forest.

Melinda and Hunter stepped next to him. "What did you see?" said Melinda.

Fear raised the pitch of Trevor's voice. "A big, dark shadow lumbering side to side. Like someone walking a refrigerator."

"Which way?" said Hunter.

"The same way we're going. Heading toward camp."

"Where is it now?" said Melinda.

"Don't know. I lost sight of it behind a tree." Trevor licked his lips and rubbed his palms on his thighs.

Hunter patted his shoulder. "Welcome to the club, Junior. Let's go. It seems to be gone."

The team resumed the hike, giving furtive glances into the forest as they marched. Trevor crossed his arms, hugging his chest. "It's like I saw Sasquatch. It's a lonely feeling."

An hour later in the growing gloom of twilight, they emerged into the clearing and entered their camp. As the team members set about their own tasks, Hunter scanned them. "Hey, where's Wiremu?"

"What?" Melinda counted heads. She cupped her hands around her mouth. "Wiremu!"

Her cry echoed and soon dampened among the trees. Only silence answered her.

Trevor stepped out of Wiremu's tent. "Hey, guys. His sleeping bag's here, but all his personal stuff is gone."

Melinda trotted over and stuck her head inside. "He's right." She stepped back and passed her gaze over them. "Just like in the first team's camp."

Hunter pointed to her. "You can run, right?"

"Yeah, I've done marathons."

"Great. We're going to the Zodiacs." He scanned the team. "The rest of you, stay here. Don't need to lose anyone else. C'mon, Mel, let's go."

Melinda raised a brow at Hunter. "Mel?"

"Sorry. Trying to ease my tension." He turned toward the trail to the beach.

The pair jogged off toward the beach with Hunter lighting their way with his Maglite. Every few minutes, they called for Wiremu. They received no replies. They found both Zodiacs where they had left them.

"Well, at least we know he didn't take off this way," said Hunter.

Bent over with hands on knees, gasping for breath, Melinda said, "Well ... then which way ... did he ... leave?"

"What part of this made you think I have any clue?"

"Nothing. Just some hopeful spit-balling."

"Well, this was a bust." Hunter jerked his thumb in the direction of camp. "Let's head back."

Melinda nodded.

The pair crept along the darkened, treacherous path to camp, calling for Wiremu as they walked. No reply came from the night-shrouded forest.

We are now five.

༄ ༄ ༄

In the morning light, the team combed the forest along the track between their camp and the ruins, leaving no fern or palm unmolested. They found no trace of Wiremu. After the exhaustive search, they reconvened at the camp and discussed the situation.

"He was acting irrational. Could he have run off?" asked Conrad.

Irdina threw her hands in the air. "We were awful to him! Paid *no* sympathy to his fears."

"I dunno. He didn't seem that irrational to me," grumbled Trevor.

Melinda said, "The fact remains, he's gone. The only fact we have. What can we do?"

Hunter held his hands wide. "Hate this not knowing." He dropped his hands to his lap. "Okay, we need to increase our vigilance, boys and girls. And clearly our eyes are not enough. I have a security camera app on my laptop. I'll set it up to monitor the camp while we sleep. When we're out in the field, we must stay in pairs, at least. No one should ever be alone."

"That will be difficult," said Irdina, holding up five fingers.

Hunter exhaled loudly through his nose. "Then a set of three and a set of two. Just no one alone, okay?"

"Your pride hurting ya, big man?" asked Trevor.

"Damn straight it is, Junior." He jabbed a thumb at his chest. "*My* job was to keep all of you safe. Wiremu's disappearance is an epic fail on my part. Now I have to prevent any further hemorrhaging."

Irdina's eyes grew big. "Do you think there could be more disappearances?"

"Don't know how the first one happened, so, yeah, it could happen again." He held a reassuring hand to her. "But not if I can help it."

"So, are we done here?" said Trevor.

"Yeah, we're done."

Trevor stood. "Good. 'Cause I got some tests to run on the cylinder." He walked toward his tent.

"Can you tell me anything about these tests? Can I help?" asked Conrad.

"Not yet. Got some crazy ideas I need to check out before I share them. Don't worry. I won't break it."

"Better not, or I'll break you, Mr. Sumner," muttered the archaeologist.

~ ~ ~

Hunter set up his laptop on a plastic tub with its camera viewing the entire camp, centered on the fire pit. Melinda led the scientists in gathering firewood, occasionally calling out to Wiremu. Trevor, the cylinder in hand, had withdrawn to his tent, flap closed.

Two hours later, his voice rose from his dome tent. "Hot damn, that's it! Everybody come here. I'm ready to share."

The others clustered near as Trevor zipped open the flap. His laptop sat atop another tub, screen facing the tent opening. Its DVD/CD tray protruded from its side with the cylinder resting on it.

"Check this out." Trevor's fingers danced on the keys with the grace of a concert pianist. The laser reader of the drive whirred, and its red beam shot upward into the stationary cylinder. Within its smoky volume, scintillating points flickered and sparkled like fireflies in a summer night. The red sparks swarmed and flowed with purposeful motion as if alive.

Irdina stopped gawking and croaked, "Obsidian doesn't do that. What are we seeing?"

Trevor beamed. "I was right. You're seeing holographically stored *data*."

"In a stone artifact?" exclaimed Conrad. "But that's impossible."

Hunter's eyes narrowed. "It's a trick."

Trevor pointed at Conrad. "Yes, in a rock." His finger shifted to Hunter. "Sorry, dude, no trick. It's real."

"How did you know?" asked Melinda.

Trevor adjusted his cap and grimaced. "Okay, that is going to get technical. I'll try to keep it simple."

"Thanks," said Melinda.

He tapped his chest. "I have a condition in my brain that causes my eyes to detect patterns as shimmering highlights. The medical name is too hard to pronounce, but this thing actually helps me. That same thing happens when a cat sees motion." He sniffed. "Anyhoo, it's how I do my work in writing code. When I looked at the sun through the cylinder, I saw the light refract in ways that displayed patterns. Logical, systematic patterns. In other words, code, data. I knew this was no plain rock. So I rigged up my DVD drive to do this test and prove what I suspected."

"And what do you suspect, Mr. Sumner?" said Conrad.

Trevor rested his hand on the cylinder. "That despite its ancient surroundings, this is an optical data storage medium."

"Can you read what's on it?"

Trevor shook his head. "Not under these conditions. Besides, this uses a data protocol I've never seen before. The data is arrayed in the three-dimensional matrix, like a multi-layer DVD, only way more complex." He handed the artifact to Conrad. "This just might be extraterrestrial in origin."

"Nonsense!"

"You've all seen it. This is no hoax. It's up to you, Doctor, to make sense of it."

The archaeologist puffed his chest. "I will."

Melinda smiled. "You were right, Trevor. You did have a crazy idea."

Hunter stalked away, snarling over his shoulder as he left. "I still think he's tricking us."

"You're entitled to your opinion, big man. But you're wrong," countered Trevor.

∽ ∽ ∽

Melinda awoke to the bright arc of her dome tent backlit by morning sky. *I had predawn watch. Why didn't Trevor wake me?* She unzipped her sleeping bag, crawled to the tent flap, and opened it. Beyond lay the fire pit, devoid of any flames. "Dammit!"

She scrambled from her tent to the fire. Finding it cold, she growled and piled logs to start a new fire.

Hunter exited his tent and joined her. "Who let the fire go out?" he said.

"Guess who."

"Fanboy?"

"Uh-huh." She scraped shavings from the firestarter onto the kindling and struck the blade against the flint mounted on its base. The shavings flared, and the kindling blazed. "He had one job. One!"

"Well, you're too nice to him." Hunter stepped to the plastic tub and checked his laptop.

Melinda stomped to Trevor's tent and thumped the side three times. "Trevor, get up!"

"What? I'm sleeping," he groaned.

"I don't care. Get out here."

His flap unzipped, and his head emerged as he rubbed his eyes. "Why so cranky?"

She jabbed a finger toward the campfire. "You let it go out, and you didn't wake me for my watch."

"You sound like we're in the army. I got sleepy!"

Hunter chimed in. "It may be because he was busy last night making another hoax."

"I haven't made *any* hoaxes. And what are you talking about, Jarhead?"

"Get it right, I was a grunt. I'm talking about what you left on my laptop." He tapped a finger at the screen.

Trevor stormed to Hunter and peered over his shoulder. "If you're messing with—" His jaw dropped, and his face grew ashen.

"Nice trick, fanboy."

Melinda joined them. On the screen, their camp at night spread before the camera's eye from its vantage on the table. Trevor sat by the fire, head nodding, eyes blinking. He yawned, stretched his arms, and stumbled to his feet. He disappeared into his tent in the background on the right. Five minutes elapsed on the time stamp in the corner of the screen.

In the left background, a motion stirred the trees. A black shape lumbered forth, waddling from side to side, and advanced toward the fire pit, its details growing clearer. Roughly human-shaped with a squat torso, thin arms folded across its belly, and an elongated head bearing a narrow, angular face, it loomed tall and ominous in their camp. Its surface glinted in the fire light like polished black stone. It stood beside the fire, aimed its gaze straight at the camera, drilling them with flaming red points of light like burning coals for eyes, set in deep-notched sockets. It raised its spindly arms above the flames. The fire flared and vanished, as did the figure. The remainder of the video showed their camp plunged into darkness.

Hunter pivoted in his seat to face Trevor, a scowl on his face. "Nice CGI, fanboy."

Trevor shook his head, backed away from the table, pointing at the screen. His face remained pale and drawn. "I didn't do that! What was that thing?"

"Looked like a statue," said Melinda. "Only it moved."

Trevor gasped and leaned forward, hands on knees. "Wait. That looked like the shape I saw in the forest. It came out ... near us."

Hunter's scowl vanished, and he blinked at the frightened tech. He turned back to his laptop and ran the video back and watched it again. The hairs on his arms bristled on goose-flesh. He whispered, "It's the same." He shot a glance to Trevor. "You swear you didn't make this, fanboy?"

"I said no. I don't even know what that thing is, so how could I fake it?" Trevor said, waving his hand at the laptop.

Melinda leaned in close to Hunter. "I heard you. What's the same?"

He nodded at the screen. "That thing and the moving shape I've seen twice before."

She pulled away. "But you said it was nothing."

"I was wrong."

Trevor glared at him. "So that's what you meant by 'welcome to the club.'"

"Yeah," replied Hunter, eyes downcast.

An awkward silence hung in the air.

Melinda glanced about the camp. "Guys, where's Irdina and Conrad?"

Hunter's eyes grew large. "Oh, crap."

The three darted to the scientists' tents to find them absent. Melinda said, "Their personal effects are still here. But the dig equipment is gone."

"Hey, there's a note clipped to Hunter's tent.

Melinda snatched the slip and read it aloud. *"You were all still sleeping. There's work to be done. We're at the dig site. C and I."*

"That's a relief," said Trevor.

"Is it?" snapped Hunter. "They could've vanished, for all we know."

"Only one way to find out, guys. We hike out to the dig. Let's grab some chow for the walk."

"But what about the thing on the video?" said Trevor, his voice quivering.

She shrugged. "What about it? It's gone, and we can't do anything about it right now. But we do need to check on the scientists."

"She's right, Junior. Let's go."

~ ~ ~

The trio emerged from the forest at the ruins to find the scientists inspecting a break in the tree line at the far side of the site.

"Why did you take off without us, in contradiction to my instructions?" said Hunter with an annoyed edge in his voice.

Conrad turned to face him. "Young man, you are not the boss of us, as the lingo goes. You were all oversleeping, and we needed to continue the dig."

"Be that as it may—"

"Mr. Marx, we did stay as a pair, as you suggested," said Irdina.

Conrad waved his hands before them. "That's all immaterial. You arrived at a good time. We made a new find. Look." He pointed into the gap in the trees.

Melinda, Hunter, and Trevor followed his direction. Through the gap, a narrow parting in the canopy wound into the depths of the forest, the path marked out by an interlocked pavement of flat volcanic stones.

Conrad beamed at them. "It's a road. We were going to follow it when you showed up. Now, we can all explore it."

Melinda tapped Hunter's shoulder. "Maybe Gresham's team went that way."

He sighed and gestured down the path. "We may as well go."

The five made their way along the serpentine road through the forest. Eight kilometers farther on, the trees ended and they stood at a vast clearing, their eyes wide in amazement.

A nearly three-kilometer-wide dish-like depression spread before them, its edges ringed with palms and acacias. The road continued into this dale, curving to the north. Clearing a low hill, they gawked once more. Trevor gasped and took a step back.

The road straightened toward the side of the dale's rim and disappeared beneath a trapezoidal arch built into the hillside. On either side of the path stood rows of statues, five on one side and three on the opposite, tall and imposing, their worn, haughty expressions aimed to the sky.

In a hushed voice, Conrad said, "Those look like moai, only smaller than the ones of Easter Island."

"It's the thing from the video! All of them," Trevor croaked, backing away from the sight.

Melinda caught his arm before he could run. "Oh, no you don't. They're only statues."

Irdina stepped to the nearest one and ran her hand over it. "It looks like obsidian. But these are worked into detail that that stone can't hold. It shatters."

"Yes, the Easter Island moai are volcanic stone, not glass," said Conrad. "Wait … what video?"

Hunter pulled his laptop from his backpack. "This one. We had a visitor last night." He tapped the keys.

The scene of the eerie nocturnal visitor replayed for the two scientists, whose jaws hung slack. At its conclusion, they pivoted and gazed at the eight statues.

"They *are* the same," whispered Irdina.

"Legends of the inhabitants of Easter Island say the moai walked from the quarries. Never imagined it might be true," said Conrad.

"So, what is this place?" said Melinda.

Conrad shrugged and shook his head. "A temple perhaps? The statues are arrayed along the path to the arch. Seems a ceremonial arrangement. But why build an arch into a hillside? It goes nowhere."

"Looks like there's space for two more moai," said Irdina.

"Yes, they're missing. I wonder where they are?"

"Stalking the woods for us!" screamed Trevor, breaking into a run back the way they had come.

"Dammit. We're done here. We can't let him get out of our sight." Hunter broke into a trot in pursuit.

"He's right. C'mon. The three of us will bring up the rear," said Melinda.

❧ ❧ ❧

Hours later, as the sun sank, the three entered their camp to find Hunter tending the fire, scowling at Trevor's tent as whimpers escaped from it.

Melinda pointed toward it. "He in there?"

"Yup," said Hunter. "Beat me back here. He's been hiding ever since."

"Poor guy," she said, and stepped to the tent. "Trevor, you okay?"

"No! We're on an island with monsters!"

Conrad sighed, sat at the table, and set up his laptop. "Superb. Now he's being irrational. What is it about this island?"

Irdina slipped onto a chair beside him. "You're being insensitive, Dr. Van Lauer. He's traumatized."

"Over what? Statues? Mr. Marx is right. Trevor faked that video."

"Then why is he terrified?" asked Melinda, eyes narrowed at the archaeologist.

"Who knows? Artistic temperament?" He tapped at the keys of his computer.

Irdina shook her head and scowled. "So insensitive."

Conrad sat up. "Aha. I knew it."

"Knew what?" said Hunter.

"I checked the coordinates. The flash that brought us here came from the same spot as the statues, which I'm naming the Glen of the Moai."

"But how can that be?" asked Melinda. "There's no sign of an explosion."

"I know. And that's what we need to find out tomorrow. With or without Mr. Sumner."

⌇ ⌇ ⌇

That night, Melinda persuaded Hunter to join her once again on the bluff overlooking the sea. The glowing blue surf shimmered and danced below them. She sat, hugging her knees. "We need to talk."

"I agree. You start."

She exhaled. "Things are spiraling out of control. I think we're all out of our depth here. We need to call the boat."

"I concur. Especially since I don't think Trevor faked that video."

She jerked her gaze to him. "You don't? What changed your mind?"

He held his hands wide. "You and Irdina are right. I've fought in Iraq and Afghanistan. I know the look of terror in men's eyes. Trevor is scared to his bones. He's not that good an actor. He genuinely doesn't know what we're seeing in the video."

"Good, that makes things easier. Tomor—" She jumped upright and pointed to the shore. "Where's the glow?"

Hunter looked where she gestured. Below, only darkness lay, the hiss of rising and falling surf lost to the blackness.

He stood. "What happened to the plankton phosphorescence?"

"I don't know. It just vanished like someone flipped a switch."

"Does it normally do that?"

Her face drew long and white. "No."

"That's it. Let's get back to camp."

Later, Melinda thrashed in her sleeping bag, her dreams plagued by red-eyed, obsidian moai swaying to and fro, murmuring gibberish as they loomed above her. She awoke with a start during the night upon hearing a multitude of whispers outside her tent. But she blinked as silence filled her ears. *It's getting to me. Just a bad dream, that's all.*

⌇ ⌇ ⌇

Over breakfast, Melinda and Hunter made their announcement. Melinda said, "People, we're not in control here. Things are happening we don't understand, and we're making no headway in solving them. Hunter and I agree. We're calling the boat back early."

Conrad rose with a huff. "Ridiculous. We only just found the Glen of the Moai but ran away before we could examine it closely." He glared at Trevor, who sank under his scowl. "You three do what you like. Irdina and I have already decided to resume the investigation of the glen today."

Irdina nodded. "Yes. It is far too significant a find to abandon."

Hunter stood and locked eyes with the archaeologist. "I think that's a bad idea."

Conrad puffed his chest. "You have your job, and I have mine. I'm doing mine today, and that's it."

Hunter sighed and resumed his seat. "You're right. I can't order you. But we're still calling the boat. You have till it arrives to finish up."

"Fine. You do that. Let us be off."

Irdina shoved her empty food packs into the trash bag. "Yes. I am quite done with this company."

The two scientists hefted their packs on their shoulders and set off down the trail.

Melinda gazed at their retreating backs until they vanished into the depths of the forest. "For better or worse, there they go."

She pulled the satphone from a side pouch of her backpack and poked at the keys. "What the ...?" She nudged Trevor with the device. "I can't get a signal. What's wrong with it?"

Trevor turned the phone in his hands and pressed a series of keys. "Battery's charged, and all functions are up and running. There's nothing wrong with it. There's just no signal."

"But it's a satellite uplink. How can there be no signal? It's directly above our heads," said Hunter.

Trevor hung his head, dejected. "I don't know. After yesterday, I don't know anything."

"Let's try this one." Hunter pulled his satphone and worked its keys. "Damn. Same thing. Can't connect."

Melinda spread her hands on the table and exhaled loudly. "My God. We're stuck."

"Warned ya," muttered Trevor.

Hunter ran his hands through his hair and swallowed. "What do we do now?"

Melinda held her palms up in surrender. "No choice. We wait 'til the scheduled pick-up."

Hunter squeezed his eyes shut. "In almost three weeks."

"Yeah."

Trevor rocked back and forth, hugging himself. "We're so screwed."

⌇   ⌇   ⌇

Later that morning, Hunter led Melinda and Trevor on the extended hike to the glen. Trevor grumbled. "Again, why are we doing this?"

"I don't feel comfortable leaving those two alone. Under the circumstances, I think we all should stay together. Separated like this, we're vulnerable."

"To be snagged by the monsters."

"Fine. Whatever floats your boat, Junior."

"Knock it off, you two," snapped Melinda.

"Yes, ma'am," replied Hunter.

Trevor grunted.

They arrived at the arch and moai. The two scientists were nowhere to be seen.

Hunter called out, "Hello? Dr. Van Lauer. Dr. Ishak. We're here to help."

Silence greeted his cry.

"Oh, crap. This doesn't bode well," said Melinda, her gaze darting about.

Hunter replied, "Fan out. Look for any signs of a struggle. Or any clue."

The trio scoured the site. Trevor kept a wary eye on the moai the entire time. The team found nothing.

Hunter called them together. "Okay, let's head to camp before nightfall. Maybe they made their way back, and we missed them."

"On those narrow paths? How? We can't even walk side-by-side on them."

Hunter rubbed the back of his neck hard. "Mel, I don't know. Let's just do it, okay?"

"All right, I understand."

"I'm way cool with that," said Trevor, pointing toward the statues. "Because there's only *seven* moai here now."

Hunter glanced at them. "Damn. He's right. Let's get out of here."

Hours later, they arrived at the camp. They searched the scientists' tents, but found no sign of them.

Melinda stepped from Irdina's tent. "Like Wiremu, their personal effects are gone but not their sleeping bags. It's happened again."

Hunter balled his fists and pounded the table. "Epic fail," he growled.

"And then there were three," said Trevor.

"Shut up."

❧ ❧ ❧

In the morning, Melinda and Hunter heated breakfast without a word. She called out. "Trevor, wake up. Time to eat.'

Nothing stirred, silence covered the camp.

"Trevor?" She walked to his tent and open the flap. "Hunter, I think he's gone too."

"What?" He stomped over to her, and they searched the tent. Emerging, Hunter walked to the table and collapsed in a chair. He pinched the bridge of his nose. "Like the others, all effects gone. What's happening, Mel?"

She squeezed his shoulder. "I think we're about to find out. Look."

A snap of a stick and the rustle of leaves came from the forest edge. Three moai lumbered from the brush in a swaying gait, stumpy legs swinging forward with each sideways shift.

Hunter rose to his feet and backed away from their approach. "My God, they're real. They're alive." He drew his pistol and aimed at the hulking figures.

"What are you doing? They're made of stone."

"Oh, yeah." He holstered his weapon.

A deep voice, shaped from the rumble of a rock slide, grated from the lead moai. "You are the last. We have come to speak to you."

Melinda stepped toward them. "Who are you? *What* are you?"

It spread its thin arms wide. "We are the Servitors. We tend the Doorway to Refuge."

"I also asked what you are."

"I answered both questions. Who we are and what is one and the same."

Hunter found his voice. "The door to what?"

It leaned in his direction. "Refuge. From the rising of the sea."

Melinda asked, "Is that where you're from?"

"No." It pointed a finger to the ground. "We are from here. We are made of the earth below. Our energy comes from it and the life in the sea about us."

"How? By whom?"

"By the People-Before-the-Flooding. They who dwelt in this world when the ends of the planet were heavy with ice."

"You mean the last ice age?" asked Melinda.

"If that is your words for it. Yes. Long ago."

Hunter cut in. "I still don't understand what you mean by *refuge*."

"Our creators knew many secrets of energy and the weave of space. They learned how to step sideways into another universe. On this island, a high mountain in their age, they opened the Doorway into such a realm to escape the rising oceans when the ice caps melted. As is happening again."

Hunter and Melinda passed a glance between them.

"You mean global warming?" said Melinda.

"The seas never sank after the last melt. They will not fall again. Land taken by the sea will never know the touch of air again."

She cast her eyes down. "Yes. We know."

The lead moai shifted its weight. "That is why we reawakened. To open the door and offer refuge to our creators' children."

Hunter raised a finger. "How is it you speak our language?"

"The others before you accepted our offer. We learned from them."

Melinda's brows shot up. "You mean our friends?"

"Yes. And the others who arrived before you."

Hunter raised his chin. "Dr. Gresham's team?"

The moai raised its hands. "If that is what you call them.

"So they're in Refuge?" said Melinda.

"Yes."

Hunter stepped back. "How do we know we can trust you?"

"We can show you. Through the *Doorway*, you can see."

Melinda crossed her arms. "Listen, that sounds wonderful. But if this refuge is to serve the purpose of mass evacuation, we must tell others."

"Can you do that?"

She held her satphone up. "With this. But we can't get a signal out. You know anything about that?"

A shimmering of light danced inside a semi-cylindrical projection on its chest. *So that's where Trevor's data cylinder goes.* The moai leaned back.

"Our drawing energy may disrupt your radio emissions."

"Can you stop that long enough for me to get a message out?"

"Yes, but not for long. We need that energy to function."

She nodded. "Do it, and we'll come see your doorway."

Hunter touched her elbow. "Mel?"

"Easy, Hunter. We've got to get the word out. Our mission, remember?"

"It is done," said the moai.

Melinda's thumbs danced on the satphone's keys. "There. Done. We'll come with you now."

"You know the way." The three moai turned and lumbered toward the trail.

Hunter cut in front of her, blocking the path. He faced her. "Mel? Can we trust them?"

She gave him a level gaze. "I don't know, but our answers are where they're going. C'mon."

⌇ ⌇ ⌇

Hours later, the five figures arrived at the arch. All nine moai raised their arms in a circular motion, and the arch shimmered. Through it, their missing companions appeared, standing before an alien cityscape of twisted spires that resembled no known architecture. The two groups' eyes met, and the four beckoned to Melinda and Hunter.

Hunter rubbed his stubbled chin. "So there they are. They seem safe." He drew close to Melinda and spoke so only she could hear. "So do we accept their offer?"

She gazed at the scene in the arch. Melinda pursed her lips then asked the moai. "What reason did our friends give for going?"

"Curiosity," replied the lead moai, nodding its great head.

She glanced back through the arch. "Not good enough."

"So, Mel, what're you thinking?"

"I think we need to explore our options." She faced him and rested a hand on his shoulder. "While the oceans *are* rising, this is too big an opportunity to come down to just a Go/No-Go solution. We need to ask questions." Melinda turned her face to the moai. "Is this a one-way trip?"

The moai rumbled, "We do not know. Our creators did not need to return."

"But light is coming through the gate, so it should be possible, right?" added Hunter.

"Yes, but we see no need."

"You're not us," said Melinda. "Your creators could move to other dimensions. Could they find a way to change the world's atmosphere?"

The moai's chest cylinder sparkled. "Possibly."

Hunter chimed in. "Are the creators still on Refuge?"

"We believe so. They have not spoken to us since they left."

Melinda's brows shot up. "So you're doing all this on your own?"

"Yes."

She whispered to Hunter. "They're capable of independent action. That opens more options."

"Such as?" he asked.

She smiled. "That perhaps we do more than one thing. That maybe not all of us need to leave."

"It did feel like we were running away. You've made up your mind, haven't you?"

"Pretty close. One of us has to step through and talk to the others. The other has to stay behind to meet the boat and tell the world about this. Just in case the gate isn't two-way."

He grinned. "You want to go, don't ya?"

"Yeah."

"Then go. I've got this."

Melinda patted his shoulder and faced the moai. "I want to step through and return. Will you hold the doorway open for me?"

The lead moai bowed. "Yes."

"What do I need to do?"

The lead moai extended a hand toward the arch. "Simply step through."

"Okay, here goes," she said to Hunter. Melinda walked under the arch and a cool tingling ran the length of her body, as if she'd stepped through a waterfall. A heartbeat of vertigo spun her head then was gone. She stood before Irdina, Conrad, Trevor, and Wiremu. An odd, sweet-sour floral scent tickled her nostrils. Her stomach lurched as she felt as if she'd float away on the breeze.

Lower gravity?

"Welcome to Refuge, Melinda!" cheered the others as they crowded around her.

"I can't stay," she murmured.

"Hey. Why isn't the big man stepping through?" asked Trevor.

"What do you mean you can't stay? Nonsense!" objected Conrad.

Irdina chimed in after him. "Yes, why not?"

Melinda held up her hands. "Please, one at a time."

The four quieted.

She smiled. "Thanks. This has to be quick." She rubbed her hands together. "Hunter and I are going to stay behind so we can explain all this to Diogenes. We need you guys to find the moai creators and ask them to reduce the CO2 in our air. *Anything* to reverse climate change. We'll lead evacuees back here. We must try a two-prong solution. Can you do that?"

"Yes, sure," the four replied.

Melinda smiled and squeezed Trevor in a bear hug. "You take care of yourself. Okay, kiddo?"

"No worries," replied Trevor.

She pointed at Conrad and Wiremu. "You two have the most outdoor experience. You keep Trevor in one piece, or I'll kick your butts. Get me?"

"Yes, ma'am," they replied in unison.

"Good. See you all when we get back." She turned, steeled herself, and stepped through the archway. The cool wash played across her skin, and a leaden weight pressed down on her.

Yup, different gravity.

"Good, it worked," said Hunter.

"Now you know," she said to the moai.

They nodded.

"And now we wait for the boat so we can tell the world."

Hunter raised a brow. "Tell them exactly what?"

"That we have a chance for a new hope."

❧ ❧ ❧

In the Diogenes Foundation's center in Christchurch, a technician called out, "We have a transmission from Melinda Banks' satphone."

"Put it on the big screen."

Friends on Spirit Island. Don't fear them. They offer ways to deal with the oceans' rise ... and recover from our mistakes. Send the boat.

THE END

Born in suburban Los Angeles, Joseph Y. Roberts describes himself as "a small town boy from a big city." His transplantation to the Pacific Northwest successfully took and he's been merrily writing away. He's had six short stories published in five anthologies, including this one. Another eight have been self-published. Their genres are wide-ranging, like Joseph's eclectic interests which reflect an ongoing fascination with the less-traveled places of the world and history.

His pursuits have included college radio DJ, actor, resort sketch artist, and newspaper graphic artist. Like a watermelon dropped from a great height, he's all over the map.

https://www.amazon.com/Joseph-Y.-Roberts/e/B014QAFNTC

Crystal

Contemporary Fiction
Fire, Water, Air, and Earth

Ferrell Rosser

The slender, sandy-haired young woman sat under the rocky overhang and watched the water cascade in front of her. Lightning flashed and she waited, anticipating an impressive boom. She wasn't disappointed. Shivering in the damp mountain air, she wrapped the survival blanket around her shoulders. Her expression turned glum.

Well, I knew it might rain ... beginning of fall, after all ... should have brought my heavier pack ... crappy hindsight ... it's gonna be cold tonight ... I shouldn't have come up here ... just needed to get away from all the damn drama at home ... besides, it's the last weekend before I become a nine-to-five worker bee ... Maybe in a few months I'll be able to move out and find my own place. Stupid George ... been almost two months since he walked out on me ... leaving me pregnant ... those screaming matches at the end ... neighbors called the cops ... twice ... damn it, don't cry again. Living with Mika seemed like a good idea at the time ... yeah, move in with my sister and niece ... that should be fun ... teenagers ... and Patti isn't even as big a drama queen as her mother ... it'd be funny if it wasn't so soul sucking ... every day and half the night, every little thing, they're screaming at each other about something stupid or petty ... or both. Ooh, that was close ... whoa ... that was a big boom ... I think the lightning is getting closer ... it's gonna be a long night. I gotta try to not think of the other thing on Monday ... damn it ... the whole point of coming out here was to not think of it ... well, maybe that nice forest ranger will rescue me ... ha! ... like I need rescuing ... gonna be a long, muddy walk tomorrow ... I should get some sleep ... glad my middle isn't hurting ... much ...

She set up her tiny collapsible camp stove in the corner of the opening, close enough to vent but not too far outside to get splashed by the water falling like a curtain in front of the shallow depression in the rock. Crystal settled uncomfortably in her blanket, fatigue overcoming her pain and disquiet.

Water in front of me ... rock behind me ... fire next to me ... damp mountain air around me ... all four elements ... Suzie would tell me I was at the perfect conjunction of the mystic ... something ... don't know ... this is probably some metaphor ... I hope the doctor's appointment doesn't take long Monday ... I'd hate to be late on my first day of work ...

She yawned, derailing her train of thought, and drifted off to sleep. She dreamt. *Silly room ... made of rock ... looks like a waterfall outside the window ... two doors ... fire beyond both ... wind's howling so much I can't hear ... why am I so cold? ...*

Crystal awoke with a shiver. It was dark, the rain had slacked off to just a drizzle, and her little camp stove had gone out. She climbed stiffly to her feet and braved the mountain slope beyond the overhang to empty her bladder. Afterward, she settled back on the ground in her small shelter and replaced the burned-out stick of fuel with a fresh one. It took only a minute to get it glowing. She filled the cup from her canteen and warmed a mixture of water and powdered broth. As she waited for it to heat, she watched the sky lighten. Dawn was in full bloom when she finally had her cup of soup.

So prefer coffee ... must have drank the last packet last time I was up here ... gotta restock ... not sure when I'll be up here again ... I'll try again when it doesn't look like rain ... I'll wait until it's full light before I pack up and hike down to the car ... I should enjoy this as much as I can, while I'm able ...

Crystal shook her head and made a conscious effort to stop thinking and just enjoy the quiet dawn. An hour later, she packed her stuff, put her shoes back on, slipped on the light pack, and began the hike down the mountain to where she'd parked the old beat-up jeep. She stopped twice for several minutes each, waiting for the pain in her lower abdomen to subside before continuing. It took just over two hours to reach her ride, then another hour to get into town. By then she was hungry again.

I'll stop by and talk to Beth at the diner ... bacon and eggs sounds good ... or maybe a waffle ... haven't had a waffle in ages ... wait, this is Sunday ... Beth might not be working ... well, the food is still good ...

She pulled into the little diner's equally little parking lot and went inside. Her friend wasn't working, but the food almost made up for the lack of conversation. When Crystal finally got home, it was a little after ten. Her sister and her niece were awake and bitchy.

"Why didn't you call us to tell us you were ok?"

"On top of a mountain. No service."

"Then why didn't you tell us you might camp overnight?"

"I did. Twice. You weren't listening."

"Uh ..."

Crystal ignored her as she made her way to the stairs.

"I need a shower. See you in an hour."

Crystal took a luxurious shower and spent a good long while dressing. She even touched up her nails, the dark green polish a nice complement to her eyes. Looking in the mirror, she tugged at her hair.

I can't decide if I want to color it or chop it all off ... brown ... black ... platinum blonde? ... don't know ... maybe grow it out past my shoulders ... or get it cut in a pixie? ... hell, purple braids down to my ass ... or maybe I'll get that tattoo I've always wanted ... well, I can decide after tomorrow ... better get dressed and go referee ... damn family ...

As she got dressed, Crystal could hear Mika yelling at Patti about cereal, of all things.

The rest of the day was as stressful as the morning. By the time Crystal gave up and went to bed she was exhausted, but the irritating ache in her abdomen had come back so her sleep was restless. She woke up Monday morning to her alarm buzzing at her, still wanting more sleep.

Ugh … no energy this morning … unpleasant is an understatement … damn it, I've got to go back upstairs … forgot to brush my hair … took me three tries to make coffee … where the hell are my keys? hanging on the hook by the kitchen door, like always … damn it, I'm gonna be late … don't cry … don't cry … gotta go … someone's moving around upstairs …

Crystal took several deep, slow breaths to try and calm down. Just as someone was coming down the stairs, Crystal left the house. It only took a few minutes to drive to the doctor's office but several more to find a parking place. She did make it inside and signed in with a whole minute to spare. Crystal sat in a comfortable chair directly opposite the reception desk. She calmed down and took in her surroundings as she relaxed.

Beige stone walls … two water features … cool, scented air … some sort of hypnotic instrumental music … I think the scent comes from the candles … dim lighting … that massage place on West 4th should take lessons from here … I hope they can tell me this pain is nothing serious.

A nurse in light blue scrubs opened the door next to the desk and called out Crystal's name. The short Hispanic woman was businesslike as she showed Crystal to a small office and left her there, seated in front of a modest desk. The walls were covered with diplomas and bookshelves. Before she could read any of the book titles, the doctor entered and greeted her.

Hm … grey streaks in his short brown hair … built like a professional athlete … a deep, calm voice … nice … pleasant … oh, what the hell? …

"Mrs. Lowry, I'll come straight to the point. The pain in your abdomen isn't associated with your pregnancy. It's cervical cancer. The pain is caused by the pressure of the tumor. It's not very fast growing at this point, and if we treat it now we can get rid of it and it most likely won't return. I have the details here." He reached for a stack of papers on the side of his desk.

"Cancer. That involves radiation, chemo, surgery?"

Crystal's question stopped him in mid reach. The doctor folded his hands. "Yes. It will need to be a very aggressive program of treatment to ensure we get all of it. At this point, we'd probably have to use both external and internal radiation."

Her face became a mask. "What would that, I mean, how would it affect my pregnancy?"

"You would almost certainly lose the baby. It will also most likely leave you sterile."

She swallowed, hard, the muscles of her jaw tightening as a quiver entered her voice. "Would my baby be healthy if I delayed treatment until after I gave birth?"

The doctor leaned forward and steepled his fingers as he spoke. "Almost certainly. However, if you delay for that many months, your chance of survival goes down significantly and the chance of it returning goes up just as considerably."

She saw his expression change, subtly, as he watched the struggle with her decision reflected on her own face. After a minute or so, Crystal gave a long shuddering sigh, and the doctor's shoulders slumped a tiny bit. His expression of sadness didn't change when she spoke again.

"So, if I delay, my baby will have a chance at life. If I don't, my baby will probably never have a chance at life. If I delay treatment, I will probably die. If I don't delay, I'll probably live, but I most likely won't be able to have any more children. Does that about sum it up?"

The doctor nodded.

Crystal squeezed her eyes closed to prevent the tears from leaking. It didn't work. She took a deep breath and held it for a few seconds, trying not to panic.

"How long do I have to make my decision?" The quiver in her voice was still there.

"You have another appointment next Monday."

Crystal went to her first day at her new job, archiving other companies' important documents, in a blur. She spent the first four hours filling out HR paperwork, then a half-hour break for lunch. The last four hours of the day was in a training class. She wrote everything down, being rightfully distracted. When she finally left she was hungry, so decided to stop at her favorite diner on the way home. After a light meal of tomato soup and a tuna sandwich, Crystal talked to her friend, Beth, but didn't mention the cancer. They talked about family instead as Beth filled salt and pepper shakers.

"So, you thought about staying with your sister or moving out on your own?"

"Yeah, I'm thinking about staying. I won't be able to afford a place of my own for months, unless I get a roommate. Or two. What do you think?"

"I think it'll get better." She nodded and grinned as Crystal snorted and rolled her eyes melodramatically. Beth recommended the blueberry pie as she got up to end her shift. Crystal was normally enthusiastic about their pie.

... eating this should be bliss ... feel so numb ... I'm going to hate it when it all catches up with me ...

When she got home, Mika had made a chicken dinner with salad and pasta. Mika and Patti were sniping at each other about how it tasted. Crystal ate a small plate just to avoid getting sucked into an argument. During dinner, Mika and Patti argued with each other about men and boys, hair and makeup, and Patti learning to drive. Afterward, Crystal told them she was tired and went to bed. However, she was up several times that night, nauseated and vomiting. She finally got some sleep, but less than she wanted.

Damn, last night was rough ... still queasy ... so stressed ... maybe that blueberry pie was a mistake ... maybe too much arguing ... not nearly enough sleep ... maybe too much worrying ... hope I can keep this job for a while ... Gotta make a decision by my next doctor's appointment ... gonna have lots of them ... damn it ... damn groin hurts ... I feel so disconnected ...

That day at work was a dull and dim memory by quitting time. On one of her breaks, she went to the admin floor. She told Human Resources about her pregnancy and gave the woman the doctor's note. The faded woman asked Crystal how long she could work.

"As long as I'm able. This isn't a physically demanding job. I just wanted you to know I'd be having lots of medical appointments, but I can work them around my schedule."

That seemed to satisfy the HR woman, and Crystal went back to shuffling other people's papers. The rest of the week went by about the same, a constant battle to concentrate on the job and not the dull ache. Before she knew it, it was Friday and she was free for the weekend.

By Friday afternoon Crystal was tired and stressed. She tried to take a nap when she got home, but Mika and Patti were yelling at each other about some school dance, so she gave up. Instead, she decided to go to a movie, even though she really didn't feel like it. It was late by the time she got there and nearly midnight before it ended. Walking back to her car, she tried to decide what to do next.

Everything is closed ... except for the bars and a couple of fast food places ... maybe I'll get a burger before going back to Mika's house ... The nearest burger joint is on my way back into town, across the street from that loud-ass bar ... the one Mika and I used to sneak into ...

She pulled into the drive-thru, and then parked across from the bar. Crystal watched the patrons drinking on the patio and smoking in front of the place as she ate.

Bars never really were my thing ... that was Mika ... nice to have a few drinks with your friends, now and again ... not gonna be doing that ... wish Mika and Patti wouldn't yell at each other ... wish Mika wasn't so mad about not knowing who Patti's father was ... makes her crazy ... I'll have to tell them something ... about the baby ... and about the cancer? ... after Monday's appointment ... god, did I ever wear clothes like that? ... probably ... another thing I'm not gonna do again ... it was a place like that where I met George ... hell, that might have been where I met him ... another reason never to go clubbing again ... this burger tastes funny ... probably just me ... soda always tastes funny ... that can't be her real hair ... the hell was that movie about? ... I can't even remember the title ... waste of ten dollars ... hope Mika and Patti are asleep when I get home

... tired of their noise ... maybe I'll go to that art show Sunday afternoon ... tomorrow is the ninth ... I'll go over to Jill's tomorrow ... she always has that get together for all us girls from high school ... see who's there tomorrow... might be nice ... it will get me out of the house ...

She finished her burger and soda, tossed the trash, and got back in her car. Twenty minutes later she was back at Mika's. The house was dark and quiet, so she finally got some rest when she went to bed.

Saturday morning, Crystal awoke to her sister and niece screaming at each other about toilet paper. Rolling over with a groan, she tried to block out the sound with her pillow, but she couldn't get back to sleep. As she sat up, she realized her lower right abdomen was aching again. Giving up on more sleep, she climbed out of bed and staggered to her bathroom. When she finally made it downstairs, her sister and niece were once again arguing.

"What the hell are you two screaming about now?" she asked as she wandered into the kitchen.

"Aunt Crystal! Momma said I can't get a tattoo!"

"No kid of mine is getting a tattoo! Ever!"

"State law says that you have to be 18 to get a tattoo without parental consent. You got four more years until you can get one, so the both of you stop arguing about it until then!" Crystal screamed back and then smirked at their confused, shocked faces as she drank a glass of milk. It wasn't until hours later that she actually thought about it.

... I think that was the first time in ten years that I've raised my voice to her ... If I knew that would shut them up, I would have yelled back way before now ... I'll tell them something Tuesday morning ...

Crystal went out to her car, pausing for a moment as the pain in her side throbbed. Letting out a gasp, she climbed into her car as the pain subsided to a manageable level. By the time she reached her friend Jill's house, it was still a struggle to pretend she was ok.

Ok ... smile and nod ... no idea what Jill just said, but nobody is laughing ... nod and smile ... hope I don't cry ... At first, she didn't think anyone noticed.

The afternoon was a wonderful mix of old and new faces. Crystal chatted with several people she hadn't seen in a while, nibbled on Jill's delightful pastries, and drank a lot of sparkling water. She almost got away with fooling everyone she was fine. However, Beth was there, relaxing before her shift, and she noticed.

"Hey, honey! You feeling all right? You usually snag a mimosa, not a fizzy water. What's up? You looked tired the other night, but now you seem ... I don't know, off your game, or something."

Crystal sighed at the taller brunette woman. She held Beth's hands as she spoke.

"Um, no. Don't tell anybody. Seriously. I'm pregnant, but I have ... complications. I have a doctor's appointment Monday before work, so I'll know more then. You're the only one who knows. I haven't even told Mika or Patti yet, so just don't say anything until I do, ok?"

Beth's face went from worried, to joyful, to alarmed, and back to worried as Crystal spoke. She just nodded at her friend, and Crystal gave Beth's hands a squeeze before letting go and wandering off to refill her glass. Beth spent the last hour she was there watching her friend. Crystal saw Beth's thoughtful frown several times that afternoon, but pretended not to notice.

Crystal stayed at the get-together for a couple of hours after Beth left for work before driving to a park near downtown. It was busy, so it took her several minutes to find a parking place. As she was feeding coins into the meter, she noticed a sale sign in one of the little shops that lined the block. On an impulse, she walked in.

Oh ... old electronics ... what do they call them? ... vintage ... ha! camcorders ... Dad used to have one ... I wonder if they work ... I'll ask ... huh, here's one that's still in the box, never opened ... I wonder how much it is? ... well, there's the guy, I'll ask ...

A little old man, scrawny and bald, sat behind a huge old-fashioned cash register in the middle of the crowded shop. Picking up the camcorder, Crystal stepped over to him.

"Hi!" She smiled at the man.

The old man smiled back at her.

"Yes, young lady, are you interested in that old camcorder? It should be in working order. Did you have a question?" His smile and voice reminded Crystal of her grandfather.

"Yes. Well, two questions, really. First, can these recordings be easily converted to a more modern format?"

The old man chuckled as he replied.

"Yes. Yes they can. Most camera or computer shops can do it for a very modest fee. What's your other question?"

Crystal smiled back at him.

"How much does it cost?"

He chuckled again.

Later, with her purchase safely hidden in her locked car, she strolled under the trees in the park on the next block. Sitting on a carved stone bench, she watched some children play in a sandbox in front of a fountain. A light breeze picked up the scent from the food trucks across the street. Crystal couldn't decide if she was hungry or nauseated. As she thought, she noticed a small crowd gathering around a street performer.

Well, I think hungry is winning ... hmm ... stone bench ... water fountain ... scented air ... some guy doing tricks with fire ... now all I need is for a spirit to appear and tell me something cryptic ...

With a sigh and a creak of her knees, an old woman sat down beside Crystal. After a moment, she started a conversation. Her voice was happy and mellow.

"So, dear, which one of them is yours?" The old woman waved at the children.

Crystal snorted, good-naturedly. She surprised herself with her reply.

"Oh, none of them. I won't have one of my own for almost seven months."

The old woman patted her arm. "Well, you're in for the adventure of a lifetime! Children are what makes life worth living."

Crystal looked at the older woman with a startled expression.

Well ... someone's lifetime ... great ... I almost stopped thinking about it all ... well, no need to be rude ...

After another minute or two of thinking, Crystal got up and smiled at the older woman.

"Well, I've decided I'm hungry, so I'm going to go pig out at those food trucks. Very nice to talk to you!"

"No need to worry about your diet now!" The old woman chuckled.

Crystal laughed and waved at her as she walked off toward the cluster of food trucks. As she waited for the light to change at the corner, she realized she felt almost normal.

Weird ... other than feeling starved, I'm feeling better than I did before things went south with George ... before I discovered that special parting gift he left me ... and what I don't want to think about ... Those kids were adorable ... eww ... stomach growled ... maybe I'll sample a little of each ... don't know how Latin and Asian go together ... or eastern European ... guess I'll find out! ... hope I don't puke all night .

The light changed, and she hurried across the street to the food trucks. Reaching the back of the shortest line, she decided to have dessert first. While eating an ice cream cone, she contemplated what to have next.

A cup of hot and sour soup? ... one of those meat stuffed bread things? ... ooh, a Cuban sandwich ... Mmm ... that barbeque smells wonderful ... well, ice cream's done ... I'll wash down a couple of sandwiches with the soup ... damn I'm hungry!

She did exactly that. Over an hour later, slurping down the last of her soup, Crystal heard a shriek of laughter from the park across the street. It made her smile, then she frowned.

Life is good ... I feel wonderful today ... watching kids play in the park ... I gotta make a decision by Monday ... damn it ... every day should be a day like today ... I won't have many days like today ... everyone should have a chance at having a day like today ...

She wiped tears from her face before returning to her car. Climbing in, she remembered her purchase. She smiled sadly. Suddenly her expression changed to a more decisive one.

Fuck it ... no one knows what tomorrow brings ... that old woman was right about those kids ... it would be an adventure ... and like that fortune cookie I read a couple of weeks ago ... what was it? ... 'Life is a series of challenges' ... well, life, challenge accepted ...

... 15 Years Later ...

Amanda walked out of school, cheerfully chatting with her friends as they wished her a happy birthday. She waved at the woman in the old blue sedan as she reached the parking lot. Her friend, Alice, snagged her arm and pointed at the car.

"Is that your mom?"

Amanda's smile faded as she answered. "No. That's my cousin Patti. She's fifteen years older than me, so she's kinda like a mom. Anyway, I have to go. I'll see everyone later at the bonfire!" As she broke from the pack of schoolmates, her habitual smile and sunny disposition returned. She waved to her friends as she climbed into the car. Patti gave her a sad smile as she greeted her.

"Hey, kiddo, how was school? Excited about homecoming? We're gonna go over to my mom's house and have a little celebration before you go out to the spring bonfire tonight." There was a tiny catch in Patti's voice. Amanda pretended she didn't hear it as her older cousin started the car and they drove off.

The ride to Aunt Mika's house only took about 10 minutes. As they rode, Amanda chatted about her friends, related a funny story about that day's gym class, and finally confided she hoped a certain boy would be at the homecoming pregame celebration that night. Patti took it all in with a wistful smile. Again, Amanda pretended not to notice. They reached the small house in the quiet neighborhood, and Patti parked across the street. A minute later, they walked through the door. A tiny squeal of joy greeted them as a golden-haired toddler raised her arms. Patti scooped up her daughter and gave her a hug before passing her over to her younger cousin.

"Hey, Lynnette! You having a good time with your grandma?"

The little girl laughed and gave Amanda a hug, then started to play with her long sandy hair. The little girl's grandmother came out of the kitchen, and Amanda greeted her.

"Hi, Aunt Mika!"

The older woman gave Amanda a hug and took the baby from her so she could sit down. Once everyone sat, Patti removed a cardboard box from beside the couch and pulled out a smaller wrapped box, handing it to Amanda. The teenage girl made a squealing noise that everyone laughed at and unwrapped her birthday gift. A minute and a photo later, Amanda was handed one wrapped box after another. After the combs, hair clips, and nail polish were examined, photoed, and oh'd and ah'd over, Patti reached in and took out one last gift. It wasn't wrapped in bright paper, or even decorated, just a heavy box in a plain paper bag. It didn't even have a tag. Amanda looked at it curiously. Aunt Mika cleared her throat, and Amanda looked at her.

"Amanda, dear, that's your mother's old camcorder. It has a couple of videos you'll want to watch. I'd suggest you get them transferred to something a bit more modern so you can keep them better. Let me show you how the playback works."

Amanda opened the package, and her aunt demonstrated how to use the old device. Lynnette started squealing about cake, so everybody went into the kitchen.

Later, as Amanda got ready to go to the bonfire rally, she dumped all the other gifts on the end of her bed, but she ever so carefully placed the camcorder on top of her dresser and made sure it and the cartridges were secure before going out.

Amanda met up with her friends at the bonfire in the big field on the edge of town. She laughed at the kid with the bullhorn making terrible jokes about their opponents in the next night's ball game, laughed even louder at an off-color joke about the dance after the game, and they all giggled as they flirted with several boys they knew.

Just keep laughing ... hope Alice doesn't notice ... she notices every-thing ... I can lie and tell them the tears are from laughing ...

By the time Amanda got home, she was exhausted. Her dreams were about a bizarre mix of baseball and dancing. She woke early.

After breakfast, she took the old camcorder and went to her favorite place. It was a quiet meadow with the stone sticking up out of the grass in front of her and the little fountain behind her. After she settled on the grass with her back to a tree, Amanda brought up the video on the tiny screen. The sound was low, so she had to concentrate on what the woman in the recording was saying.

"Hi, kiddo! I'm recording this ... just in case we don't get a chance to see this together. So, look at this view!" The sandy-haired woman swung the camera around, first showing a shallow depression in the rock wall of the steep slope, but then the changing perspective came around to show a breathtaking view of a mountain vista in late winter. After a moment the scene went back to the tired looking woman, and she spoke again.

"Honey, I've always loved this place and I wanted to share it with you. By the way, this is you." The picture shifted to the woman's rounded belly before moving back to frame her face. She was smiling but clearly in pain.

"Yeah, that's you, Amanda. This will be the last time I'll be able to come up here, no hiking after the seventh month! I hope you'll be able to visit here in person sometime. I love you, Amanda. I wish we could see this view together. Promise me you'll enjoy life." The recording went on, but Amanda couldn't see it with her eyes blurry from tears. Carefully placing the camcorder in her lap, the girl picked up a tiny candle and lit it. She placed it next to the stone with the name and dates.

Finally, she reached over to the other tape cartridges, caressed them and whispered, "I love you too, Momma."

THE END

Ferrell Rosser has lived in Colorado since the early '90's. Writing short stories since 2002, he has self-published several collections, mostly fantasy. He lives with his wife, works at a mundane job, and they share an apartment with their oldest daughter and two very bossy cats. The author needs enough readers to buy this book so he can afford to buy a round in his favorite drinking establishment in celebration. The bar owners would be ever so grateful. He also enjoys an occasional bit of dark humor and playful sarcasm, with it often showing up in his creative works.

Pearls of Rhyce

Middle-grade Literary Fiction
Water and Fire

Deborah S. Vlick

Mom chose the stupidest time to tell me something devastating today. Right as our boat nosedived over the edge of the highest drop-off of the log flume at Hersheypark, she blurted out, 'Rhyce, your father died.'

I thought I didn't hear her right because of the air pushing against my face, and I *might* have been screaming a little bit. Plus, the water in my left ear didn't help.

After the boat came to a complete stop and we climbed out, she said, 'Rhyce Decker Foley, did you hear me? Your father died.'

I ignored her, thousands of thoughts swimming around in my mind. A few months ago, my best friend Linc and his dad took me to see the Harlem Globetrotters at the massive arena in town. Time with Linc and Dr. Henderson, sharing popcorn and laughing at the goofy basketball players, showed me how much I've been missing in life. I promised myself I'd find the father who abandoned me as a baby and make him proud enough to want me, to love me. Then he'd come home to stay and I could call him Dad and he would call me son.

Now it will never happen. He left me behind once more, but this time he's gone forever.

"My mom thinks I'm mad at her. Does she expect me to just bounce back like nothing happened?" I drop my skateboard onto the pavement and plop my left foot near its nose. "I'm going nuts, Linc."

He glances up at me while tying his shoelaces. "Dude, you're not the one who's nuts. She told you on the freakin' log flume!"

"Which happened to be the best ride ever ... until then." I push off with my right foot and glide across the parking lot. "She ruined it for me."

Lincoln jumps onto his two-wheeled board—one of his many awesome blue-and-black Razor RipSticks—and speeds past me. "You'll get over it."

"Uh-huh. Right. Sure I will. Like being told your father died is an everyday occasion." I pivot my wheels, lose my balance, and slam into a Tesla parked under the long portico in the charging station lot.

"I just meant you'll get used to riding the flume again." He points at the candy-red Tesla. "You're lucky the alarm didn't go off."

"Yeah, especially with my *luck* today." I rub my elbow and drop to my knees to retrieve my skateboard from beneath the car. "Subject change. I need a break."

Lincoln kickflips his board onto the sidewalk and belts out the old jingle for the Kit Kat bar—we found it on YouTube a few months ago when he typed kit instead of kite.

I stare at him and grin, shaking my head.

"What? You said you needed a break. We're in front of Chocolate World. Dude, admit it. It was perfect timing."

"At least you're good at skateboarding because you have a zero-percent chance at being a famous comedian when we grow up."

"Oh, I see how it is. You're buying your own freakin' candy bar today, Crispy."

The Muppets version of "Bohemian Rhapsody" blares from his cell phone. He yanks it out of the back pocket of his shorts as he rocks the deck of his board back and forth under his lime-green Nikes.

"Dad says I need to be home by four. We're meeting my sister Loren and her boyfriend Cody for dinner. He said you can come along if your mom says it's okay."

I peer at my watch and jut my jaw to the right, thinking.

"Come on! Grab your pterodactyl flip and text her. Then we can hit the rides for a few hours. It'll help get your mind off—"

I glare at him and signal the throat-cut.

"Crud. Wave pool and waterslides? Or we can hang out in the arcade."

The green-and-yellow trolley pulls under the portico and around the corner. Tourists climb off, and a bunch of girls snap selfies in front of the welcome sign.

Linc winks at a blonde. She giggles and whispers to one of her friends.

"Ew! What are you doing? Girls are gross!"

"Are not."

"Are too! Yuck."

"Foley, did you text your mom yet?"

"I don't need to text her. She started work twenty minutes ago. Let's go ask." I tuck my skateboard under my right arm.

Lincoln hesitates, examining the girl, then flips his RipStik in the air and catches it as it descends.

"Show-off."

"Whatever!"

We zig-zag through the crowd, lug open the milkshake-spattered glass door—at least I *hope* it's from a milkshake—and head to the customer service desk.

"Hello, boys! You know the routine." Mom's manager gives us a slight nod and eyes our skateboards. "Rhyce, your mom is stationed down on the rotating floor today."

"Thanks, Nova Leigh."

We lay our boards, wheels up, on the bottom shelf behind the desk, squirt our palms with sanitizer, and head for the entrance of the tour.

"Dude, this place is as bad as Times Square on New Year's Eve. Did the rest of the world explode and everyone evacuate to Hershey?"

"Trust me. *This* is a science-class colony of ants when you compare it to the crowd in Manhattan on *any* day."

The rubber soles of Lincoln's Nikes screech like compressed brakes on a race car. "When did you go to New York City? Isn't it too *normal* of a place for your mom to choose for a vacation destination?"

My uncontrollable laughter causes people to turn their heads. "Mom wanted a baked bagel from her favorite shop called Ess-a-Bagel."

"What? Are you sure you're not adopted? Seriously, you traveled to NYC for a baked bagel?"

"Yup. Nope. Yup."

Linc and I shuffle past a mammoth-sized group of Girl Scouts and a double stroller, two chocolate-covered toddlers tucked inside hugging stuffed plush cows.

"A baked bagel?!"

"Hush. There's my mom."

Lincoln raises his eyebrows. "A baked ba—"

I elbow him in the ribs.

"Okay, okay. I'll stop. Geez."

My mom glimpses in our direction. After guiding a wheel-chair-bound man into one of the mahogany-colored tour cars, she walks over to Linc and me.

"Boiled." Mom rubs her mouth as if she's trying to hide some-thing.

"Huh?" I ask, confused.

"The bagel. It was boiled. Boiled then baked."

Mom laughs and I feel like leaping into one of the triple-linked cars and pretending I'm just a visitor, not her son. Her laugh is the most embarrassing thing ever. It's this high-pitched giggling and pig-snort combination.

"Linc, do you ... where'd he go?"

"He's over there." She points to the open-aired pod entering the tunnel. "Go join him. We'll chat after you get off the ride."

I sprint over to Linc, my mom's giggle snorts echoing as we disappear into the storyland of dairy cows and chocolate.

"Dude! How do you live with her?" The wide whites of Linc's eyes have this bluish tint from the lighting in the signs above our heads. "I'm glad I was born a Henderson."

"Like I had any choice in whose you-know-what I popped out of. She's not insane all the time—"

"Foley, your mom is not like any mom I've ever met. I mean, listen ... her ears hear all, her mouth says all, and her brain is so far out there. Straitjacket material. Seriously."

I smash my fists against the pod's seat and scowl at the conching machines on my left.

"Diarrhea."

"What?"

"Nothing."

The slimy brown liquid—supposed to represent chocolate liquor—sloshes against the walls of the tubs. In the mirror behind the equipment, Linc's scrunched-up facial expression reflects back at me. I lean against the seat and focus on the displays around me as the pod shimmies along the track in the floor. Out of all the times I've been through this demonstration, I never realized until now how much chocolate looks like poop. And today, life-sized piles of poop are suffocating me.

"I guess I'm no better than her. I shouldn't have said those things. I just … I don't know." Linc picks at the alligator on his Izod socks. "Plecostomus?" His lips form a cautious smile.

Plecostomus. It's our way of apologizing when we make each other feel like moldy fish-tank scum. I don't know whether or not to forgive him right now because I'm feeling *way* beyond moldy fish-tank scum. More like full-blown crap.

Lincoln stares at his shoes. "I'm sorry."

Those two words—or the way he whispered them—hit me hard. The extreme tenseness I have dealt with all morning lightens a smidgen.

Our car edges closer to the final part of the ride where a camera snaps souvenir photographs. I whack Lincoln on the head and holler, "Plecostomus!"

His fingers wrap around my neck in a fake choke right as the camera makes the clicking sound. "I guess I owe you a candy bar after all."

"After such torment, you owe me the five-pounder, Henderson, but I'll settle for a bag of Reese's Pieces."

"Deal. You ask your mom if you can go with me for dinner. I'll go get our stash and boards."

We scramble out, and Linc bolts past my mom and up the steps.

"What's his rush?" Mom paces backward on the rotating floor to stay in line with the staircase. "Everything okay?"

I shrug my shoulders and change the subject. "Dr. H invited me to go out to eat with them. Can I go, please?"

She escorts the next cluster of sightseers to the slow-moving trio of cars. "You can go, but don't get the most expensive meal." Mom pulls our house key out of the pocket of her beige uniform pants. "I work 'til eleven. Make sure to lock the door after you get home. And don't leave the key in the lock. I have the spare in my purse. Oh, by the way, tomorrow afternoon we're flying to California."

"What! *Why?*" I stomp my foot and cross my arms. "I don't want to go to California for one of your stupid vacations. Can't I stay here with Linc?"

Mom's shoulders slump. "It's not a vacation, Rhyce. Your father lived there. He's left his est—"

"Hello? We'd like to see the tour today if you don't mind." A rotund bald man in a tree-themed Hawaiian-style shirt waves his hand toward the pods and tunnel.

"I'm sorry, sir. I'll be right with you." Mom lowers her voice. "Honey, I have to work. We'll talk later. Go have fun with the Hendersons."

"How long will we be in California?"

"I don't know. It could be a week or a month or longer. There's paperwork and such, and the memorial service, but don't worry about it today, all right?"

"Yeah, right. Pretend like *nothing* happened, again. I get it."

Mom furrows her brows. "I love you, Rhyce. I'm sorry, but I'll see you later."

"Yeah, uh-huh. Later."

An attendant next to the door throws me a kiss—the chocolate kind wrapped in silver-colored foil—on my way out. I traipse across the lobby to the front desk where Lincoln is sitting on a bench next to the window, our candy and skateboards beside him.

"So? What'd she say?"

I dangle the house key in front of him.

"Whoop! Whoop! It's one o'clock. Want to hit the arcade? I freakin' want to hook the killer whale and jellyfish in Harpoon Lagoon."

I sigh and try to think of a way to tell Linc I'm leaving tomorrow. He's not going to be happy our summer plans have changed.

"What's wrong?" He tears open his Kit Kat, snaps a piece off and takes a bite.

"My life, but never mind. Harpoon Lagoon is boring." I roll my eyes and slide my skateboard back onto the bottom shelf of the desk. "But Hydro Thunder!"

"Dude! Hydro is like five years older than us." He slithers his RipStik onto the shelf. "Totally beyond ancient in video-game years. And how can you say Harpoon is boring? It gave us *ten thousand* tickets so far this summer and it's not even July yet!"

"We could go get my five-pound chocolate bar ... with your big, fat allowance." I start walking backward toward the candy section.

"Or we could freakin' win it in the arcade!" He taps his left foot. "Tick, tock, tick, tock."

"Henderson, you're a dweeb." I slip out the door and Lincoln follows me. "Dweeb, dweeb, dweeb, dweeb!"

Once past the main gate, we break into a run toward the arcade and away from my pile-of-poop life.

I'm eating French fries and a grilled cheese under a Corvette. The classic car is bolted to a bright red four-post car lift. There's a Yamaha motorcycle dangling from the ceiling over the table next to ours. Quaker Steak and Lube is the coolest vehicle-themed restaurant in the whole world.

"Dude! A grilled cheese?" Linc jabs me with his bony elbow before taking a bite of his bacon cheeseburger. "You ... should ... mmm ... this. This!"

"What's wrong with a grilled cheese?" I take a sip of my chocolate milk.

"We're not little kids anymore! Adult menu, duh!" He waves his burger so close to my face I can smell the disgusting onion slivers and melted Swiss cheese. "We'll be twelve in three months!"

My jaw juts to the right. "I know, but my mom said—"

"Yeah, sure. Blame the weirdo."

"Lincoln Ulysses Henderson! Mind your manners." Mrs. H glares at Linc.

"Sorry, Ma."

"Your mother isn't the one you should be apologizing to." Dr. H nods in my direction.

"Sorry, Foley." Linc rolls his eyes. "You know my dad doesn't care what you order. You could have gotten the baby back ribs or *this* bacon burger! Grilled cheese is for babies."

"Oh, Lincoln Logs, you are so wrong." Loren drizzles ranch dressing on her salad and pops a crouton into her mouth. "Some eateries specialize in grilled cheese sandwiches."

"... And some even use glazed doughnuts for the bread!" Cody blows his straw wrapper in Linc's face. "Get with the times, Logs."

"Hey, stop calling me Logs!" Lincoln crinkles up the thin white paper, rubs it in the condensation on the side of his glass, and flicks it back at Cody.

Loren laughs. "You're the cool one, Rhyce. Burgers are so yesterday. Hey, Ma, do you remember the cheesy goodness we ate when we visited Los Angeles? Wasn't the diner named Fred 62 or some other number? Oh. My. Gosh. They were *the* best!"

At the mention of California, I slip down on my chair and stare at the chassis of the Corvette, the conversation around me morphing into the voice of Charlie Brown's teacher. I wonder what kind of vehicle my father drove. Did he love cars as much as me? What did he do for a job? What would it have been like to live with him? Why did he abandon me?

Someone tugs on my arm, jolting me out of my thoughts.

"Rhyce? Are you feeling all right?" Dr. H presses his hand against my forehead. "You don't have a fever. Something on your mind? We can go for a little walk."

I straighten up in the chair. "I'm okay. It's just ... it's ... my mom and I are leaving for California tomorrow, and when Lor—"

Orange soda spurts out of Linc's mouth. "You're what? You can't go! Harpoon Lagoon, Foley!"

"I don't have a choice. We're going to my father's ... his ... memorial." I jump up from my chair and run to the front door, teardrops blurring my vision.

Once outside, I lean against an antique gasoline pump. After a few moments, the door opens and Loren's gentle hand comes to rest on my shoulder.

"Life has some really tough moments, doesn't it? I'm not going to say I know how you feel, because I don't. I still have both my parents. But I do know there are times we need to allow ourselves to sink below the surface of the raging seas."

"Sink?"

"Not literally, but ... you know. Our minds are like the ocean. Unpredictable. Sometimes they're peaceful and we float about, not a care in the world. But other times, they're like a hurricane, a typhoon. They knock us off our feet and bury us alive."

She wipes some of my tears away with a tissue. I remain silent, staring at the fabric-lined hose attached to the nozzle.

"What I'm trying to say, Rhyce, is sometimes good things come from bad things. We'd never notice the colorful coral reef or find a breathtaking pearl if we didn't plunge ourselves into the unknown. Think about it." Loren plops down onto the ground and shields her eyes from the sunlight. "I think there are a lot of pearls in California just waiting for *you* to discover them."

I sit down next to her, my chin quivering. "You really think so?"

She leans into me, playfully knocking against my shoulder.

"I know so. And I'm sure your dad was a wonderful gem, despite whatever happened in the past."

"I really wanted to meet my father. Why didn't my mom ever talk about him?" I attempt to sigh but the hiccups take over.

"Hold your breath. One Mississippi, two Mississippi, three Mississippi. Boo!"

I laugh out loud. "Work ... ked."

"Or maybe not." She giggles and wraps her hand around mine. "I can't promise your trip out west will be all sweet milk chocolate, because some bites will be bitter or dark. I'm not sure why she never spoke to you about him. She probably had good reasons not to, though. But I'm sure you'll find answers to the questions you have. Jump in with both feet. Dive in head first. You'll either sink or swim, but you have to give it a whirl."

Loren yanks me to my feet. "Ready to go back inside?" She winks, pulling me toward the entrance.

I stop, clinging on to the pump.

"What's wrong?" She lets go of my hand.

"Thank you." I engulf her in a gigantic bear hug. "I feel a little better."

Loren rubs the top of my head. "My dad will be pleased to know my psychology major is worth his every hard-earned penny. Come on, dessert time."

When we return to our table, Lincoln is snuggled up next to his mom, his eyes puffy and wet. He shoots upright when he sees me.

"Dude, don't get the wrong idea. I ... I ... my straw poked my eye."

"Yeah, I hear you. And I was just draining the ocean to make it easier to find pearls."

Nova Leigh's Chevy Cruze smells like stale cigarettes and wet puppies. Dog biscuits and a discolored rawhide bone lay broken on the floor. Black and white hairs cover the blanket on the back seat. I scrunch up my nose in disgust.

"Wait. Let me move the blanket before you get in." She rolls it up and tosses it on the floor behind the passenger seat. "There you go."

On the way to the airport, back roads, dairy farms, and fields fade away behind us as highways, factories, and a convoy of eighteen-wheelers takes over. After signaling one of the truck drivers to honk his horn—which he does three times—I rest my head against the seat cushion and close my eyes.

"Looks like he's sleeping," Nova Leigh says. "This whole ordeal must really be wearing on him."

"It's all my fault, Nov." Mom sniffs.

"Don't blame yourself, Ramey. You had nothing to do with your ex's death."

"I know, but every now and then I wonder if I made the right choice to leave Lake Tahoe twelve years ago."

What? My eyebrows crease and my jaw shifts.

"I don't think you ever told me why you left him."

Mom blows her nose. I open my eyes a tiny bit and see Nova Leigh's right hand on Mom's left shoulder. She glimpses into the rearview mirror, so I close my eyelids again.

"Scott was an amazing man. He was hardworking, patient, and his heart was full of so much love, Nov. But after—"

His name was Scott?

"But after Scarlett drowned ..."

The ticking of the turn signal echoes in my ears right along with Mom's words. She never mentioned anyone named Scarlett before, but my heartbeat is racing faster than a Lamborghini.

The car swerves to the right and stops. I wonder if we're at the airport, but I don't want to risk looking around.

"Oh, hon!"

"A month later I found out we were expecting. I was three months along. I couldn't tell Scott. I just couldn't. He wouldn't talk, wouldn't get out of bed. Refused to eat. I got so overwhelmed, I needed to get away from it all. If I stayed I would have gone crazy.

He never knew about me?

"It's just all too much. Going back to the lake and the house, having to face the past, the present, and the future all at once."

"I'm so sorry, hon. I wish there was something more I could do to help you. Sometimes adulting sucks, doesn't it?"

Quiet tears run down my cheeks. I'm not sure who Scarlett was, but I now know my father didn't abandon me. You can't abandon a son if you don't even know he exists.

⌒◯ 𝔷 ◯⌒

It's been two hours since Nova Leigh dropped Mom and me off at Dulles International Airport. Concourse D smells like coffee, tomato sauce, popcorn, and soft pretzels.

"I'm going to get us some pizza."

I yank off my backpack and toss it beside a row of connecting chairs. "I'm not hungry."

"You're always hungry. What's wrong with you?" Mom tugs a twenty-dollar bill from her wallet. "What do you want to drink?"

"I said I'm not hungry!" I flop down onto one of the chairs and twist around to face the window. Airplanes taxi to the runway, and airport personnel load baggage onto waiting aircraft.

Mom's skirt makes a ruffling sound as she walks away. "Fine, grouchpuss. I'll get you a Dr. Pepper."

Don't bother. The only thing I want is to know why you're keeping secrets from me about my own life!

There are three missed texts on my phone. Two from Linc and one from Loren.

12:32 p.m. - Dude! You missed it. I pooned the jellyfish!

12:47 p.m. – Yo, did you get my text? I freakin' pooned the jellyfish, Foley.

1:06 p.m. – Hope you have a safe flight. Remember, the pearls are waiting just for you.

Even though Linc texted me first, I click to respond to Loren's message. Maybe she can help me reel in my anger.

2:14 p.m. – Secrets. Lots of them. I'm mad.

The windowpane behind me shakes from the rumbling of a 737 rushing down the runway. A second later, my phone vibrates in my hand.

2:15 p.m. – Dark chocolate. It's tough, but you'll make it.

2:16 p.m. – She left and didn't tell him. Someone drowned.

2:16 p.m. – ??

2:17 p.m. – I don't know. Too mad to think.

2:18 p.m. – Breathe. Take a deep breath. One Mississippi, two ...

Mom returns holding a tray. She sets it on the chair next to me and grabs her drink and a slice of pizza loaded with mushrooms, onions, and green peppers. I glare at my slice to make sure it doesn't have the same nauseating toppings. It doesn't. Just cheese and sauce. My stomach growls, but I ignore it and go back to texting.

2:21 p.m. – Why didn't she tell me? It's MY life!

2:22 p.m. – But it's hers, too ...

My jaw shifts as I watch Mom take a bite of her crust. She glances at me and smiles. Her eyes look sad, though. They don't have the normal crinkles around them.

The phone vibrates multiple times. Three messages one right after the other.

2:25 p.m. – uddy pearls. Just need a good washing.

2:25 p.m. – *Muddy

2:25 p.m. – KILLER WHALE BELLY UP! Whoop! Whoop!

A deep voice on the loudspeaker startles me and I drop my cell phone.

"United Airlines Flight 696, departing for Denver, now boarding at gate D1. United Airlines Flight 696, departing for Denver, now boarding at gate D1."

Mom chucks her paper plate and cup into the trashcan. "That's us. Grab your stuff, and eat as we walk."

"We're going to Denver? Since when is Denver in California?" I snatch up my pizza slice, phone, and backpack. Mom throws my plate and soda away.

"We have an hour layover in Colorado. From there we fly to Reno."

"But Reno's in Nevad—"

"I know. It's the closest airport to your father's house. We'll drive the rental car to California. It takes approximately an hour."

I chomp on my pizza, and wish Mom wouldn't have thrown my drink away.

Once we reach D1, I use the bottom of my shirt to wipe sauce from my chin.

"Rhyce Decker Foley!"

"Sorry!" I press my lips together and stretch them as wide as they can go.

"Your father used to do the same thing."

"He did?"

After a lady scans our tickets, I follow Mom through the airbridge and into the plane.

"He did. You do a lot of things he used to do." She gently runs her fingers through my hair. "And you look just like him."

My chin trembles. "I do?"

"You do." She hugs me as the plane taxis out to the airstrip.

2:49 p.m. – On the plane. Found another pearl.

2:49 p.m. – Text me when you and the pearl land.

My phone vibrates as the nose of the plane lifts.

2:50 p.m. – Ahem …

2:50 p.m. – 737 WHEELS UP. Boeing beats killer whale.

As I'm about to switch my phone to airplane mode, a photo of Linc biting into a five-pound chocolate bar appears on my screen, a three-word sentence below it.

See my *pearl?*

Mom veers the rental car—a boring black Ford Focus—around a sharp bend, passing a green-and-white sign for Tahoma, California. When the road straightens again, she pulls into a gravel alcove and turns off the engine. Nothing but trees surround us.

She drums her thumbs against the steering wheel. "Your father treasured this spot." A tear slips down her cheek. "Come. I want you to see something."

Mom drapes her arm over my shoulders. She leads us a little ways into the woods and stops in front of an enormous tree.

"This one was his favorite in the whole forest." Mom sniffs the cracked bark, rubbing her fingers along two adjoining hand-carved hearts—one with an S in the center, the other an R. "Put your nose against the crevices. Take a whiff."

At first, the aromas of pineapple and vanilla fill my nostrils, but the second sniff sort of smells like the taste of a butterscotch Lifesaver. My body quivers from the awe-inspiring thoughts of my father standing in this exact spot and smelling this particular tree.

"It's a Jeffrey pine." She skates her fingers across the yellowed trunk, her eyes focusing on the hearts. "His name was Scott Jeffrey Gallagher."

I gulp and soak in the new information. Going from knowing nothing about him my whole life to learning so many special details in a three-day time is causing my thoughts to twist into a mangled mess.

"I'm sorry, Rhyce. This is—"

"So, the S and the R stand for Scott and Ramey?"

Mom nods then quickly shakes her head. "Yes and no, but more no, I think."

"Huh? You think? I don't understand."

Her gaze meets mine before drifting back to the carvings. "I only knew about the S. Let's head back to the car and finish the drive."

I touch the tree one more time and take in a deep lungful of the fragrance. "How long until we get to where we're going?"

"It's a few minutes' drive. Not far." She sighs. "Rhyce, this isn't easy for me, either."

I rest my head against the bucket seat and gaze out the window as we whiz past a trillion trees. Loren *is* right. It's Mom's life, too. In fact, I'm starting to realize it was her life first.

Mom turns right onto a winding, paved lane lined with moss-covered pines. I can see two stone chimneys peeping out from a black shingled roof. The lane divides and we take the narrow road on the left. An immense log-and-stone structure comes into view.

"Whoa." The Henderson's mansion is puny compared to this place. "Just whoa."

Mom bites her bottom lip as she parks between an orangey-brown Jeep Renegade and a gold Studebaker Challenger—a 1964 model.

All the breath whooshes out of me. "He liked cars?"

"He loved cars. I told you the two of you had a lot in common."

I don't know whether to laugh or cry. My mind is on overdrive. I inspect the Studebaker. It's perfect. Not a single scratch or smudge. Tears stream down my face. I never knew him, but yet I miss him ... a lot.

Mom guides me toward the front of the house where she crouches and retrieves a key from under a terracotta planter. She places it into my palm, wrapping her fingers around mine. "This key unlocks *your* world."

If my brain wouldn't automatically tell my lungs to breathe, I'd be out of luck right now. With blurred vision, I wiggle the key into the lock and the door swings inward.

Along the far wall, twelve massive windows—four rows, three high—display the most spectacular view of Lake Tahoe. Two yellow-orange lounge chairs sit near the edge of a long pier. Boats tied to wooden beams and buoys bob up and down with the ripples.

"This ... all this ... is my father's?"

"Yes and no."

I park myself on a leather couch and scan the immense room. "He lived here?"

She nods, running her fingertips along the edge of the slick cushion. "I used to live here, too. Before you were born. I loved it here until—"

"Mom, I wasn't asleep in Nova Leigh's car."

She rocks back and forth, her eyes full of emotion. Tears sting my eyes, but I blink them away.

Mom crosses the room to a sturdy oak desk. She picks up a silver frame and returns to the couch.

"This is Scarlett. Scarlett Deziree."

She slides the photograph into my hands. A little girl with reddish-blonde hair—as curly as Mom's—stares back at me, her jaw jutting to the right ... exactly like mine.

"I had an older sister? She drowned? I thought I was an only child."

Mom closes her eyes and nods several times.

"She was two. I put her down for a nap and started dinner—chicken cordon bleu. I thought she was in her crib. Your father was fixing one of those glass panes before the snowstorm hit. A bird had smacked into one and caused a spider-web crack. Your father hollered 'Scarlett, no!' and I saw him running down the pier. But it was too late. She'd slipped and fallen into the cold water. He couldn't revive her." She dabs her nose with a tissue. "I didn't know how to tell you, and every time I thought I was ready, it wasn't the right time for you."

"You left him. Did he even know about me?"

I set the picture frame on the coffee table. Pacing around the room, I stop at a bookshelf near the desk. A bright yellow Post-it note catches my attention. It's stuck onto a worn leather-bound book. When I open the cover, a wallet-sized snapshot of me falls onto the floor. I pick it up and read the back. *Rhyce Decker Foley, age 5 – Kindergarten.*

Mom attempts to smile. "A year ago, I told him about you—and sent him an album filled with photos of you at various ages." She clasps the photograph of Scarlett and cuddles it to her chest.

Resting against the bookcase, I flip through the pages of the journal. At the top of each sheet are three simple but overwhelming words: *My Dear Son ...*

"It's been an emotional day for both of us. I'm afraid tomorrow won't be much different, with the memorial and all." Mom yawns. "Are you hungry?"

I shake my head.

"All right, then. Time for bed."

I tuck the journal under my arm and follow Mom up the spiral staircase to the third-floor landing. Four doors line the right side of the hallway. There's no wall on the left side, just a glossy wooden banister. I grasp the shiny railing and peek over it at the living room far below. Mom opens the last door and flips on the light switch.

I can't help but grin. The room is filled with shelves of books, display cases with die-cast model cars, and a substantial collection of Matchbox and Hot Wheels Studebakers and Corvettes.

"Cool!" I sigh deeply, but for the first time all day, it isn't a sad sigh. It's a sigh of ... I don't know how to explain it. He called me son.

"I'm glad he never changed this room. I remember bickering with Scott about how to decorate it. He wanted a space for his car collection, but I wanted a guest bedroom. We came to an agreement and as you see, it became both. Now, I just remembered we didn't bring the suitcases in from the car. I'll go down and get them, then we can get ready for bed."

Mom slips out the doorway and down the stairs. I crawl onto the bed and open the journal to the first page.

> *April 16th, 2013*
> *My Dear Son,*
> *I love you.*
> *I love you more than words can describe. More than I love antique cars, Cessnas, and pedal boats. More than I love lakes, mountains, and Jeffrey pines. More than I love blueberry pie, chocolate pudding, and pistachio ice cream.*
> *I love you now and I'll love you always.*
> > *Daddy*

Ten. I was ten when he wrote this. I flip to the next entry.

> *April 22nd, 2013*
> *My Dear Son,*
> *Everyone makes mistakes. No one is perfect.*
> *Sometimes our mistakes are huge and cause problems for other people; people we love.*

Have you ever played the game Dominoes? When one of the tiles falls, it starts a chain effect, and every single one connected to it falls shortly after.

Your mother and I made some wrong choices—mistakes. And I'm sorry for the chain effects it has caused you.

But just know I love you. And I can only hope one day you'll love me, too.

Daddy

A loud crash echoes on the hardwood floor downstairs. I close the book and hop off the bed and out into the hall. Poking my head over the handrail, I see Mom rubbing her ankle, the contents of her open suitcase all over the floor.

I trek down the steps to the living room. "I can carry mine up. Are you okay?"

Mom waves her hand toward the room on her left. "They're in there beside the fridge. Yeah, I think so. I shouldn't have worn these heels."

"You said his service is tomorrow. What's a memorial like? Will his body be in a casket? Will I see him at least *once* in my life?"

Mom sits down on the floor, a polka-dotted sock clutched in her hand. "Family and friends of your father—"

"My dad ... he was my dad."

"Family and friends of your *dad* will gather together to celebrate his life. There will be no casket, no body. The minister will say a blessing for him, and ask if people in the congregation would like to share a special memory they have of him. There may be piano music and singing of hymns."

I scrunch my brows together. "Do *I* have other family members I never met? Why did you wait until after he died to tell me anything about him!?"

Mom tosses the sock into her suitcase and breathes deeply. "Rhyce ..."

"What! I went all my life thinking he didn't love me, didn't want me. But today—in his journal—I learned he *did* love me and he apologized for his mistakes. For *your* mistakes. Why didn't you—"

"Rhy—"

"No! Shut up."

Mom's eyes widen and her mouth drops open.

"Why didn't you ever bring me here? After you told him about me, did you tell him not to contact us? Is that why he never came to Hershey to see me? I'm supposed to sit through a memorial and listen to complete strangers who know more about him than I *ever* will?"

"Rhyce, you don't know the—"

"What else is there to know? *You* left him. *You* waited ten years to tell him he had a son. Ten years *I* was without my daddy. You ruined my life. I hate you!"

I grab my bags and run up the stairs as fast as I can, slamming the bedroom door behind me. Pulling my phone out of my pocket, I check my missed texts. One from Loren.

9:26 p.m. – Flights okay?

9:42 p.m. – Yes.

9:43 p.m. – You okay?

9:44 p.m. – No. Furious.

9:45 p.m. – One Mississippi, two Mississippi ...

9:46 p.m. – Screw Mississippi.

9:47 p.m. – Ouch. How about the other 49 states?

9:48 p.m. – I HATE HER!

My phone rings and Loren's name blinks on the screen. I push the answer button.

"Talk, Rhyce. I'm listening."

"I'm so mad. Because of her, my dad and I suffered. She ruined my life! Oh, and guess what else. I wasn't ever an only child."

Loren coughs and clears her throat. "So you learned a lot of things at once. A lot of negative things. Remember I said there will be moments of bitter and dark?"

"I know, but ..."

"Did you find some positive things, too? Happy things?"

"Yes, but ..."

"Good things come from bad things, remember. Did you have a brother?"

"No, a sister. Scarlett."

"Nice. What was her middle name?"

"Deziree." I take a deep breath. "She drowned in the lake. I wonder if she found any pearls."

Loren is quiet.

"You still there?" I ask, tapping my fingers on the journal.

"Yeah. So I'm guessing your mom needed her space ... you know, to heal."

"To heal? What do you mean?"

"Losing a child is tough. Really tough. A parent should never have to deal with burying their children. It hurts ... a lot. Everyone mourns in different ways and for different lengths of time. And it never leaves you."

"My dad wrote a journal."

"Oh, yeah? Did you read it?"

"Some. I'll read more tonight. He called me son."

"I told you he was probably a gem. That's fantastic, Rhyce."

"Yeah. He has ... had? ... a Studebaker Challenger. It's gold. And there's this room in his house filled with amazing car collections."

"Awesomeness! Hey, hold on a sec, okay? Linc wants to say hi."

I switch the phone to my other ear, listening to Loren and Linc bicker with each other. *If Scarlett was still alive, would we fight, too?*

"Dude! I thought you said girls are gross. F.Y.I., Foley, my sister's a girl!"

"Hey, Henderson." I lean back against the headboard and pick up the blue Corvette from the bedside table. "What are you doing awake?"

"Waiting for you to text me." He groans loudly. "And my stomach hurts."

I huff a laugh. "How much of that five-pounder did you eat?"

"Hush it, Crispy."

"Whatever, Logs."

"Twenty big bites, but anyway, I wish you were here. Winning those tickets wasn't as fun without you. You okay?"

My jaw shifts to the right. "Not really."

"Do you need Loren again? She's right here."

"Nah. I think I'm going to head to bed now." I spin the Corvette's front tires with my fingertips. "Linc? Wait. Yeah, put her on, okay?"

"Yeah. Just a sec. And Foley? I'm sorry about your father."

"Thanks."

In the background, I hear Lincoln sniff. "Here's Loren."

"Rhyce?"

"Tomorrow is his memorial. I don't know what to do." I set the Corvette back onto the nightstand. "What do I say? What do I do?"

"You breathe and take it as it comes. I know you never met him, but it might make you feel better if you share your feelings with everyone. But only you will know when it's the best time. Go get some sleep. I'll check on you tomorrow evening."

"Loren?"

"Yes?"

"Thank you."

"Anytime, Rhyce. Anytime."

"Night."

An usher seats us in the front pew of the church and hands Mom a light-green sheet of paper. I edge away from her, leaving a wide gap between us. Glancing over my shoulder, I watch as people enter and take a seat.

A tall woman in a nursing uniform assists a gentleman whose eyes are covered with gauze. They slide into the bench directly behind me.

Within a few moments, the main doors close, and a man's voice echoes around the room. I shift on the bench and face the stage where three metal folding chairs sit empty.

"Good afternoon, I'm Pastor Tom. Today we gather to honor the life of Scott Jeffrey Gallagher. I had the privilege to be at his bedside when he took his last breath on the tenth of June."

People in the congregation sniff, and an older woman next to me dabs her eyes with a tissue. I fight off the heavy feeling in my eyes. I don't want strangers to see me cry.

"Scott was born in Incline Village, Nevada on the twelfth of May in the year nineteen seventy-seven. He graduated from Washoe County School District in nineteen ninety-five and emerged from University of Nevada in Reno several years later with a Ph.D. in Hydrogeology. He enjoyed boating, fishing, and the great outdoors. He succeeded in obtaining his pilot's license and spent many hours flying his Cessna above the Sierra Nevada. He was preceded in death by his father, Samuel Decker Gallagher, and a daughter, Scarlett Deziree Gallagher. He is survived by his mother, Melody Roseville, and a son, Rhyce Decker Foley."

Wait. I have my grandfather's middle name? And ... he just said my grandmother is still alive?

I wiggle in my seat and look over my shoulder. *Is she here?*

"At this time, I'd like to call three people to the platform. Edward Lyle, Melody, and young Rhyce. Please, join me."

I crease my brows and jut my jaw to the right, glimpsing at Mom. She nods at me, a weak smile forming on her lips. The man with the gauze-covered eyes whispers something to the nurse and they make their way up front. The older woman beside me also leaves her seat and joins the pastor.

Whoa.

"Rhyce? It's okay. Will you come?" the pastor says, smiling.

I slide past Mom and into the aisle where I stop and look around the room. Many kind eyes glisten back at me.

One Mississippi, two Mississippi ... I put one foot in front of the other and somehow arrive at the stage.

The pastor gestures to the chairs behind him. "The three of you may be seated."

We sit, me in the center. Instantly, my grandmother's cool fingers clasp around my right hand. The nurse guides Edward's hand into mine. Once she steps behind his chair, the pastor smiles at us and then at the audience.

"Let us bow our heads in prayer. Lord God, we come into your presence this day to mourn the passing of Scott Jeffrey Gallagher: son, father, friend, and brother in Christ. We come to celebrate a life well lived. We come to be comforted in our sorrow, and pray you would grant us peace beyond understanding. We know just as you walked with Scott throughout his life, you are walking with him now in his new heavenly home. Grant us all courage and strength to face the days ahead. Be with Melody and Rhyce; give them a new sense of your comfort and peace. Be with his friends and give them an extra source of your love and understanding. Be with our community here in Lake Tahoe as Scott has moved on. Allow us to never forget the efforts, both big and small, Scott made on your behalf in this world. In the name of our Lord and Savior Jesus Christ. Amen."

Pastor Tom lifts his head.

"Would anyone like to share a memory of their time with Scott? If you do, please stand, one at a time, and tell us your name and memory."

A man in the back rises to his feet.

"My name's Ryan Kefauver. I met Scott when my family moved from Fort Worth, Texas to this area in my fourth-grade year. No one gave me the time of day, but Scott did. One day, when we were seniors in high school, we got hiking permits, stocked our backpacks with water and snacks, and trekked the trail up Mt. Tallac." He pauses and stares at the five of us on the platform. "Once we reached the summit ... ten rough miles later ... I sat down on a rock and a little creature popped its head up and made me practically jump out of my skin. Scott said, 'It's just a pika, not a black bear, doofus.'"

People laugh and then Ryan sits and a woman rises from her seat, teardrops drenching her cheeks.

"I'm Audra." She swipes her shirt sleeve across her face. "Sorry. Scott was my high school sweetheart. My first love. We used to spend hours and hours on pedal boats out on the lake near King's Beach. He ... I'm sorry." She sits back down and lowers her head.

Mom's staring toward the ceiling of the church and rubbing her upper arms.

"Pastor? May I?" Edward says.

"Yes. Go ahead."

"I never met Scott, but he means the world to me. Because of his generosity, in more ways than one, I have hope to see clearly again. For the past several years, an eye disease called Kerato-conus caused my eyesight to become blurred and extremely sensitive to light. June eleventh, the day after Scott died, I had corneal transplants at no cost to me. Rhyce, is it?"

"Yes, sir."

"One moment. Stacey, please remove the bandages."

The nurse slowly peels the tape and gauze away.

"Your father may be gone from this life, but his corneas are right here." A single tear slips down his right cheek. "And I promise to take care of them."

"Whoa. You have my dad's eyes?"

"Not his whole eyes. Just the corneas. The clear part that shields your eyes." He crouches in front of my chair, and I hear numerous sniffs in the room. "Your dad is now my protector."

Letting go of my grandma's hand, I give Edward a hug. "Thank you for coming."

"You're welcome."

I lean back against the chair and Melody clutches my hand again.

"You look like my Scotty did at your age. Those blue eyes, the blond hair. It's wonderful to finally meet you, Rhyce. Thank *you* for coming." She glowers at my mom. "Despite never meeting him."

It's time.

"My name's Rhyce Decker Foley, and Scott was my dad. Like Mr. Lyle, I never met him, but he's my world. I thought he abandoned me as a baby. I was wrong. He wrote a journal to me, and through his words I've come to learn how much he loved me. He wrote in one of the entries, 'people make mistakes.' It's true. We all make mistakes. We all say or do things that hurt the ones we love the most." I pause and look around at the people in the pews. Some dab their eyes, and others smile at me. "My mom's name is Ramey Foley. She's right there. I may get mad at her at times, but I love her."

Mom's chin quivers. "I love you, too, Rhyce. I'm sorry. So, so sorry."

Pastor Tom clutches the pulpit. "Before Scott passed, he said, 'Tell Ramey I forgive her.'" He smirks at me. "He also said, 'Tell Rhyce not to drive his Studebaker until he's sixteen.'"

The congregation laughs.

My jaw shifts to the right and I stare at Pastor Tom.

"*My* Studebaker?"

"His exact words, kiddo." He gazes up at the congregation. "Thank you for coming today. There are refreshments in the fellowship hall and a display table with photographs of Scott through the years. If more of you wish to share memories with the family, feel free to do so. I'm sure they would love to hear them."

Mom rests her arms along the backs of the wooden lounge chairs on the pier. After a few minutes, she stoops and gently swirls her hand back and forth in the water.

I edge closer but halt when I hear her singing words to a tune she used to hum to me every night. I never knew it had lyrics.

She removes her hand from the lake and curls strands of hair behind her ears.

"Mom? Are you okay?" I rest my fingers on her shoulder. "Is this where Scarl—"

"Yes, it is. And I owe you a few explanations. Yesterday you asked me some questions, and I replied 'Yes and no.' Is it too late to explain my answer?"

A white pebble shimmers below the water's surface.

"The S on the tree stands for Scarlett. The R ... it stands for Rhyce, doesn't it?"

Mom nods. A tear falls from her eye and lands on the pier.

"Rhyce, when you asked me if all this belongs to your father, I didn't know how to respond. Yes and no was the honest answer. It *belonged* to him. Not the lake, of course, but the house, cars, and property."

"Belonged? Who does it belong to now?"

She looks up as a large bird soars above us. "You."

"Whoa."

Mom's giggle snort echoes across the lake, and for the first time, I love hearing her laughter.

We've been in Lake Tahoe exactly one month now. Over the past three weeks since the memorial, I've spent lots of time with Grandma Melody, zip-lining through the trees, hiking parts of the Tahoe Rim Trail, and swimming in the lake.

One day last week, she took me to Fannette Island in Emerald Bay. We hiked to the tea house—it doesn't serve tea anymore, and it doesn't have doors or a roof—and then we toured this cool Scandinavian castle called Vikingsholm. It sits along the lakefront.

Today we're going miniature golfing and later we're meeting Edward for ice cream. He can see clearly now. It's kind of neat to peer into his eyes and know I'm looking at Dad, too.

Mom has met several times with the lawyer. She says the title of the Studebaker will be in Grandma's name until I turn eighteen, but Grandma says I can drive it whenever I'm old enough and have my driver's license. Dad left the Jeep Renegade to Mom, and we're planning on driving it home tomorrow. The GPS says it's approximately twenty-seven hundred miles from here to Hershey.

The house and the trust fund, though, will be mine on my eighteenth birthday. That's only a little over six years away. It's all a bit daunting, but Mom and Grandma are on speaking terms now, and with their help, I'm adjusting to all these sudden changes in my life, both good and bad.

Loren was right when she told me I'd find pearls. I think she herself was the very first pearl I found, though.

ᘖ ⚬ ᘖ

"Melody's here for you. You ready to go?" Mom musses my hair and massages my shoulders.

I look out the windows at the lake. "Even though I'm excited to see Linc again, I'm going to miss it here."

"I promise we'll come back many times. No more keeping you from what was stopping me."

Grandma opens the front door and pokes her head in. "Time to hit the Magic Carpet. Want to take Ol' Gerty?"

"Gerty? Who's Gerty?"

Mom and Grandma laugh as I stand there baffled.

"Your dad named the Studebaker after his great-grandma. She was a feisty thing."

My eyes widen, but before my jaw has time to shift out of position, Grandma Melody struts across the living room and tugs on my arm, pulling me through the kitchen and into the garage.

Am I dreaming? I have to be dreaming.

"Are you just going to stand there? Get in the car!"

There is no way to describe the feeling deep inside me when its engine purrs to life.

"Whoa."

"Put your seat belt on and let's get to gettin', shall we?"

The buckle slides into the constraint, and Grandma backs the car out of the garage. I wave to Mom until she disappears from view.

"It's our last day together, for now, Rhyce Decker, so let's make the best of it."

I roll down the window, lean my head against the back of the seat, and do nothing but smile.

⤷ ⚭ ⤶

After forty hours on the road—not including overnight stops in Utah, Nebraska, Illinois, and a flat tire in the middle of nowhere Ohio—Mom pulls the Jeep Renegade into our apartment's parking lot. I climb out and sniff the air.

Chocolate.

I yank my cell from my back pocket, and snap a photo of me, the Trailblazer roller coaster behind me. Attaching it to my best friend's number, I click send and wait for his reply.

Five minutes later, Linc whizzes down the hill on his RipStik, Loren and Cody running right behind him.

"Dude! You're back!" He jumps off his board, kickflipping it into the yard as he eyes the Renegade. "Wow. Nice ride!"

Loren embraces me, and I feel a weird warmth on my face as she lets go.

Linc rolls his eyes. "Better be careful there. You might catch her cooties."

"Henderson, you're still a dweeb."

"Whatever."

Loren wraps her arm around Cody's waist. "It's great to have you home again, Rhyce. Logs was driving us nuts."

Cody slaps my back. "You are *not* allowed to be gone that long ever again."

"Maybe next time you can all come with us."

Loren beams. "I'd love to hear all about the pearls of Rhyce."

Lincoln grabs my skateboard from beneath the porch and shoves it under my arm. "Yeah, yeah. Later, sis. He's got a date with a racing boat over in Minetown Arcade." He tilts his head toward the amusement park's fence across the street.

I bite my top lip as Loren winks at me.

"Dude, seriously. Cooties. Come on."

"Wait. There's something I need to do before we hit the arcade. Here, hold my board."

I walk over to Mom as she sets the last suitcase inside the door. "Hey, feeling up to riding the log flume with me?"

Teardrops cascade down her cheeks as I wrap my arms around her. "I thought you'd never ask."

THE END

Deborah S. Vlick grew up in Pennsylvania but a part of her will always remain in her birthplace in Michigan. Her immediate family is English, originating from London, which has had a positive impact on her writing style. She is an accomplished writer of Middle-Grade fiction, including several published short stories under her adoptive name. Deborah recalls the trials and tribulations of being a young teenager, and enjoys weaving them into fiction.

From the publisher and all the authors—thank you for reading. We hope you enjoyed our creative dive into the elements.

Reviews are the life-blood of an author. We would very much appreciate a short review wherever books are sold.

Also, please check out each of the authors' pages which are posted in their biographies at the end of each story. Many have other works on offer and would appreciate your patronage.

CPSIA information can be obtained
at www.ICGtesting.com
Printed in the USA
LVHW032327250219
608758LV00002B/243

9 780967 018539